ALSO BY RADU R. FLORESCU AND RAYMOND T. MCNALLY

In Search of Dracula: A True History of Dracula and Vampire Legends

Dracula: A Biography of Vlad the Impaler, 1431–1476

*The Essential Dracula: A Completely Illustrated and
Annotated Edition of Bram Stoker's Classic Novel*

Dracula

PRINCE OF MANY FACES

VLADISLAVS DRACVLA. WALLACHIÆ WEIWODEN.

Painting of Dracula recently discovered by Dr. Virgil Cândea of the Romanian Academy of Social and Political Sciences, secretary of the International Association of Southeast European Studies. The painting was in the possession of Nicolaus Ochsenbach, governor of the castle of Hohen Tübingen. It is presently located in the Library of the State of Würtenberg in Stuttgart, and dates back to the early seventeenth century

Dracula

PRINCE OF MANY FACES

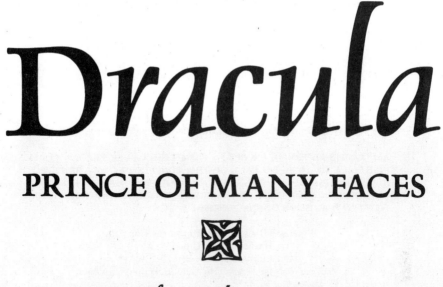

His Life and His Times

Radu R. Florescu

Raymond T. McNally

BACK BAY BOOKS
LITTLE, BROWN AND COMPANY
NEW YORK   BOSTON   LONDON

Back Bay Books / Little, Brown and Company
Hachette Book Group USA
237 Park Avenue, New York, NY 10017
Visit our Web site at www.HachetteBookGroupUSA.com

FIRST PAPERBACK EDITION

Library of Congress Cataloging-in-Publication Data

Florescu, Radu.
    Dracula, prince of many faces : his life and his times / by Radu
R. Florescu and Raymond T. McNally. — 1st ed.
        p.   cm.
    ISBN 978-0-316-28655-8 (hc)
    ISBN 978-0-316-28656-5 (pb)
        1. Vlad III, Prince of Wallachia, 1430 or 31–1476 or 7.
    2. Wallachia — Kings and rulers — Bibliography.   I. McNally, Raymond T.,
    1931–   . II. Title.
    DR240.5.V553 F58   1989
    949.8'201'092 — dc20
    [B]   89-8164

                    HC: 10   9   8   7   6   5   4   3   2
                    PB: 20   19   18

                                         Q-FF

                         Designed by Jeanne Abboud

                    PRINTED IN THE UNITED STATES OF AMERICA

DEDICATION

This book is dedicated to those undergraduates of Boston College who in the spring semester of 1988 were curious enough to enroll in a course entitled The Life and Times of the Historical Dracula. *The co-authors gratefully acknowledge the tough criticism, the invaluable suggestions, and, above all, the enthusiasm expressed in the final examinations — the ultimate satisfaction of the teacher-scholar.*

Contents

(Illustrations appear following pages 74 and 170.)

Acknowledgments

I T would be difficult to acknowledge the names of all those who were responsible for aiding in the preparation of this book. One way of doing it collectively is to acknowledge all those authors who contributed important works on the occasion in 1976 of the five hundredth anniversary of Prince Dracula's death.

The co-authors would like to pay a tribute to a few scholars, among many to whom we are indebted, who made substantial contributions to this work and helped us resolve some problems connected with the life story of Dracula. We owe special thanks to our fellow Dracula hunter Dr. Matei Cazacu of the Centre National de Recherches Scientifiques and the University of Paris (Sorbonne) for having generously placed at our disposal the research of his most recent monograph on the German and Russian narratives. We warmly thank Dr. Cornelia Bodea, senior research associate at the Nicolae Iorga History Institute in Bucharest (and Fulbright Exchange Professor at Boston College from 1987 to 1989), for her many suggestions concerning Stoker's folkloric and historical research. We gratefully recognize the leading expert on the history of the German Saxons of Transylvania, Dr. Adolph Armbruster, presently associated with the Institute for South East European Research at Munich University, for his help in making vital material available to us, from both his personal collection and that in the Munich State Library; Dr. Ştefan Andreescu of the Iorga Institute, the author of an insightful biography of the historical Dracula (1976), who helped us locate Castle Königstein, the place of Dracula's arrest in 1462; Dr. Mihai Pop, the former director of the Institute of Folklore in Bucharest, who, with his team, Dr. Constantin Eretescu and Dr. Georgeta Ene, was our chief "anchorman" in researching the Dracula castle epic. The original inspiration for this study and our methods of research we owe to the late Constantin C. Giurescu, the dean of Romanian historians, and to Radu Florescu's uncle, the late George D. Florescu, former director of the Museum of the History of the City of Bucharest, the country's leading genealogist.

We recognize the contribution of detailed information on various points, which we incorporated into our text, from the following scholars: Dr. Nicolae Stoicescu of the Iorga Institute, the author of the first modern Romanian scholarly monograph on Dracula (1976); Dr. Radu Constantinescu of the Romanian State Archives for his invaluable research at the History Museum at Bucharest on the German Saxon code of laws; Dr. Octavian Iliescu, an eminent numismatist, who placed at our disposal the original Dracula coin bearing the effigy of Halley's comet; Dr. Dan Cernovodeanu, now in Paris, well-known heraldist, for his discovery of Dracula's Hungarian descendants, a study more recently completed by Dr. Paul Binder of the Iorga Institute; Dr. Pavel Chihaia, who teaches French in a Munich gymnasium, for his study on the evolution of the dragon symbol in Romanian iconography; Dr. Virgil Cândea of the Academy of Social and Political Sciences in Bucharest for his discovery of a new sixteenth-century portrait of Dracula, which he generously made available to us; Radu Ştefan Ciobanu, a high-school teacher in Bucharest, for his insights into Dracula's youth and the quaint folkloric anecdotes he has gathered.

In our research we utilized many libraries and archives that deserve recognition. We are most grateful to Dr. Iancu Bidian, director of the Romanian Library and Research Institute at Freiburg-im-Breisgau, the richest resource on Romanian history in the west, and to his able assistant, Irina Nasta, for their time and especially for making an exception to their lending rules by sending rare materials to us across the Atlantic. Dr. Ştefan Ştefănescu and his senior research associate at the Iorga Institute, Dr. Paul Cernovodeanu, were responsible for sending countless materials for our benefit from their rich collection. Dr. Mihai Ionescu, associate director of the Institute of Military History (Bucharest), was our link to the excellent resources of the Institute, particularly useful for questions of tactics, uniforms, and weaponry. Freiherr von Adrian-Weiburg, chief archivist at the Nuremberg Archives, provided invaluable bibliographic guides on the Order of the Dragon. P. Gottfried Glasner, chief librarian of the Lambach Benedictine Library in upper

Austria, made two separate attempts to locate the original Lambach Dracula manuscript. Dr. Wilfred Kowavich, chief archivist at the Benedictine Abbey of Melk in lower Austria, supplied transcripts concerning the Romanian prior who mentioned Dracula in his chronicle. P. Ochsenbein, the librarian of the library at Saint Gall, offered informative remarks on the original Dracula manuscript in his collection. Dr. C. Göllner, distinguished scholar from Sibiu, placed some important materials of the Transylvanian Museum at Gundelsheim at our disposal — this being the most important museum in the west on the Transylvanian Saxons and housed in the ancient Teutonic fortress of Horneck in Bavaria. Güngör Dilmen, Filiz Cağman, and Ghengis Köseoğlu of the Topkapî Palace Archives in Istanbul made available original Greek and Turkish sources. Professor Charles "Ted" Ahearn, our colleague at Boston College in the Classics Department, translated some Latin texts for us.

We are also indebted to the Heidelberg University Library for the original photostat of Michael Beheim's poem on Dracula, as well as the poem on the Varna crusade. The curator of the Philip H. and A. S. W. Rosenbach Foundation Library, Leslie Morris, allowed us a second look at the folkloric and historical titles Stoker used in the composition of Dracula. We were given permission by the Vatican to use and microfilm the unabridged report to Pope Pius II from the papal legate Niccolò Modrussa, in the Corsiniano Collection of the Vatican Secret Archives.

With regard to the photographs, reproductions, and artwork, we are indebted to Alexandra Altman for her acumen in pointing out the surviving fifteenth-century portions of the old fortress of Belgrade and for a visit to the Military History Museum at Belgrade. The Kunsthistorisches Museum in Vienna gave us permission to reproduce both the Dracula portrait and those of some contemporaries, located for the most part at the Ambras Castle Museum in Innsbruck. Baroness Ileana Franchetti (Radu Florescu's niece) obtained permission to photograph the paintings of Pope Pius II located at the Cathedral in Siena. Lodging at her castle in the Dolomites afforded us the opportunity to visit the tomb of one of Dracula's Romanian descendants, at Bolzano, a few miles away. Hélène Maumy-Florescu (Florescu's daughter-in-law), a graduate of the École Nationale Supérieure des Arts Décoratifs in Paris, drafted the two maps.

The co-authors' recent travels to Romania are owed to two awards by the Council on the International Exchange of Scholars (Fulbright Research Fellowship). Our typists, Ellie Waal of Cohasset, Massachusetts,

ACKNOWLEDGMENTS

and Karen Potterton of Boston College, deserve a strong note of commendation for putting up with messy and at times nearly indecipherable manuscripts. Above all, this book is a much better one for the patience, diplomacy, and enthusiasm of our editor at Little, Brown, Debra Roth, who in the end helped put it all in proper focus, while making the experience enjoyable, and Glea Humez, our copy editor, whose exceptional knowledge of languages and eye for detail helped resolve many a problem that this polyglot manuscript entailed.

To our respective families, particularly our wives, Nicole and Carol, we owe a note of apology for having been mostly absent from domestic duties in thought, in work, and in travel. In the end, the co-authors pay a very special tribute to Radu Florescu's son John, for his interest in our work, the many helpful suggestions he made, and his constant words of encouragement. By an odd coincidence, his present employer, the English television personality David Frost, was responsible for introducing the historical Dracula to the American television audience.

Introduction

AFTER some twenty years of research and three books about Dracula (both the legendary and the historical figure), the authors feel they owe some words of explanation for their long-term commitments to this subject, as well as their reasons for writing the present book. Both writers have deep and genuine roots to the topic at hand, traced through their forebears. Radu Florescu is the descendant of an old Romanian noble family whose ancestry may be followed back over five hundred years to the times of the real, historical Dracula. One of his ancestors, Vintilă Florescu, was Dracula's contemporary and joined the opposition to him by supporting Dracula's brother, Radu the Handsome, who had seized the throne after Dracula's capture by the Hungarian king in the year 1462; Vintilă became a member of that prince's council. He later served as a court dignitary under Dracula's half-brother Vlad the Monk, who ruled from 1482 until 1495. As for the co-author of the present book, Raymond McNally, his paternal ancestors came from County Mayo in the West of Ireland, very close to County Sligo, where the mother of Bram Stoker, the author of the novel *Dracula*, was born. It was an area where Stoker's mother imbibed the well-preserved Gaelic folklore, which she transmitted to her son and which inspired his writings. This common background in Ireland with the author of *Dracula* may also help to account for McNally's lifelong interest in fairy tales and those stories of the imagination that have a basis in reality. It was Professor McNally's inspiration and flair for research into the historical facts behind legends that led the two authors on their initial search for the historical Dracula. McNally's mother's ancestors came from a German-speaking village near Ljubljana, the present capital of Slovenia. The village is close to the monastery that once housed the Benedictine monk Brother Jacob, author of one of the first authentic fifteenth-century Dracula horror stories. Beyond these personal connections, both authors of the present book are professional historians, who have discovered much new and valuable material since the publication of their previous works on this topic.

It seems like a lifetime since the two co-authors embarked on their Dracula hunt, which led to the publication of their best-seller *In Search of Dracula*. By design, that book was a miniature encyclopedic and pictorial pioneer work that included a brief historical sketch of the fifteenth-century Romanian prince who inspired the novel, an examination of the ancient and various vampire beliefs of eastern Europe, the setting of Stoker's novel in its gothic literary tradition, and a short analysis of the better-known Dracula films.

As a result of our search, several books have been published, in both Europe and America, that attempted to make scholarly a subject hitherto simply dismissed as the product of Stoker's imagination. Reviewers described this quest for genuine sources and prototypes of the Dracula legend as "a minor publishing phenomenon." Even today, there sometimes appear newspaper articles referring to disclosures pertaining to the true story. Our discovery of the actual location of the real Castle Dracula, described in our first book, perhaps unwarrantedly generated the kind of publicity associated in some sensation-seeking newspapers with Howard Carter's unearthing of Tutankhamen's tomb.

In bestowing a musical-sounding name upon his fictional vampire count, Bram Stoker added a word to the language of mankind. It evokes the ugly, gaunt, emaciated vampire with pointed ears and long fingernails portrayed by Max Schreck in the 1922 silent classic film *Nosferatu;* the sophisticated continental-lover type of count, invariably dressed in his tuxedo and black cape, speaking English with a thick Hungarian accent, immortalized by Bela Lugosi in the 1931 Universal movie *Dracula;* the bloody technicolored six-foot lusty demon with fangs played by Christopher Lee in the 1958 Hammer film *Horror of Dracula;* and the suave, sexy, velvet-voiced, handsome tempter presented by Frank Langella in the 1978 Universal International picture *Dracula*. The late poet Ogden Nash paid Dracula the supreme compliment of simply mentioning his name in his *Terrible People,* knowing that the reader would instantly recognize it.

Because of the success of our previous book, the historical prototype of this fictional Dracula, a truly extraordinary, flesh-and-blood Romanian ruler of the fifteenth century, began to acquire an identity of his own, propelled to fame partly because of his name's being identical with that of the vampire. Our search for the details of his life story carries the excitement of a genuine discovery. And, in this case, as in others, truth is stranger than fiction. A fortuitous coincidence, the visit of former president Richard Nixon to Bucharest in 1969 (the first visit by an American president to that country), brought two hundred newspaper and media people there just at the time when we began our search; this event resulted in the first newspaper headlines attesting to the authentic historical figure called Dracula and to the existence of the real Castle Dracula. In time, the genuine historical personality acquired dimensions and an identity distinct from that of the vampire. He is remembered best for his unusual method of imposing death — impalement — a fact that is particularly important because it bears an uncanny resemblance to the traditional manner of disposing of vampires by driving stakes through their bodies. The use of the stake may well have helped to establish the separate recognition of the real Impaler by his nickname. This notice was exemplified by a recent Boston radio broadcast in which Daniel Ortega, the strong man of Nicaragua, was referred to as "not as bad as Vlad the Impaler." There are references now to the historical Dracula in encyclopedias, *Reader's Digest*, comic strips, and high school and college texts. Historical monuments associated with the real Dracula have become major tourist attractions in Romania. Our book has been used as a guide by the Romanian National Tourist Office.

The present book is far more than a response to those who can no longer consult our earlier books. It represents the first comprehensive attempt at putting the life story of Dracula into the broad context of fifteenth-century European history, in the century of the Renaissance, a period of remarkable change. Even a cursory glance at those times may show points of comparison with our contemporary world, which is one reason why historians have often labeled it as marking the beginnings of the modern era. The century is certainly "modern" in terms of the brutality and cruelty of its wars. It also mirrors our century in its ideological confrontation between east and west (Islam vs. Christianity in the fifteenth century), as well as the amorality of politics within and among nations, mass extermination of political enemies, and the anxiety caused by unstoppable plagues, which resembles our own fear of uncontrollable new diseases and nuclear annihilation. Moreover, Dracula's contemporaries, Pope Pius II, the German Holy Roman Emperors Sigismund and Frederick III, Sultan Mehmed the Conqueror, the warrior John Hunyadi and his son, Matthias Corvinus the Hungarian king, and George Poděbrady, king of Bohemia, were extraordinary personalities by any standards. But whether seen as a new-style Renaissance despot, a pre-Machiavellian patriot, a tactician of war and terror, or even a sadist, Dracula commanded great attention even in his lifetime, amid all the talented people that the 1400s produced. He was certainly one of the most controversial personalities in the history of eastern Europe during that period and the subject of more anecdotes and historical narratives than most of his contemporaries.

After tracing his extraordinary life, we shall follow the growth of the Dracula legend after his death. Most relevant was the transformation of anti-Dracula propaganda tracts into best-sellers of fifteenth-century German horror literature. In contrast to those legends, the evolution of oral Romanian folklore made Dracula a national hero, a kind of George Washington of Romanian history, while in the emerging Russian state he served as a political mentor. In the end, we shall resolve the problem of the many faces of Dracula and arrive at conclusions of our own.

Over the twenty years that have elapsed since the writing of our first book, both authors have continued and deepened their search into the details of the life of the historical Dracula. This exploration has taken us to a number of libraries and archives in western Europe, the United States, Romania, Yugoslavia, Russia, and Turkey. With the help of two Fulbright Research Exchange Fellowships, we have examined the genuine Dracula archives that are centered in the library of the Romanian Academy and the specialized books and articles at the Nicolae Iorga Historical Institute in Bucharest, as well as the Bruckhental Library at Sibiu and the Braşov Archives in Romania. Oddly enough, principal contributions to this book came from research done outside Romania. Visits to the Bayerische Staatsbibliothek in Munich and consultations at the Nuremberg State Archives were useful in obtaining additional information about the origins of the name Dracula and Dracula's father's investiture in the Dragon Order. We came across a series of some thirty-two Dracula stories in manuscript form, located at the library of the former monastery of Saint Gall, in Switzerland. We followed up this discovery by studying the complete poems of Michael Beheim, a minnesinger of the late fifteenth century, whose works are housed at the Library of Heidelberg University. These poems proved important, because they were based on firsthand information about Dracula given to

Beheim by a certain Benedictine monk, referred to as Brother Jacob. In a separate trip to the Soviet Union, we probed into the Dracula story by Fedor Kuritsyn, ambassador during the late fifteenth century from Moscow to the Hungarian court, who learned there about Dracula, since Dracula had lived there for over a decade, barely ten years before Kuritsyn's arrival. The authors also worked on documents in other western and eastern libraries and archives. These included the Vatican Secret Archives in Rome (Archivio Segreto Vaticano), especially the Corsiniano Collection, where we studied the accounts of Niccolò Modrussa, the papal legate to the Hungarian court, who had met Dracula personally and who wrote about him in a manuscript that has only partially been published in our day. We consulted historical documents in the Topkapî archives in Istanbul, especially the works of the Byzantine historian Kritoboulos, and compared the original texts with the standard translations. Study of the chronicle by the Byzantine historian Chalcondyles yielded important information and anecdotes about Dracula's campaign against the Turks. Reading the published reports of representatives from various Italian republics such as Venice, Genoa, Ferrara, Bologna, and Milan was significant in our toning down the negative image of Dracula. In America, at the Rosenbach Foundation Library in Philadelphia, we discovered the notes Bram Stoker used for the composition of his novel. Those provided additional evidence that the novelist framed his story within a solid historical and geographical context.

Where the actual documents or narratives failed, the co-authors studied the oral traditions preserved by the Romanian people in those regions where Dracula's name is best known, as in the villages surrounding his famous castle. Even allowing for the rich variety of documents in a number of different languages, the extraordinary coincidence of the Dracula sources, whether in terms of theme or basic plot, proves beyond doubt that they are rooted in historical fact.

Beyond the search in archives and the gathering of Romanian folklore at first hand, we engaged in extensive fieldwork with the help of local historians, those natives who are usually the best informed. In this endeavor, a few episodes stand out. Following in the footsteps of Brother Jacob, who had met Dracula, we were able to trace the changes his original atrocity story underwent in the course of his peregrinations from one Benedictine abbey to another. We located the grim and desolate fortress of Egrigöz in Asia Minor, where Dracula was imprisoned as a child. We found the tomb of one of Dracula's descendants, who had brought Dracula's portrait to the west. We visited Bistriţa in northeastern

Transylvania and discovered the remnants of a small fort at the Borgo Pass. We climbed to the fortress of Belgrade to experience its strategic location as a bastion of Eastern Orthodox Christendom. We located Königstein Castle along the road from Braşov to Cîmpulung on the ancient border between Transylvania and Wallachia, where the historical Dracula was taken prisoner in 1462.

As on past occasions, our search was a collaborative, interdisciplinary effort, which involved specialists from a wide variety of fields. Folklorists helped us gather Dracula narratives. Historians of art drew our attention to a number of new Dracula paintings, including one that may be a depiction of Dracula's father, recently discovered in the course of repairs to Dracula's homestead. Specialists in numismatics have discovered relevant old coins, including one showing Halley's comet on one side and Dracula's insignia on the other. Genealogical research has uncovered a Hungarian branch of the Dracula family in eastern Transylvania. Archaeologists aided us in probing into the remains of churches and castles associated with Dracula. All this work was facilitated by the research and publication program initiated by the Romanian government on the occasion of the five hundredth anniversary of Dracula's death in 1976.

Note on Spelling

S PELLINGS and variations of personal and geographical place names, when dealing with a multitude of languages, many of them unfamiliar to the English reader, always present somewhat of a problem. For the spelling of most of the well-known names, whether places, surnames, first names, et cetera, we have relied on Webster's *New Geographical Dictionary* (1984) and Webster's *New Biographical Dictionary* (1983). Most of the well-known historical figures as well as the internationally known place names are given in the way they are known best, usually with the Christian name anglicized. Thus we shall use Bucharest (rather than Bucureşti) and John Hunyadi (rather than the Hungarian Hunyadi János or Romanian Iancu de Hunedoara), to give two extreme instances. In the case of Transylvanian place names that have Romanian, German, and Hungarian equivalents, we shall use the modern Romanian form, except in the case of quotations, where the old German form will be substituted. To avoid confusion, all other place names will be given in their current forms. Christian names will be given in the form presently in use in each country, thus John in English, Jean in French, Johann in German, János in Hungarian, Ion in Romanian, Jan in Polish, et cetera. All diacritical and other accents will be used in the various eastern European languages, using the most recent forms. The Romanian ţ, for instance, which transliterates into English in *ts* sounds, while the ş is pronounced *sh;* thus the Impaler Ţepeş is pronounced *Tsepesh*. A special difficulty has been presented by the name Vladislav or Ladislas, which occurs frequently in our book, being the name of at least three major personalities. We shall use Ladislas for the Hungarian king (Ladislas V Posthumus), Ladislas for the Polish Jagiellonian kings Ladislas II and III, and Vladislav for Prince Vladislav II and III of Wallachia.

Dracula

PRINCE OF MANY FACES

PROLOGUE

From the Fictional to the Factual

W H E N they first read Bram Stoker's novel *Dracula,* the two co-authors were not convinced that this famous vampire plot belonged simply to the classical traditions of the Gothic horror romance, traditions of ghosts and rattling chains established in the late eighteenth century by Ann Radcliffe, Horace Walpole, and even John Polidori, with his imaginary vampire, Lord Ruthven, modeled on Lord Byron. Still less did they believe the theory advanced by Stoker's best biographer, Harry Ludlam (*A Biography of Dracula,* 1962), who informed his readers that the idea behind *Dracula* came from a nightmare caused by "a too generous helping of dressed crab at supper one night," a nightmare in which Stoker envisaged "a ghoul rising from the grave to go about its ghastly business." Nightmares, after all, have always been favorite literary devices, used by Mary Shelley and Robert Louis Stevenson, among many others, to camouflage all traces of borrowings from prior readings connected with their subjects. The claim of dream inspiration was meant to highlight the creative genius and originality of the author. For different reasons that will be explained in this book, many of our Romanian colleagues supported this explanation of the novel's genesis: *Dracula* was the product of the wild imagination of the author; the only thing the vampire shared with any historical prototype was the name. The reading public, on the whole, had endorsed these assessments.

Even a cursory glance at the novel reveals a significant difference from other gothic novels: *Dracula* mentions specific geographic locations, in both eastern Europe and in England, such as Whitby and sites in the greater London area. Most readers, however, believed that Transylvania, where the count's castle is located, was a "Ruritania," a "Never-Never-Land."

The story is first told through the diary and notes of an English solictor's clerk, Jonathan Harker, who is journeying from the west to the mysterious east, symbolized by northeastern Transylvania. He is going to complete a real estate transaction with a certain Count Dracula. Following a series of melodramatic encounters with Dracula at the count's castle on the Borgo Pass, during which the purchase of a property at Carfax Abbey near London is completed, Dracula sets out on his famous quest to vampirize England. He leaves Harker, who escapes from the count's castle and recovers slowly from his trauma in a hospital bed in Budapest, where he eventually marries his fiancée, Mina (Wilhelmina) Murray. In the meantime, the count travels, accompanied by seven boxes of his native Transylvanian soil, by boat from the Bulgarian port of Varna to Whitby in northern England. Shortly after landing, the count, who has already vampirized the whole crew of the boat in which he traveled, claims his first victim on English soil, Lucy Westenra, Mina Murray's best friend. Dracula then takes up residence at Carfax Abbey, hiding his boxes of Transylvanian soil at various locations along the Thames.

Once settled in, the count is finally ready for his horrific undertaking. Stoker compares Dracula's attack on London to a plague that causes instant death — for only a few choice victims attain the nirvana of the vampire's immortality. One can follow the count's deadly activity by means of the eccentric conduct of a patient called Renfield (who eats flies, spiders, et cetera) in a nearby insane asylum; Renfield is increasingly excited at the vampire's approach and clearly under his sway. This behavior, in turn, arouses the attention of Dr. John Seward, the director of that institution.

Eventually the "Dracula hunters" become organized, to ward off this insidious menace. They include Harker, Dr. Seward, Lucy's suitor, a Texan by the name of Quincey Morris, and lesser characters. They are led by Dr. Abraham Van Helsing from Amsterdam, a distinguished scholar and specialist in rare illnesses. The latter, the real hero of the novel and the character with whom Stoker secretly identifies, is able to convince his colleagues that conventional medicine is of little avail against the vampire and that they must rely on ancient folkloric rites involving herbal medicine, specifically garlic, and the religious ritual of the cross for added protection. Above all, they must find the seven hidden boxes containing the count's native soil, without which, according to genuine folklore, the vampire cannot rest during the day. (Stoker indulges in a lapse concerning this point when he mentions the vampire walking in broad daylight on Piccadilly.) All else failing, they must dispose of this living corpse in the traditional manner reenacted on the screen so many times: by driving a stake through his heart into the soil. Following a number of confrontations between hunted and hunters, Dracula feels sufficiently insecure to decide to flee back to his native castle in Transylvania. There he is finally killed at sundown by the Texan Quincey Morris, who plunges a bowie knife into his heart and puts the world at ease.

As previously remarked, it is the specific and detailed geographic context that sets this novel apart from earlier gothic novels and gives it its peculiar flavor. In challenging the conventional explanations of the novel's origins, the two co-authors were particularly impressed by the wealth of geographic, topographic, folkloric, historical, and even culinary details contained in the novel, but hardly ever explained. These are particularly evident in the gripping introductory and concluding chapters. Such details convinced the authors to challenge the predominant view of literary critics and historians. To begin with, we believed that Stoker did considerable research on eastern Europe and Romania in particular in preparation for his novel — particularly since he had never traveled to this part of the world.

Our sleuthing technique, at a century's distance, was to use Bram Stoker's novel as a guide, and to follow in the footsteps of the London lawyer's clerk, Jonathan Harker, as he set out on his extraordinary nineteenth-century journey from London, stopping initially at Munich. Like him, we stayed at the Hotel of the Four Seasons (Vierjahreszeiten Hotel), mentioned by Stoker in a chapter that was originally intended to be the introduction to the novel — but that ultimately appeared instead as a separate story, under the title "Dracula's Guest" (a few editions of the novel do in fact include it). We followed Harker's example and traveled on the express train from Munich to Vienna, which took us only a few hours — less than the "one night" mentioned in Harker's diary. From Vienna we went on to Budapest — which Stoker correctly spells in the old-fashioned way, "Buda-Pesth," since the two cities sit across each other on the Danube, the old capital being Buda. In Harker's words, the city represents a gateway to eastern Europe, dividing two worlds, though the traveler is hardly conscious today of "traditions of Turkish rule," mentioned by Harker. The journey from Budapest, Hungary to "Klausen-burgh" (Cluj), Transylvania (Stoker chose the anglicized German spelling of Cluj since in his time it was located within the Habsburg Empire), took us about six hours. We were loyal to Harker's selection of "the Hotel Royal," today called "Continental." German was no longer as useful a language there as it had been to Harker, since most of the Germans have gradually left Transylvania since World War II. Today the city contains large Romanian and Hungarian populations. Amazingly enough, the fare on the menu a century later was strikingly similar. One can still order "*paprika hendl*," chicken spiced with the hot paprika, though it is much more of a national dish for the Hungarians than the Romanians.

At Cluj, the largest city, we were in the heart of Transylvania. We noted the general correctness of Stoker's remarks about the ethnic composition of the country: "There are four distinct nationalities: Saxons in the south, . . . the Wallachs [the Romanians], who are the descendants of the Dacians; Magyars [Hungarians] in the west, and Szekelys in the east and north . . . who claim to be descended from Attila and the Huns." Harker is familiar with the historical fact that the Magyars settled the country in the eleventh century and that King Arpad was the founder of the dynasty (of whom the greatest ruler was St. Stephen, crowned by the pope in the year 1000 when Stephen converted to Catholicism). Unaware that he was tackling a most controversial issue of national precedence, Harker notes that when the Hungarians initially invaded this land, they found that Szeklers, the "so-called descendants" of the Huns, had already settled there — a moot point. He is more accurate in remarking that to these same "Szekelys" (Szeklers) was entrusted by the Hungarians "the guarding of the frontier . . . [the] endless duty of the frontier guard."

The following day when we got up, like Stoker's daring Englishman, we found that paprika chicken was readily available at the hotel, though not normally served with breakfast. The "*mămăligă*" that Harker describes as a "sort of porridge of maize flour" is still the national dish of the Romanian peasant (rather like polenta for the Italian). The eggplant "impletata" (*umplutură* in Romanian), however, though still a good native fare, was impossible to order at this early time of day. (We took Harker's advice and obtained the recipe, which is included in the latest Dracula cookbook published in the United States: *The Dracula Cookbook,* by Marina Polvay (1978).

During the day-long ride eastward from Cluj to "Bistritz," Harker has ample time to peer outside his carriage window and can make out enough of the countryside to describe it. His description, taken by Bram Stoker from the various travel guides of the period, is a far cry from the sinister, stark, and primeval landscape that has delighted movie scenarists and subsequent sensation-seeking writers of vampire tales. Quite the opposite is true and thus recorded by Harker: "the country . . . was full of beauty of every kind. Sometimes we saw little towns or castles on the top of steep hills . . . sometimes we ran by rivers and streams." He notices the density of forests: "oak, beech, and pine." (We were both heading toward Bukovina, which historically is known as beech-tree country.) We also saw the haystacks neatly laid along the hills "held by two or three stakes set in the ground."

As we observed the peasant types, we agreed with Harker's view "that the women looked pretty," even though "very clumsy about the waist," a characteristic from middle age onward, the result of a rich protein diet and physical labor. Harker admires and accurately describes the native national dress. "They had all full white sleeves of some kind or other, and most of them had big belts with a lot of strips of something fluttering from them like the dresses in a ballet but of course petticoats under them." The presence of the Czechs and particularly the Slovaks whom Harker encountered is perfectly plausible at a time when all these lands were part of the Austro-Hungarian Empire, and Slovakia a close neighbor controlled by Hungary. The solicitor's clerk notes the fact that the people are both religious and superstitious, which is still the case especially among the older generation. Harker notices "by the roadside . . . many crosses." Superstitions of all kinds actually do abound, particularly in this northern, more remote area of the country, where the peasants still believe in a strange dichotomy between the forces of good and the power of evil against which they must protect themselves. They fear the "*nosferatu*" (*necuratul,* literally "the unclean one," meaning in Romanian the devil); Harker mentions *Ördög,* the Hungarian word for Satan, and *pokol* (hell), "*stregoica*" (*strigoiacă,* female vampire, in Romanian), as well as the Slovak word *vrolok* and the Serbian *vlkoslak,* "for something that is either were-wolf or vampire." For some reason Harker chose to limit his remarks to the Romanian female equivalent *strigoiacă,* perhaps because they are said to be more mischievous than their male counterpart. (The more commonly accepted word *vampire* is Slavic rather than Romanian.) Van Helsing, who uses the word *nosferatu* in chapter XVIII, is well aware that the peasant has recourse to the powers of the church (the use of holy water, the symbolism of the cross, et cetera) and to various forms of herbal medicine such as garlic, wolfbane, or the petals of wild roses, and makes use of all of them in combating the vampire. The stake (made of wood or iron) must be relied on only as a last resort.

We finally reached the town of "Bistritz" (today Bistriţa). We found that Harker was correct in his description of its general location "in the extreme east of the country, just on the borders of three states, Transylvania, Moldavia, and Bukovina, in the midst of the Carpathian mountains." (At the time Transylvania and Bukovina belonged to the Austro-Hungarian Empire, while Moldavia was part of the old kingdom of Romania. Today, of course, Stoker's Dracula country is part of the modern Romanian state, though half or Bukovina was ceded to the Soviet Union at the end of World War II. The traveler, at this point, is thus not too far distant from the Soviet-Romanian border.)

At Bistriţa Harker was aware of recent tragic events that had left their mark on the city at the time of his visit. "Fifty years ago a series of great fires took place, which made terrible havoc on five separate occasions. At the very beginning of the seventeenth century it [Bistritz] underwent a siege of three weeks and lost 13,000 people, the casualties of war proper being assisted by famine and disease." All traces of this specific nineteenth-century calamity, which is known only to local historians, have long since disappeared. Superstitious peasants "crossing them-selves" and discouraging anyone from proceeding eastward are a thing of the past — if they ever existed. We should note, however, that an abandoned fortress giving off flames of various hues at night is still looked upon as an evil place and avoided by the local people.

As you proceed toward the Borgo Pass, which in Romanian is known as Prundu Bîrgăului (Stoker, in fact, mentions "Borgo Prund"), the description of Jonathan Harker is as authentic today as it must have been at the time. He did not find the region particularly gloomy. Indeed quite the opposite was true: "Before us lay a green sloping land full of forests and woods, with here and there steep hills, crowned with clumps of trees or with farmhouses, the blank gable end to the road. There was everywhere a bewildering mass of fruit blossom — apple, plum, pear, cherry; and as we drove by I could see the green grass under the trees spangled with the fallen petals." At the Borgo Pass Harker finally reaches Count Dracula's castle. He speaks of a "vast ruined castle, from whose tall black windows came no ray of light, and whose broken battlements showed a jagged line against the moonlit sky." The adventures of the Dracula hunters led by Van Helsing at the novel's conclusion are described with the same eye for geographic and topographic detail as is found in the introductory chapters. The meticulous details of these final peregrinations, like those of Harker's first journey into Transylvania, are truly amazing for the period and imply consultation of a very detailed map of the area, not readily available today.

Given such geographic minutiae, and quite accurate descriptions of the countryside and the ethnic origins of the people, we wondered why Stoker would be any less conscientious in researching a possible historical prototype for his vampire count. Indeed, there is a great deal of evidence, which Stoker hints at by way of his characters, particularly Dr. Van Helsing, that he consulted genuine historical sources about the man, as about all else. Van Helsing makes this point by emphasizing the knowledge that he has gained "from the researches of my friend Arminius of Buda-Pesth," referring to Arminius Vambery, a notable scholar and orientalist in his own right, who often traveled from Budapest to London. Van Helsing, as Stoker's alter ego, goes scurrying for information to the British Museum, at that time the largest library and source of knowledge in the world. From this research and other historical sources to which we shall refer there emerges a composite picture — admittedly sketchy — of an authentic historical character who bore at least some of the characteristics of the historical Dracula. This living prototype was sufficiently intriguing for Stoker to embark on what might be described as a mini-research, derived from a variety of books available at the time that focused on some of Dracula's more memorable deeds and various aspects of his complex personality. The result of such readings is an adequate physical description of Dracula the vampire, not too far removed from the authentic physical traits of Dracula the man, which we shall later describe. Stoker sees him as "a tall old man, clean shaven save for a long white moustache." He has a waxen face, a high aquiline nose, and parted red lips. He was "clad in black from head to foot" — a description not unlike the dragon cape of the real Dracula. Stoker is aware of Dracula's aristocratic origins: Dracula says, "Here I am noble; I am *boyar;* the common people know me, and I am master." The word *boyar,* borrowed from Slavic lands, in Romanian signifies a member of the landowning nobility. Harker has a "long talk" with Dracula, poses "questions on Transylvanian history," and notices that "he warmed up to the subject wonderfully." Dracula explains his enthusiasm for leading figures in Transylvanian history by saying that "to a *boyar* the pride of his house and name is his own pride." Occasionally Dracula seems so confident of his fame that he dispenses with titles altogether, simply styling himself "Dracula," as did the historical personality, who signed correspondence without using any title at the end of his career. Beyond

knowing Dracula's noble origins, Stoker is also acquainted with the title
voivode, a Slavic word that the Romanians translate as "prince," by
which the historical Dracula was also known; *hospodar,* was also used
frequently as late as the nineteenth century and meant "ruler" or
"governor." It is yet another historically correct denomination used in
the novel. Though Stoker is quite right in pointing out that Dracula's
ancestry goes back to "wolf country" (the Dacians or ancestors of the
Romanians often described themselves as "wolfmen," and their standard
was the head of a wolf with the body of a snake), he is mistaken in
considering the count a descendant of the Szeklers who carried the blood
of Attila in his veins — but this is an error which we will try to account
for at the end of this book.

Beyond accuracy, there is unqualified admiration on Stoker's part,
expressed through the words of Van Helsing, for many of Dracula's
character traits and for his truly exceptional preparation for rule. Van
Helsing speaks of his "mighty brain," his study of "new tongues," a
"learning beyond compare," in politics, law, finance, and science, even
of "the occult" which "the Draculas" learned at Sibiu "over lake
Hermanstadt" (at a place where young students known as *Şolomonari* in
Romania were introduced to the science of alchemy). Harker is struck by
the count's hospitality ("Welcome to my house"), a traditional character
trait of the Romanian people, particularly vis-à-vis foreigners. He agrees
with Van Helsing that the count "was in life a most wonderful man" with
"a mighty brain" and an "iron resolution." Van Helsing categorizes
Dracula's various roles as a "soldier, statesman, and alchemist." But he
accurately stresses his capacities as a warrior and leader of men, "a heart
that knew no fear and no remorse."

Through Van Helsing, Stoker is most explicit about the historical roots
of his fictional count. Van Helsing thinks he can identify Dracula the
vampire's historical prototype: "He must, indeed, have been that
Voivode Dracula who won his Name against the Turk, over the great
river on the very frontier of Turkey-land [meaning the Danube]. If it be
so, then was he no common man; for in that time, and for centuries after,
he was spoken of as the cleverest and most cunning, as well as the bravest
of the sons of the 'land beyond the forest.'" Dracula speaks of "one of
my race who as Voivode crossed the Danube and beat the Turk on his
ground." Stoker is not quite as charitable when referring to Dracula's
brother Radu the Handsome: "Woe was it that his own unworthy brother,
when he had fallen, sold his people to the Turk and brought the shame of
slavery on them!" All of the above are essentially correct references to

events directly or indirectly connected with the authentic Dracula, and Stoker makes many other such allusions. In the novel, for instance, he cites the fact that the Hungarians experienced a defeat at the hands of the Turks, "the shame of Cassova," drawing the reader's attention to the second battle of Kosovo Polje in 1448, as a result of which Dracula began his brief first reign with Turkish help. Stoker also displays acquaintance with the events leading to the defeat of the Hungarian army at Mohácz in 1526, a prophecy the historical Dracula clearly made because the Hungarian king was unwilling to come to his help in 1462. Toward the end of the novel the Dracula hunters testify that Dracula as a last resort relies on being defended by gypsies, a fact not entirely removed from historical truth. Stoker even discovered an indirect descendant of Dracula's important enough to be mentioned twice in the text: ". . . was it not this Dracula, indeed, who inspired that other of his race who in a later age again and again brought his forces over the great river into Turkey-land; who, when he was beaten back, came again and again, and again, though he had to come alone from the bloody field where his troops were being slaughtered, since he knew that he alone could ultimately triumph?" Possibly the author was referring to Michael the Brave, the prince who first achieved the unity of all the Romanian lands, an indirect descendant of one of Dracula's half-brothers, Vlad the Monk. Thus Dracula, irrespective of his obvious vampire characteristics, is hardly the by-product of a nightmare or an overwrought imagination of an author obsessed with the occult. Though admittedly a composite character, he is in part the product of serious readings on Stoker's part that we shall analyze in detail. Stoker was, in any case, sufficiently inspired by his research to give a historical dimension to his famous count, which added an important element to his personality. Prince, statesman, war leader, endowed with a cunning, mighty brain, a resolute politician, a linguist . . . Dracula the man sounds enticing enough, even in the novel. In one final document allegedly discovered by Arminius Vambery, Dracula is also referred to as a " 'wampyr,' which we all understand too well," which in essence means blood-drinker. Given a tantalizing character such as this, whose creation required extensive research by the novelist, we are ready to take up Stoker's cues and embark upon the life history of the real Dracula, a fifteenth-century ruler remembered by Romania's first nineteenth-century scientific historian, A. D. Xenopol, as "one of the most fascinating personalities of history." Indeed the fictional vampire pales by comparison.

CHAPTER I

The World of the Real Dracula

The Crusade against the Turks

THE real Dracula, who ruled the territories that now constitute Romania, was born in 1431, the year that Joan of Arc was burned as a witch at the stake in Rouen, France. He died in 1476, two years before Spain was united as a kingdom under the rule of Isabella of Castile and Ferdinand of Aragon. He was very much the by-product of the Europe of his day — the Renaissance, essentially a period of transition. Though the Renaissance helped usher in the modern age, with its accent on nationalism and secularism that is still very characteristic of our epoch, the old medieval structures of feudalism and the all-pervasive authority of the church had not as yet, in Dracula's time, entirely broken down.

Europe, from the Atlantic Ocean to the Black Sea and the Baltic coast, represented during this period much more of a single civilization, connected by solid dynastic and cultural ties, than the contemporary world, or even Europe, does today. The notion of an east and west division, which still permeates our college courses in "western civilization" and our current "iron curtain" way of thinking, dividing western democracies from the eastern European socialist states, would have made little sense to a contemporary of Dracula. There are those who tend to reduce European history to a clash of forces between the west, with its legacy of high culture inherited from Greece and Rome, and the despotism of Asia. Since time immemorial, that conflict had been waged on the borderlands of this common European civilization against various destructive alien nomad forces coming from Asia. In Dracula's day, the latest and most crucial manifestation of this conflict was represented by the Ottoman Turks, who initially set foot on European soil in the middle of the fourteenth century.

The designation *Ottoman* is derived from Othman, one of their early leaders. The Ottomans had been converted to the fundamentalist teachings of Islam by Turkoman tribes of Asia Minor whom they subjugated. Our image of the Turks may still be largely colored by nineteenth-century attitudes formed when individual sultans, attempting to stave off the inevitable symptoms of internal decay of their empire, massacred Greeks, Armenians, and Bulgarians on a massive scale. These subjugated peoples were subverting the Ottoman Empire, in the process of attempting to form nation states of their own. This oversimplified negative image of the Turks ought not to be applied without serious qualifications to Turkish rule in Dracula's time.

In fact, quite the reverse was true: the two great sultans of the Dracula era, Murad II (1421–1451) and, more directly, Mehmed II (1451–1481), in whose company our young prince was brought up, were, like their predecessors, splendid, worldly, and cultured personalities who patronized Italian artists and married the daughters of Balkan and Byzantine rulers. They were also farsighted politicians who taught Europe the lessons of religious toleration, by granting asylum to Jews and members of other minorities at a time when these minorities were being persecuted by the Roman Catholic church.

The Turks first crossed the Dardanelles Straits, which separate Europe from Asia, in 1353, summoned by the emperors of Byzantium to resist pressures from the Balkan states, particularly the Serbian kings, who had their eye on the imperial title. To strengthen their bonds with the Turks, several Byzantine emperors actually gave their daughters in marriage to sultans. Once having set foot on European soil, however, the Turks were not easily dislodged. Initially they turned on Bulgaria, which had at one time been a most powerful Balkan state. Bulgaria was partially defeated in 1371. Northern Serbia offered greater resistance, but on June 15, 1389, Sultan Murad I's son Bayezid, "the Lightning," destroyed the armies of the Serbian prince Lazar at the first battle of Kosovo Polje (the Field of Black Birds). This decisive defeat opened up the rest of Bulgaria, Albania, and most of the Balkan peninsula to Turkish penetration. All that was left of Serbia was a semiautonomous state under the rule of George Branković, who bore the Byzantine title of *despot*. Branković survived on sufferance, because he had given his daughter Mara as wife to another sultan, Murad II. For safekeeping, he handed his capital, Belgrade, to the Hungarians in 1420.

In effect, the Turks had advanced their frontier to the Danube, the border of what would eventually be Dracula's land, which at the time represented the frontier of European civilization. Although the Ottoman conquerors were Muslims, they did not force the subjugated people of the Balkans to convert to Islam. In fact, the majority of the subject peoples remained faithful to Eastern Orthodox Christianity. Nevertheless, the Christians of the Balkans, reduced to second-class status, resented the domination of an alien creed under a sultan who combined supreme political and religious powers. Many were also outraged by the Turkish system of recruiting the finest among the Christian male children of the Balkans, taking them away from their parents at a tender age, forcibly indoctrinating them in the new religion, and inducting them into the army. These special troops were called janissaries; some of them fought in infantry corps — though technically slaves could rise to the level of their abilities in either military or civil service — and many of them ended up as viziers (prime ministers) to successive sultans. It was, however, the induction of the most gifted youth of the conquered territories that drained the Balkans of the flower of its manhood and at the same time gained for the Turks their military supremacy. This was considered one of the most devilish, and perhaps unique, methods of world conquest among all those yet devised by humankind.

The east (Turkish) versus west (Christian) confrontation was looked upon by some as a conflict between two systems of values and two cultures, much as the conflict between communism and western democracy is seen today. However, since in frontier areas values were at times hopelessly intermingled, it is best to view the struggle of the Dracula era as arising from the inordinate ambitions of Mehmed II, a conqueror of the stamp of Alexander the Great, who was ready to invoke the spirit of a Holy War to achieve world domination. Dracula, Mehmed's contemporary, educated by the same tutors and holding identical sets of values, perhaps understood the crucial importance of this struggle better than any of his European contemporaries did. Had the surviving free states of eastern and central Europe not been determined to resist these ambitions, it is just conceivable that the Muslim world would have extended from the Bosporus to the Atlantic seaboard.

It was in the age of Dracula that the notion was introduced of Balkan crusading, the efforts of the lands on the fringes of the Ottoman conquest, the borderlands of Europe, to resist the power of Islam in the name of the cross. It represented a struggle in defense of Europe quite as significant as the Spanish resistance to the Moors, which had preceded it. In many

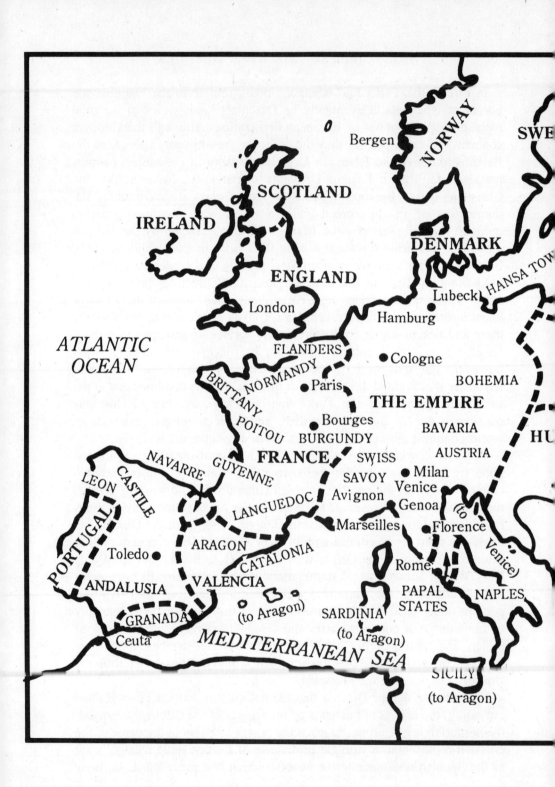

EUROPE
IN DRACULA'S TIME

DEN

NS

TEUTONIC ORDER

Novgorod

DUCHY OF MOSCOW

LITHUANIA

POLAND

• Kiev

• Krakow

TATARS' GOLDEN
HORDE

MOLDAVIA

NGARY

TRANSYLVANIA

WALLACHIA

CRIMEA

CAFFA
(to Genoa)

Belgrade

Danube R.

BLACK SEA

SERBIA

BULGARIA

Constantinople

TREBIZOND

OTTOMAN TURKS

AEGEAN SEA

CRETE

(to Venice)

60 miles
100 km

Budapest

Hungary

Cluj

BISTRI

TRANSYL

VAN

AMLAS

SIBIU

Mures R.

CARPATHIAN
MOUNTAINS

FAGA

HUNEDOARA

BANAT
OF
SEVERIN

TURNU
ROSU

COZIA

TISMANA
SEVERIN

WALLACHI

Belgrade

GLAVACIOC

SMEDEREVO

Olt R.

Turkish Serbia

Danube R.

Turkish

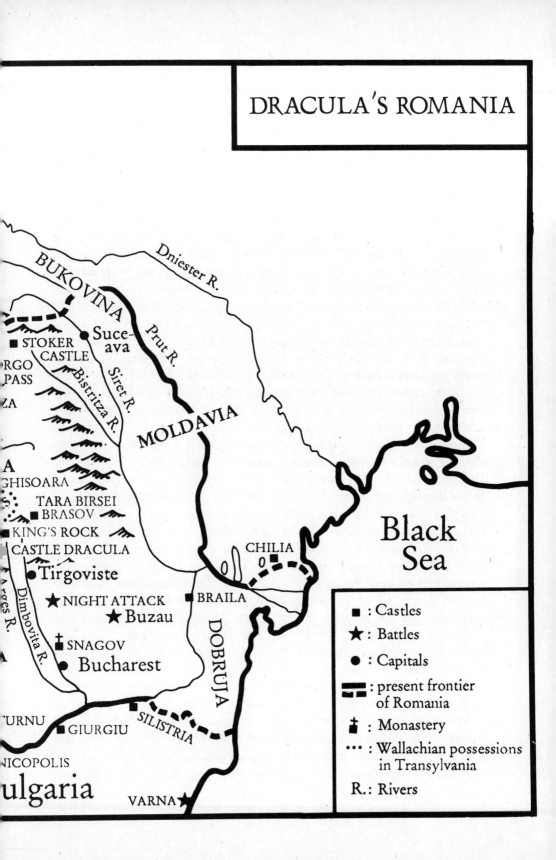

DRACULA'S ROMANIA

BUKOVINA

Dniester R.

Prut R.

Siret R.

Bistritza R.

Suce-ava

STOKER CASTLE

RGO PASS

ZA

MOLDAVIA

A

GHISOARA

TARA BIRSEI

BRASOV

KING'S ROCK

CASTLE DRACULA

Tirgoviste

NIGHT ATTACK

Buzau

Dimbovita R.

Arges R.

SNAGOV

Bucharest

BRAILA

DOBRUJA

CHILIA

Black Sea

URNU

GIURGIU

SILISTRIA

NICOPOLIS

ulgaria

VARNA

■ : Castles

★ : Battles

● : Capitals

▬▬ : present frontier of Romania

† : Monastery

••• : Wallachian possessions in Transylvania

R.: Rivers

respects it was more significant than the crusades of the eleventh and twelfth centuries, aimed at delivering the holy places in Jerusalem, because the defense of the European continent itself was involved.

At the gates of Europe stood the skeletal remains of the once mighty Byzantine Empire, with its proud leading city of Constantinople, built by Constantine in the year 330 at the site of Byzantium, a former Greek city-state at the Bosporus. Though heir to imperial Rome and thus often referred to as the East Roman Empire, its spoken language was Greek. The Byzantine church had separated itself from Rome in 1054 because the bishop of Constantinople refused to be subordinate to the bishop of a rival city that had fallen into decadence and barbarism — theological differences were manufactured later to justify the split. Extremely proud of its thousand-year-old history, Constantinople also claimed cultural and political superiority to the ''upstart'' medieval emperors, who had initially been established by the pope with Charlemagne's coronation in the year 800, and their successors. The empire was still immensely prestigious in the early 1400s, and the city acted as a magnet for powerful would-be conquerors from both the east and the west. They were all the more attracted because the city had lost its reputation for military invincibility since its occupation by Venice in 1204. The Eastern Orthodox emperors of Byzantium had frittered away their strength, fighting Roman Catholic crusaders and their Balkan rivals, specifically Bulgarian and Serbian rulers intent upon securing the imperial crown. When Dracula was born, Constantinople and its European hinterland still survived, like a salamander with an enormous head and an elongated body, that included the holy mountain, Athos, the despotate of Mistra, Thessaloniki, and a few islands in the Aegean Sea.

One of the more tragic aspects of the Turkish onslaught on Europe was the western powers' reluctance to defend the frontiers of their culture in eastern Europe. This extraordinary failure of moral fortitude was not intelligible in the fifteenth century, since French ruling families had originally consolidated the Polish and Hungarian states; Venetians, Pisans, Genoese, and Spaniards ruled in the eastern Mediterranean and Aegean seas; and countless western adventurers occupied a string of threatened colonies along the disputed eastern coast and on the islands near what are now Yugoslavia and Greece.

The pretexts for the fifteenth-century failure of the west to respond to successive crusading appeals were no different from those that had awakened such deep emotional response during the heyday of the crusades, in the age of faith. Charles VII, king of France, the oldest daughter of the Catholic church and foremost crusading power, had just emerged from one of the most crucial conflicts in his country's history, the Hundred Years' War. He and his soon-to-be successor, Louis XI, "the Spider King," who had a predilection for hanging young boys from the branches of trees and placing his enemies in cages to consolidate royal power, had just liberated their country from the English. The French kings were also busy fighting the dukes of Burgundy for supremacy in the French state. The semiroyal dukes of Burgundy were in fact the only rulers within the actual territories of what is now France who for a time remained true to the crusading tradition. Their generous participation in Dracula's father's crusade in 1446 atoned somewhat for the ineffectiveness of their cousins in Paris.

England was to be no more closely drawn than France into fighting the Muslims; the traditions of Richard the Lionhearted were entirely forgotten. Two rival families there were locked in a desperate struggle for survival, the Wars of the Roses (1455–1485). (The white rose was the symbol of the followers of the Duke of York and the red rose represented the House of Lancaster.) This last of England's feudal wars dragged on throughout Dracula's lifetime. The only Englishmen connected in any way to our plot were individual soldiers of fortune who enrolled as volunteers in various crusading armies. (One of these veterans, John Tiptoft, Earl of Worcester, later used the impalement technique that he had learned in eastern Europe to kill his Lancastrian enemies. He was executed for his crimes.)

Medieval Spain, apart from a few northern kingdoms that had survived as independent states, had actually experienced the trauma of Muslim conquest, though the Arabs, unlike the Turks, had their own sophisticated form of civilization, which still survives in the finely sculptured mosques of Córdoba, at that time a center of learning more advanced than Paris and Oxford, particularly in the disciplines of science and mathematics. These free kingdoms had gradually succeeded in liberating the territory in a series of wars, the Reconquista, which had deeply stamped themselves upon the character of the people, particularly in the kingdom of Castile: the inhabitants were fanatically Catholic and intolerant and were prepared for almost any sacrifice in defense of their land. Though they were crusaders at home, the Castilians, once freed of Muslim control, were not equally concerned about the struggle in the east against the Turks. Geography undoubtedly had a great deal to do with this reaction. Like the Portuguese, who, under their navigator king, Henry, looked westward to the sea for expansion — the circumnavigation of Africa, exploration of the Far East — the Castilians were eventually also led to the discovery and conquest of a new continent, under Queen Isabella. She was to become the patron of Christopher Columbus, born ten years before Dracula became prince.

Of the lands of the future Kingdom of Spain, only Aragon faces eastward. In particular, the Catalans of Barcelona, an important Mediterranean port, were concerned by the Turkish menace, because it threatened ancient commercial routes and their appetite for eastern expansion. Even before Dracula's time, an effective group of military adventurers had been formed, the famous Catalan Company, to defend the Byzantine emperors against all their enemies, though in effect the Catalans fought for themselves. The Aragonese wished, through Balkan crusading, to forge commercial and political contacts with the Aegean, the Adriatic, and the Black Sea. The ambitions of the Aragonese king, Alfonso V, are best exemplified by the decision of his bastard son Ferrante to make Naples — closer to the eastern theater of war — the center of his power. Ferrante managed to perpetuate his rule through the use of terror: having killed most of his political opponents, he had his victims mummified and placed in the royal museum, where they were shown to his guests.

Fifteenth-century Italy was the headquarters of the Renaissance. Although Niccolò Machiavelli was not born until 1469, the amoral principles he would set out in *The Prince* (1517) were being applied well ahead of publication. There was certainly little evidence then of Italian patriotism among the warring republics and city-states of northern Italy, and less evidence of crusading spirit, though the straits of Otranto, at the heel of the peninsula, separate Italy from the Balkans by only some thirty miles.

In the north, the prestigious Medici were more interested in making money by establishing the first international bank in Europe, assuredly another symptom of the modernism of the age. They used the resources of the powerful bank, with its numerous affiliates in various capitals, to finance trade, indulge in the frills of a luxurious life, win political and papal elections, and buy marriage connections with the noblest of families, including blue blooded royalty. Cosimo, in a sense the founder of the dynasty, became the self-styled sponsor of the classical renaissance. Later, his grandson, Lorenzo the Magnificent, destroyed the last vestiges of constitutional government in the north. In other Italian states, political standards had sunk to an abysmal low as the medieval communes had their liberties subverted by tyrannicide. This period in Italy (and elsewhere) was also the age of the ambitious and unscrupulous autocrats sometimes referred to as the *condottieri*. These men were guided solely by ambition in seeking to acquire political power, by any means possible, even destroying whole rival families in the process.

The papacy, which controlled Rome and the central neck of the Italian peninsula as a temporal power, was in difficulties that greatly weakened its natural role in any crusade and siphoned off the prestige it had gained by having led the crusading movement in the past. At the time, the church was still recovering from the most dangerous crisis in its history, when two popes, one in Rome, the other at Avignon, vied for supremacy. The great church council summoned at Basel in 1431, the year of Dracula's birth, to resolve this conflict was followed by the danger compounded when the Holy Roman Emperor attempted to substitute "government by cardinals" for the rule of a single pope. This far more serious threat was resisted with alacrity by the Venetian pope Eugenius IV and his chief spokesman, Giuliano Cardinal Cesarini, both of whom were to be closely connected with Balkan crusading in the 1440s.

In essence, papal energies were aimed at diverting attention from the problems within the Roman church by working at healing the schism between Eastern Orthodoxy and Roman Catholicism, which had divided the two churches since 1054. Reunion, in fact, was to be the precondition for a joint eastern and western crusade against the Turks. A historic agreement was reached, at least on paper, at the Council of Florence in 1439, helped by the presence of the emperor of Constantinople, John VIII. However, many of the Orthodox bishops, notably the Russians and the Romanians, refused to append their signatures to the final document. Eugenius's successor, Pope Nicholas V, finally reasserted the authority of Saint Peter by compelling the resignation of all rival popes, thereby ending the internal danger to the papacy. He made less progress, however, in implementing the reunion between the two churches. And, rather than go crusading, this splendid figure, who made Rome the headquarters of the Renaissance, preferred to collect Greek and Latin manuscripts, founded the Vatican Library, patronized dangerous critics such as the humanist Lorenzo Valla, and reconstructed St. Peter's Church in the style of a Roman basilica. As a man of peace he showed little concern, even for the fate of Constantinople, which fell to the Turks under his pontificate. However, guilt for this neglect ultimately shortened his life.

It was the pontificate (1458–1464) of Enea Silvio de' Piccolomini, the future Pope Pius II, that most closely coincided with Dracula's reign. Piccolomini began his career as a libertine not devoid of literary talent and changed his ways only when he became a priest in 1446. He was enough of a medievalist to understand the threat inherent in the Ottoman expansion.

From 1459 onward the pope repeatedly appealed to the Christian powers to join in a common crusade, and he raised the monies to subsidize such a concerted movement. Indeed, Pius II, a thorough "Europeanist," saw the Ottoman menace not merely as a danger for eastern Europe but for Christianity itself. Dracula alone responded to his call.

The Republic of Venice faced the Balkans from its lagoon on the Adriatic; its chief commercial rival, Genoa, was located on the Mediterranean gulf bearing its name. Genoa held colonies along the Black Sea and the Crimea, and Pera, a suburb of Constantinople, lay under its control. Thwarted in the Italies, Venice also was compelled to turn to eastern conquest for commercial expansion in the Levant. The Venetians were a Balkan power by virtue of having annexed a string of cities along the Adriatic coast, of which Ragusa (now the Yugoslav resort town of Dubrovnik) was the queen city. With their fleet in absolute control of eastern Mediterranean waters, the Venetians also secured, by purchase or otherwise, a number of colonies on the tip of the Greek peninsula, including Athens, Salonika, and many islands in the Aegean Sea. In essence, Venice controlled most of the southern and western tier of the Balkan peninsula, and its merchants made the Venetian ducat legal tender throughout the Balkans. Yet the ruling senate was reluctant to challenge the Turks, relying on diplomacy to keep the republic out of war. However, as Turkish expansion began to threaten their bases, some of the republic's diplomats began to show interest in Dracula's determination to resist the Turks — though Venice joined the crusade only in 1464, when it was already too late to save the prince.

Though it was more immediately threatened by the Turks, the Holy Roman Empire, as well as the surviving powers of northern central and eastern Europe, was no more ready to defend its threatened autonomy, with very few exceptions. To take an example of relative apathy in the face of the Turkish menace in northeastern Europe, Ivan III (the Great), geographically distant from Dracula's country, sent occasional merchantmen into Turkish waters and patronized Renaissance artists and architects, having them build many of the imposing monuments in the Kremlin. He intended no crusading, but merely wished to deepen his knowledge of the Western world when he finally decided to establish an embassy at the court of the Hungarian king, Matthias. The mission was led by Fedor Kuritsyn, who at the end of his service wrote a fascinating political tract based on Dracula's life.

This lack of moral fiber was particularly evident in the case of the Germanies — the Holy Roman Empire, which, unlike Russia on its easternmost fringes, was more dangerously threatened by the Turkish conquest. Including bishoprics, free cities, and larger and smaller princely states, there were over three hundred "Germanies" in Dracula's time, inhabited by people of various ethnic and linguistic backgrounds. The only common denominators within this amorphous, multilingual state (which, according to Voltaire, was "neither holy, nor Roman," and which was by no means exclusively Germanic in character) were the emperor and the waning influence of the Catholic church. Unlike other western states, where the principle of primogeniture was well established, Holy Roman Emperors were elected by a special committee composed of the heads of three archbishoprics and four principalities. The tendency of these electors was to try to select weak candidates who were unlikely to interfere with the power of the feudal states. The election of Sigismund, the son of Charles IV, emperor of Luxemburg, crowned German emperor in 1411, was an exception, and he was destined to make at least one major attempt at crusading. This may have been because in 1387, before his election, he had already succeeded to the throne of Hungary (in essence an eastern European power), having taken as his wife Mary, the daughter of the last French king of Hungary and Poland, Louis the Great. Thus there was established between Hungary and the Holy Roman Empire a dynastic link that was to last until the end of World War I. In addition, on the death of Sigismund's half-brother Wenceslas in 1419, Sigismund became king of Bohemia as well.

When Sigismund died in 1437, his three kingdoms were eventually transferred to Albert of Habsburg, the ruler of the tiny Austrian duchy, who had married Sigismund's daughter Elizabeth. Never elected emperor, Albert II ruled for only two years. His son Ladislas, born after the death of his father (hence his sobriquet Posthumus), became the heir to Austria, Bohemia, and Hungary, though he could not effectively rule until he should come of age. Vienna, the seat of Ladislas's government, was located, like Buda, on the Danube and thus dangerously exposed to Turkish attack. But with Albert's passing, the real arbiter of the eastern European situation, and the leader of the anti-Ottoman crusade, became John Hunyadi, viceroy of Hungary and governor general (voivode) of Transylvania. He was also for a time the political and military mentor of Dracula.

The imperial title was next bestowed upon the Habsburg Frederick III (1440–1493), the last Holy Roman Emperor to be crowned in Rome (1452, though he had been king of Germany, as Frederick IV, since Albert's death), who showed little taste for crusading. He was more interested in maintaining the illusion that as duke of Austria he, rather than Hunyadi's son and successor, Matthias, was the legitimate king of

Hungary, since the crown of St. Stephen, which alone conferred legitimacy, was kept safely hidden in the vaults of his palace at Wiener Neustadt. (The symbolic holy crown, topped by a heavy golden cross and bedecked with precious jewels, was originally given by Pope Sylvester II to the first king of Hungary, St. Stephen, in the year 1000, to commemorate Hungary's entry into the Christian community of states through the king's conversion to Catholicism.) In order to while away the long wintry nights at his desolate court at Wiener Neustadt, Frederick engaged the services of one Michael Beheim, a soldier of fortune and German *Meistersinger,* who composed a famous poem on the subject of Dracula.

Poland was now by far the most powerful eastern European state. Its power was achieved in 1384, when the second daughter of Louis the Great of Hungary, Jadwiga (whose older sister, Mary, had been Emperor Sigismund's first wife), then barely ten years old, married the pagan Lithuanian grand duke Jagiello, on the condition that he accept conversion to Catholicism. He took the Christian name Ladislas II. With this union was born a vast confederation of states, which stretched from the Baltic coast across the Ukraine to the Black Sea, sustained by the intensive Catholicism of its people, the courage of its kings, and the chivalry of its nobles. Ladislas III, son of Jagiello, became the spiritual leader of two successive crusades, and perished in battle as a knight, fighting the Turks in the company of Dracula's older brother. His successor, Casimir IV (1447–1492), did not live up to this tradition, in part because of the threat of insurgent German pressures in the Baltic, Crimean Tatars in the Ukraine, and the ambitions of Grand Duke Ivan III of Moscow.

Thus, in a confrontational world more interested in the acquisition of political power, the accumulation of material wealth, and the elimination of the tired vestiges of the monopoly once exercised by the Roman Catholic church, whether one looked east or west, there were few states indeed ready to rekindle the Crusader spirit. Dracula's country represented one of the few exceptions.

An Era of Transition

Though assuredly Italy was the tutor and propagator of classicism, humanism, and scientific inventiveness, it would be erroneous to believe that these movements did not spread to the eastern borderlands of European civilization. At the University of Krakow, established in 1364, the mathematician Nicolaus Copernicus was now in the process of discovering a new universe that centered on the sun; thereby he advanced enormously the science of astronomy. At the University of Prague, founded by Sigismund's father, Charles IV, in 1348, the Renaissance assumed more of a theological and philosophical bent; the languages of instruction included both Czech and German, a concession to the principle of coexistence among peoples. The summer palace of King Matthias I at Visegrád, where Dracula spent many years of house arrest, was rebuilt almost entirely by Italian artisans and architects. Indeed, it was in this summer palace that Dracula's portrait was painted by a court artist, the first color and oil reproduction of a prince of the future Romanian lands.

As for the invention of the printing press, historians speculate to this day whether Johannes Gutenberg or Fust of Mainz was the actual inventor of the mobile type that made printing on a large scale possible. Regardless, printers at Buda and Krakow knew the art at least five years before William Caxton had opened up his press in England at the end of 1476. In 1463 the first broadside about Dracula was printed in Vienna; it circulated in German initially as political propaganda to justify Dracula's arrest. Later during the fifteenth century Dracula "horror stories" were printed in Leipzig, Augsburg, Stuttgart, Strassburg, Nuremberg, and many other German cities.

On a darker note, one of the most terrifying inventions associated with this period of technological progress in Europe was that of gunpowder, with its deafening noise and bright flash. It revolutionized warfare by making killing much easier than it had been during the Middle Ages, with the refined set of dos and don'ts instilled into the code of chivalry, which formed the most important aspect of the education of a young knight. The candidate was taught to respect human life, protect women and children, and observe the right of an enemy to seek sanctuary in a church. From the Renaissance onward, wars involved paid professionals who had little or no concern for the sanctity of human life. They were taught to kill, not to maim or to disarm. No distinction between soldiers and civilians was to be made any longer. The cannon, the monopoly of the tyrant, used by Dracula's armies, was the supreme instrument of destruction, and only exceedingly thick walls could save civilian populations from its devastations.

In addition to this new and more terrible kind of warfare, epidemics, following the pandemic of the Black Death (bubonic plague) in the 1300s, which had reduced by a third the population of Europe, continued to ravage eastern Europe in cyclical recurrences during Dracula's period.

Other dread diseases, such as syphilis, tuberculosis, leprosy, and smallpox, accompanied the Turkish conquest of the Balkans. Calamities such as these, along with natural disasters like floods, earthquakes, and swarms of locusts, noted by travelers particularly in eastern Europe, also fostered belief in false idols, the burning of "witches" and "warlocks," consultation of oracles and soothsayers, and other types of superstitious behavior. Given the often resultant brevity of life, and the high incidence of infant mortality, the age of Dracula was, understandably, also a period of cynicism and despair. This fact helps to explain the cruelty and the low regard for human life exhibited by Dracula and his contemporaries.

The Romanian Background

Dracula became a crusader because his country was, by virtue of geography, the one most immediately threatened by the Turks. Thus it is impossible to understand the man, the statesman, and the soldier without knowledge of the essential geopolitics of his country, which even today is rare in the west. Indeed, many of the myths and confusions connected with his name originated in the fertile imaginations of Bram Stoker and countless filmmakers who persist in describing Transylvania, a western region of present-day Romania, as a mysterious land of gypsies, vampires, and superstitious peasants.

The territories comprised by contemporary Romania have a very ancient history. Having been conquered by Rome in two successive campaigns (A.D. 101 and A.D. 105–106), natives of the land, called at that time Dacians, finally laid down their arms, while their king took poison to avoid captivity. A Roman occupation followed, involving massive migrations from all provinces of the Roman Empire. This land of opportunity beyond the Danube was labeled "Happy Dacia," because of the fertile agricultural soil of the plain and the extensive mineral deposits of gold and silver that had been mined in the Carpathian Mountains ever since ancient times. Roman Dacia, although not exactly coincident with the frontiers of modern Romania, included much of the Danube plain and extended beyond the Carpathian Mountains into the plateau of southern Transylvania. In modern terms, one can visualize the backbone of the territory inhabited by the Dacians as forming a huge inverted S that extended from the borders of what is now Czechoslovakia down to the Danube, this backbone being formed by the mountains themselves.

Roman power did not extend, however, either to the Black Sea or to the Dniester River. By A.D. 271, under heavy pressure by barbarian invaders, the military force and the Roman administration withdrew south of the Danube to what is now Bulgaria. Most historians argue that the bulk of the native population, who within this brief period of time came to speak a rough Latin dialect, stayed behind, seeking shelter in the plateau of Transylvania.

Dracula's birthplace, Transylvania, is thus the region that was inhabited from ancient times by the Daco-Romans, or, as they came to be called because of the basic Latinism of their language, Romanians. For convenience, we shall use that designation from here on. The region beyond the heavily forested Carpathian belt, which the Hungarians gradually occupied until the thirteenth century, was described by their early chroniclers in Latin as "*trans silva,*" literally "beyond (or across) the forest," a very accurate description of the densely forested mountains. The Hungarians were an essentially nomadic people who had come from central Asia; they still speak a Turkic language unrelated to that of other European peoples except the eastern Finns. The Hungarians established their kingdom in ancient Pannonia, the plain east of Romania, then extended their sway over Transylvania at the beginning of the eleventh century.

A century later, the Hungarian kings invited another Asiatic tribe to whom they were related, the Szeklers, or Székely (Stoker erroneously says Dracula is of Szekler ancestry), whom some historians describe as the descendants of Attila's Huns, to their territory. The Hungarian word *szek* means "seat" and *el* means "beyond"; they were accordingly established "beyond the seat of power," on the actual frontiers of Hungarian land. The Szeklers were followed by Germans, most of whom came from the Rhineland and Flanders and who likewise were given considerable land. These Germans eventually were allowed to establish self-governing cities and gained extensive trading privileges. They were collectively known as Saxons. In 1211, for additional protection of their lands from eastern invaders, the kings of Hungary gave charters to the renowned Germans of the Teutonic Order to defend their southeastern border for some twenty years.

The Romanians who had survived in Transylvania during the period of barbarian invasion organized in small independent fiefdoms; they tended their sheep, practiced agriculture, and kept alive their language and traditions. They maintained a precarious autonomy during the period of Hungarian domination. Then, taking advantage of the devastations wrought by the Mongol invasion of Batu Khan in 1241, which had seriously weakened Hungarian power, they began to migrate from the plateau of Transylvania into the foothills of the Carpathians, in two separate colonizations. The earlier took place at the close of the thirteenth century when Romanians founded the principality of Wallachia — the word *Vlach* is simply a German word designating all Latin-speaking peoples. (The Romanians now prefer to call the area *Muntenia,* "the land of the mountains," or *Ţara Românească,* "the Romanian land.") Around 1352 another migration took place, from the northern Carpathian Mountains into what became Moldavia, named because of the proximity of the land to the Moldova River, where the new settlers considered themselves comparatively secure from Tatar or Hungarian attacks.

When Wallachia, where Dracula was to rule, was first established as a state in about 1290, its political organization was rather crude. By the standard of the mosaic of small eastern European states, Wallachia was not a very large country, even if one considered the two Transylvanian duchies of Făgăraş and Amlaş to be under its rule. It consisted of 48,000 square miles of territory (roughly the size of the State of New York), and had a total population of half a million inhabitants, most of them Romanian, scattered in 3,220 villages and townships. The vast majority lived in the country, particularly in the hilly Carpathian districts, close to the Transylvanian plateau from which they had come. The Danubian plain to the south, in those days still covered in part by extensive forests, was sparsely populated because of the danger of Turkish incursions.

Tîrgovişte became the capital of Wallachia around 1385. Earlier capitals had been located closer to the mountains, for reasons of security. Brăila, on the Danube, was the largest commercial port. Important fifteenth-century commercial centers were Tîrgsor, an inland trading center near Tîrgovişte that has long since disappeared, and Rucăr, a northeastern frontier outpost. Bucharest, much closer to the Danubian plain, although in existence as an urban center since the early Middle Ages, was too exposed to Turkish attack to acquire much significance. Few of these towns were fortified in the western sense, being surrounded at most by wooden palisades. Some of these townships were, in point of fact, no more than extended villages. A handful of fortresses of Serbian or Byzantine design, occupying remote strategic positions on the mountains, the Danube, or the sea, at the eastern frontiers of the country, had been built by Dracula's predecessors, but on a very small scale, unlike the powerful German and Teutonic fortresses to the north. Most were intended only as places of refuge rather than as defensive bastions. One more powerful strategic fortress at the Moldavian frontier was built at the town of Chilia, on the northernmost branch of the Danubian delta outlets. Another important fortress, which fell to the Turks in 1416, was Giurgiu, built on a Danube island at great cost (with the revenues of salt mines) by Dracula's grandfather, to protect his southern flank against the Turks.

The two main classes of Wallachian society were the boyars and the peasants. One could barely distinguish the beginnings of a middle estate in the fifteenth-century. Whether these boyars were originally free landowners, wealthy village leaders, or the legitimate descendants of an old military caste, in the western European sense of the term, is a problem best left to specialists. However, the boyars' claim to represent a native aristocracy is at least partially substantiated by the fact that, from the very birth of the principality, or even before its foundation, the term *boyar* was generally associated with tenure, not necessarily ownership, of land. In that sense, boyars possessed vast domains comprising dozens of villages. They constantly extended these by purchase, by marriage, or through princely donations. On these estates, like the feudal aristocracy in the west, the boyars were truly sovereign lords.

In addition to land, members of the upper echelons of the boyar hierarchy were also granted certain titles of Byzantine origin, roughly corresponding to our cabinet offices. These titles were usually conferred in recognition of merit, military or otherwise, in the service of the ruling prince of Wallachia. The first boyar of the land was the *ban,* or governor, of the province of Oltenia. The ban, like other title holders, commanded the services of one or two aides, usually boyars of lesser importance. There were in addition countless court sinecures and minor appointments. The important functions brought substantial revenues. In the provinces other boyars were appointed governors of districts and castles. The title of "great boyar" secured for the holder of that rank a seat in the state council, which, together with the prince, ruled the land. In this duality of government, it was, at times, difficult to say precisely where true power lay.

On the surface, the prince — *domnul* in Romanian, from the Latin *dominus* (lord); the Slavic *voivode* was less frequently used — possessed all the chief attributes of power. He was the formal sovereign and the head of the central and local administration; he raised and spent taxes, collected customs and revenues, dispensed justice, minted coins, and was commander in chief of the army and the police. In spite of these formidable attributes, his power was far from being absolute. Primogeniture, one of the more important means of consolidating centralized authority in the west, had not developed in Wallachia. In practice, any son of the ruling prince, whether legitimate or not, could be selected by the boyar council and then invested by the primate. This situation often led to factional strife and anarchy, as various boyar factions supported different princely candidates. The boyar council also had to be consulted to confirm important edicts and even to witness ordinary judicial transactions, such as land donations.

A powerful instrument of princely power was the Romanian Orthodox church, loosely linked to the patriarchate of Constantinople since the conversion of the country by missionaries of the Eastern Orthodox church during the ninth century. In point of fact, from the foundation of the Wallachian principality, the Romanian church was to all intents and purposes autonomous under the rule of a native chief bishop, who styled himself "Metropolitan of Ungro-Wallachia and Exarch of the Plains." His see was at Curtea-de-Argeş, northwest of Tîrgovişte. Theoretically, his authority extended to all those of the Orthodox faith in Transylvania. Serving him were other bishops and the abbots of a number of wealthy and powerful monasteries such as Tismana, Govora, Cotmeana, Vodiţa, Cozia, Glavacioc, Dealul, and Snagov. They owned vast tracts of land and countless villages, and had a seat in the princely council. These monasteries, which enjoyed immunities and privileges and were exempt from taxation, generally supported the central power. Princes occasionally resided and hid their treasures there. In times of danger, individual monasteries were compelled to make financial contributions to the war cause commensurate with their respective importance. In addition, there were a few Roman Catholic abbeys belonging to the Dominican, Franciscan, Cistercian, and Benedictine orders, some of them offshoots of more powerful Transylvanian foundations across the mountains. A Franciscan monastery existed at Tîrgovişte, close to the prince's palace. The Roman Catholic church, however, had little influence. Roman Catholicism was always considered "foreign" and was suspect both for religious and political reasons, since the papacy was closely associated with Hungarian power.

As noted, it makes little sense to speak of a middle class in fifteenth-century Wallachia. The development of certain towns, however, inevitably entailed commerce, and much of that commerce was in the hands of Transylvanian merchants, particularly German merchants from the Saxon communities, who enjoyed a virtual monopoly in certain Wallachian trading cities. In exchange for this monopoly the German merchants had to pay customs duties, which provided a lucrative revenue for the princely treasury. There were two traditional commercial roads from Transylvania into Wallachia, which followed two river passes across the mountains: one along the Olt River from Sibiu to Turnu Roşu, the frontier point, the other from Braşov to Rucăr along the Dîmboviţa River. Along these two passes, Transylvanian-manufactured goods found their way to such marketing towns as Tîrgsor or Tîrgovişte. The obligation to buy and sell goods only in specific towns led to a considerable confluence of people during the trade-fair days of the year. From the prince's point of view it was important to be able to control foreign trade, both because of the revenues generated and because of the native artisan and mercantile class, developing at the beginning of the fifteenth century, that looked to the prince to protect its interests against Transylvanian and other competition.

In terms of origin, all Romanian peasants were originally free. In actual practice a good many of them gradually became serfs on boyar and ecclesiastical estates, though the process was just beginning in Dracula's time. In case of war, the prince would naturally appeal to the boyars, who, together with their retainers and servants, fought under their individual banners. In addition, however, the ruler of the state also relied on the free peasants, who gave the Wallachian army a definite popular and peasant character in contrast to the feudal structure of the armies of neighboring states. Also in contrast to the armies of powerful feudal countries such as France and England, the Wallachian army often reached as many as thirty to forty thousand men in size, out of a total population of only half a million, a much higher proportion of soldiers under arms.

Outside a major war, though, fought in defense of the fatherland, the prince could rely for repression on only a very small contingent of police and custom forces. There were, in addition, the prince's personal guard and the garrisons of fortresses. The absence of military power made the struggle against the nobility difficult in times of peace. A prince could certainly punish "disloyal" boyars or churchmen by confiscating their fortunes or lands, but only in certain, limited cases: treason was one, the absence of an heir another, nonpayment of taxes yet a third. When confiscation was justified by law, the prince often created new boyars from among his adherents.

As a potential crusading power, the Wallachian principality during the fifteenth century had some characteristics that clearly distinguished it from its neighbors. Unlike Serbia and Bulgaria, where the Turks had previously encountered only weak feudal armies, Wallachia had an army of free peasants and boyars determined to defend their native soil. It seemed as if the social and political framework of the country as well as its unique military institutions were awaiting a ruler able enough to exploit them against the enemy from without.

Dracula's Ancestors

Dracula came from a native ruling family the first known ancestor of which was Basarab the Great (1310–1352), a shadowy early ruler of Wallachia of whom little is known beyond his name and various legends carried in the collective memory of the Romanian people. Specialists in genealogy have noted that the name Basarab is of Oriental rather than Romanian origin; Basarab's coat of arms, with its device of three dancing black figurines, bears witness to his victory over the dark-skinned Tatars when his ancestors settled in the Romanian lands.

The best known of the early Basarabs is Mircea the Old, sometimes referred to as Mircea the Great, Dracula's grandfather, who ruled with interruption during a period of some thirty-two years (from 1386 to 1418), quite a record for the period. Mircea built an extensive Romanian state, stretching north to south from the mountains to the Danube River, and east to west from the Black Sea to the Danube bend. The region included two districts of Transylvania, the duchies of Amlaş and Făgăraş, and the Banat region of Severin to the southwest. To protect his land from Hungarian encroachment on the north, he constructed a number of small outposts along the frontier of Transylvania. He built the powerful island fortress of Giurgiu in order to halt the growing expansion of the Turks, his immediate neighbors in Bulgaria to the south. His son Vlad, Dracula's father, was fond of recalling the strategic importance of Giurgiu by saying that, once the fortress was finished, "even the women of his land armed with their spindles would be able to conquer the Turkish Empire." Dobruja, the region bordering the Black Sea that included the Danube delta, fell to Mircea in 1389. Mircea also fortified the stronghold of Chilia on the Danube delta. These achievements led Mircea to assume the bombastic title "God's anointed and Christ's loving autocrat Ioan Mircea Great Voevod and prince, with God's help ruler over Ungro-Wallachia and parts of the country beyond the mountains, the Tatar lands, the duchies of Amlaş and Făgăraş, ruler of the Banat of Severin and of both banks of the Danube up to the Black Sea."

During Prince Mircea's reign the chief danger was the presence of the

Turks, who in 1387 threatened what was left of free Serbia. Mircea probably sent a Wallachian contingent to fight alongside the crusaders at the first battle of Kosovo. Although the Turkish sultan, Murad I, was killed in that hard-fought battle, his son Bayezid took up the cause and led his troops to the victory that signaled the end of Serbian independence. When in 1393 the Turks finally completed the transformation of Bulgaria into a Turkish province, Mircea realized that the handwriting was on the wall; shortly thereafter he signed the first act of Wallachian submission to the sultan.

It was in order to avoid total subjection to the Turks that Mircea signed a treaty of alliance with Sigismund of Luxemburg in 1395. This act accounts for Mircea's participation the following year in the last great western anti-Ottoman crusade, led by Sigismund, John of Nevers, son of the duke of Burgundy, Frederick of Hohenzollern, the duke of Lancaster, and other western and eastern allies. On September 25, 1396, on the heights just outside the fortress of Nicopolis on the Danube, ignoring Mircea's advice to lead the attack with his well-seasoned infantry, Sigismund sent out the heavily clad feudal cavalry of the west. They suffered a disastrous defeat, "as the Christians fled like pigs, overwhelmed with fear," in the words of a contemporary Turkish historian. The Turks took many prisoners, including a cousin of the king of France, whom they ransomed.

The humiliating defeat experienced at the hands of the Turks might have proven disastrous for Prince Mircea, had destiny not turned to his advantage, through a fortunate diversion on Bayezid's eastern flank. Out of central Asia and Persia arose one of the last great Tatar warriors, the infamous leader Timur Lenk, known in the west as Tamerlane. After founding his own powerful state in Asia Minor, Timur was ready to challenge the power of the Turks.

It was at the battle of Ankara (Angora) that Timur's forces inflicted a great defeat on Sultan Bayezid in 1402. The latter, having been captured, preferred to commit suicide rather than survive as a captive. Mircea did his best to exploit the temporary decline in Turkish power by championing the cause of Musa Çelebi, Bayezid's weak-willed son, who had married Mircea's daughter Arina, to seize the sultanate. He managed to install the boy on the throne at Adrianople on February 17, 1411, where the latter ruled during three years. This was the high point in the career of Dracula's grandfather. It seemed that Romania might become a major eastern power like Poland, yet this was not to be. Musa, Mircea's protégé, was murdered in 1413 by his brother Mehmed I with the support of the emperor of Constantinople, Manuel II of the Paleologus dynasty. The Turks made a remarkable comeback. Sultan Mehmed captured the powerful island fortress of Giurgiu, and Mircea lost control also of the province of Dobruja, which had once given him access to the Black Sea.

By 1417 Mircea was forced to accept the inevitable: he recognized Turkish suzerainty and agreed to pay a tribute of 3,000 golden ducats to the sultan. However, unlike the total submission of other Balkan states, his land maintained its autonomy. In contrast to its neighbors in the south, Wallachia preserved its native administration and an independent church; the nobility lost none of its lands; and no Turk was allowed to settle on Romanian soil. Yet a reign that had begun so brilliantly ended in humiliation and defeat. One year later (1418), Mircea was laid to rest in the Byzantine-style monastery of Cozia in the gorge of the river Olt, where his tomb can be admired to this day.

Mircea had been married to Princess Maria, the daughter of a powerful Hungarian noble family called Tolmay, which owned important estates in the Lake Balaton area of Hungary and in northeastern Transylvania. Maria was also related to the powerful Cilli family (one of whose members, Barbara, became the second wife of Sigismund of Luxemburg). Of the many sons born to Mircea only one, Mihail, was legitimate, and from 1408 to 1418 he was co-ruler with his father, a frequent practice in those days. More important than Mihail was Prince Mircea's numerous illegitimate brood, conceived by a variety of unknown women. These sons' claims to the throne, in accordance with existing Romanian customs, were quite valid. None of them amounted to much, except for two: a certain Alexandru Aldea, who ruled briefly in 1431, and Vlad, Dracula's father.

We know very little of Dracula's father's early life beyond the fact that he was born sometime before 1395 in Wallachia. Because of Mircea's close relationship with Sigismund of Luxemburg before the battle of Nicopolis, it is likely that young Vlad was sent as a hostage to Buda, the count of Sigismund I — as a token of Mircea's good faith in maintaining the treaty of alliance he had signed with Hungary in 1395. In any case, we know that Vlad spent much of his youth in the Hungarian capital and in other German cities such as Nuremberg, where the future Holy Roman Emperor also sometimes held court. Sigismund, in fact, described Vlad as "educated at our court" (which implied conversion to Roman Catholicism).

The death of Prince Mircea in 1418 ended Vlad's forcible confinement, but the young son of the prince decided to stay on as a page of Sigismund.

He was treated with the respect due his rank, attached to the retinue that surrounded the emperor, and followed the peregrinations of this retinue from Nuremberg to Prague, Buda, Rome, and various cities of Transylvania. As a page he was given the choice education reserved for members of the imperial family, which was as much French as German in culture and character — because of the influence of Sigismund's French first wife. The emphasis lay on the values of chivalry and the precepts of knighthood, and on learning languages, since the rudiments of German, Hungarian, Latin, Greek, and Italian were essential for a cosmopolitan court. Vlad was also obliged to acquaint himself with the tedious bureaucracy of the imperial chancellery. No matter how privileged, according to a recent Romanian biographer Vlad was profoundly unhappy with the drudgery, the petty rivalries and intrigues, the uncongenial, unhealthy climate, and the Germanic surroundings of the emperor's court.

More to the point, Vlad had the conviction that after Sigismund's defeat at Nicopolis, the emperor had lost all interest in the idea of eastern crusading and had become more intent upon pursuing political ambitions in the west. Vlad's paramount objective was to secure his father's throne, which after the death in 1420 of Mihail had once again become an object of dispute among all the illegitimate half-brothers. Meanwhile, an additional rival, Dan II, the son of one of Mircea's brothers and hence a cousin of Vlad, had appeared on the scene. He and his successors maintained with the future Dracula family a struggle so bitter and bloody that historians have labeled it the Dracula-Dănesti feud. In terms of its violence it can be compared to the Lancaster-York conflict in England, Shakespeare's Capulet-Montagu rivalry, or the Burgundian-Capetian antagonism in France. Even Pope Pius II made note in his *Commentaries* of its bitterness.

Rather than continue to rely on the emperor, Vlad thought that a better avenue for securing the throne would be to gain the support of the Polish king, Ladislas II Jagiello, a sometime rival of Sigismund, who through the union of Poland and Lithuania had formed the most formidable coalition of states in eastern Europe. Thus, with a few faithful adherents, under cover of darkness, Vlad secretly left Buda in the early spring of 1423. He wished to exchange masters and find a more supportive sponsor at Krakow. However, word of this unwarranted disappearance leaked out; when his destination became known, orders were given to the brothers Márton and György Thurzó, counts of Ujvár, to pursue and catch the escapees before they reached the Polish border. They were caught, admonished, and brought back to Buda. By way of retaliation for this act of disloyalty, the emperor confirmed Dan II, who had ruled since 1422, as prince of Wallachia. However, there were to be no further reprisals, though Vlad was for some time placed under stricter surveillance.

One way of distracting this turbulent young page from rash actions of this kind was to use his considerable skills for diplomacy in negotiations that were just beginning to help pave the way for a union between the Roman Catholic and Eastern Orthodox churches, in which both Emperor Sigismund and the Byzantine emperor John VIII Paleologus had a stake. The Greek historian Michael Ducas recorded Vlad's presence in Constantinople in a perfunctory manner: "In those days there appeared one of the many bastard sons of Mircea, the profligate voevod of Wallachia. As an officer in the army he had access to the palace of Emperor John, where early on he deliberated with young men knowledgeable in both warfare and acts of sedition. At that time there happened to be certain Wallachians in Constantinople who were willing to help him along." Vlad's mission was to greet and accompany Emperor John VIII, who had landed in Venice on November 15, 1423, hoping to find military support in the maritime republic, in Milan, or with the Holy Roman Emperor himself. Vlad's mission was to explain to the embattled and beleaguered Byzantines that the essential precondition for any Western assistance was acceptance of the supremacy of Rome. He later befriended the emperor on the lengthy homeward sea journey to Constantinople.

However, the wily Romanian also had plans that deviated from his ostensible mission. He was going to Constantinople in the best tradition of other Romanian and Balkan princes: namely, to seek political support for his own candidacy and perhaps to bolster his chances by marrying a Byzantine princess. (He was only around twenty-eight at the time, and teenage princesses of marriageable age abounded.) From the emperor's viewpoint, the "export" of Byzantine princesses had been an important weapon used by successive members of the imperial family to keep the Balkan peninsula under their political control.

Vlad's first glimpse of the glamour and glitter of the dying thousand-year-old civilization of Byzantium made an indelible impression. The luxury, ritual, and the extraordinary refinery of the court, the abundance and diversity of goods at the central marketplace were impressive enough. The local bazaars further titillated the imagination with the display of exquisite articles of apparel and consumption: ornate jewelry of silver and gold, silk brocades, textiles from Flanders, perfumes, spices from the east shipped by the Genoese and the Venetians, the choicest wines from the Balkans, beautiful slaves of many races from Europe and Asia — in short, everything was aimed at impressing the unwary traveler.

Most theatrical was the mystery and complexity of the Orthodox ritual at the holy shrine of St. Sophia, which had more affinities to a mystical dialogue between celebrants and the faithful than to a religious service. This sacred drama was enhanced by the heavy use of incense, and its setting among gilt-edged mosaics of saints and emperors and indescribably edifying ikons, their eyes turned towards heaven, motioning the faithful to prayer. Pageantry such as this, in addition to cruel distractions at the hippodrome that pitted men against beasts, and the popular superstitious consultations with witches and oracles, exercised Vlad's imagination.

For Vlad this immersion was so tempting as to make him entertain the thought of defecting to Constantinople from his lackluster German court. However, open talks with Emperor John VIII about the hopelessness of the military situation at Constantinople persuaded Vlad to return. The Romanian prince, in turn, convinced the emperor that his presence was essential at the church councils that were being discussed by Emperor Sigismund to meet eventually at Basel in 1431 and at Florence in 1439, to implement the union between the two churches. Thus, during the few months that he spent in the Byzantine capital, Vlad played a small but useful role in the intricate negotiations aimed at saving Constantinople by reuniting the two churches, an essential precondition to the formation of a new joint east and west crusade to eliminate the Turks from Europe.

At a personal level, in furthering his own ambitions the young prince's efforts were far less successful. He was introduced to a number of eligible princesses of the Byzantine court, and had a brief tryst on the Bosporus with an unnamed Greek heiress. But as he left the imperial city, he realized only too well that insofar as the Wallachian throne was concerned, he could expect no more help from Emperor John VIII Paleologus than from the Polish king. In any event, Vlad's decision to remain loyal to the Emperor Sigismund was soon to bear fruit.

In the years following the death of Jan Hus, the first martyr of the Protestant cause in Europe, the Hussite heresy that he had championed began to spread. Sigismund summoned an imperial diet at Nuremberg in February 1430 to organize the fifth crusade against the powerful armies of the rebel Hussite leader Jan Žižka von Trokow, who using quite revolutionary tactics had kept four crusading armies at bay in the 1420s. Among the novel tactics of war that helped account for Žižka's success was the use of mobile fortified camps composed of wagons chained to one another. The soldiers manning each cart were organized in much the same manner as a modern tank crew. This western method of warfare was later adopted by John Hunyadi, and taught to his young ward, Dracula.

Vlad was summoned to Nuremberg one year later, together with other high dignitaries of the realm. In the early dawn of February 8, 1431, a most unusual ceremony took place in the double chapel of the imperial fortress, which involved Vlad's induction in the Order of the Dragon. The order had originally been founded by the Holy Roman Emperor and his second wife, Barbara Cilli, in 1387 and reorganized on December 13, 1408, with the character of a secret fraternal society. Like other semimilitary and religious orders of knights (such as the Knights of the Hospital of St. John and the Teutonic Order of Knights), its ostensible objectives and duties were protecting the German king and his family, defending the empire, shielding widows and orphans, and going into mourning and praying for the deceased members of the society. A principal aim entailed the defense and propagation of Catholicism against the partisans of Jan Hus and other heretics, and, of course, crusading against the infidel Turks. The reason for the "secret" character of the order, in the eyes of its founders, was the undeclared ultimate aim of gaining for the house of Luxemburg political supremacy in Europe. This also provided the principal reason for the small number of first-class members initially inducted — only twenty-four in all, including Vlad — drawn from the royalty of Europe.

Among a host of symbolic minutiae required of a new knight was the wearing of two capes, of differing colors to suit differing occasions: one green, reminiscent of the dragon's hue, which was worn over a red garment representing the blood of the martyrs; one black, to be adopted by Stoker's future vampire, to be worn only on Fridays or during the commemoration of Christ's Passion. In addition, each member of the order was given a golden necklace or collar on which appeared the insigne of the dragon in a medallion artfully designed by a master craftsman from Nuremberg. The dragon was represented with two wings and four paws outstretched, jaws half open, and its tail curled around its head and its back cleft in two, hanging prostrate on a double cross similar to the cross of Lorraine adopted by Joan of Arc. On the cross appeared in Latin the mottos of the society: "*O quam misericors est Deus*" ("Oh how merciful is God!") and "*Justus et Pius*" ("Just and Faithful "). This symbolized the victory of Christ over the forces of darkness. The medallion had to be worn at all times until the member's death, and after death, in theory, it was to be placed in the defunct member's casket.

For Vlad this was a singular honor that more than richly repaid his minor diplomatic assignments. He was certainly in distinguished company: among the twenty-four "first-class" members were heads of state such as King Alfonso of Aragon and Naples, Stepfan Lazarevič of Serbia, Prince Witold of Lithuania, and his cousin (to whose court Vlad had tried

to escape) Ladislas Jagiello of Poland. Those of the "second class"
order included members of the Hungarian nobility and other barons of the
empire.

When he eventually returned to his native country, Vlad was called
"Dracul" by the boyars, who knew of his honor, because he was a
Draconist, a member of the Order of the Dragon (*draco* in Latin),
dedicated to fighting Turks and heretics. On the other hand, the people at
large, unfamiliar with the details of Vlad's investiture in the order, seeing
a dragon on his shield, and later on his coins, called him "Dracul" with
the meaning of the "devil," because in Orthodox iconography, particularly those ikons that depicted St. George slaying a dragon, the dragon
symbolized the devil. The word *drac* (*-ul* is simply the definite article
"the") can mean both "devil" and "dragon" in the Romanian language.
It is important also to underscore the fact that, at the time, the use of this
particular nickname in no way implied that Dracul was an evil figure, in
some way connected with the forces of darkness, as some have suggested.
The name Dracula, immortalized by Bram Stoker, was later adopted, or
rather inherited, by Dracul's son. Dracula, with the *a*, is simply a
diminutive, meaning "son of the dragon." (The son inherited the title
Dracul by virtue of the statutes of the order.) Evil implications were
attached to the name only much later by Dracula's political detractors,
who exploited its double meaning. That the family itself did not consider
the epithet in any way offensive is proven by the fact that they
consistently adopted it, that Dracula signed letters by that title, and that
historians used *Dracula* to describe all members of the family (Radu and
Mircea, his brothers, for instance), as well as their descendants, who
were collectively known as the Drăculeştis.

Later that evening of February 8 a far more meaningful ceremony took
place in the throne room of the fortress of Nuremberg in the presence of
the emperor; the Burgrave of Nuremberg, Friedrich von Zolern (of the
House of Hohenzollern); the Grand Master of the Teutonic Order, Klaus
von Redwitz; the nobles of the kingdoms of Hungary, Bohemia, and the
empire; and a few other boyars from Vlad's native Wallachia. This time
Dracul, as we can now dub him, swore allegiance to the emperor, whom
he referred to as "my natural Lord and Sovereign, at whose Court we are
assembled to accomplish very great things." He was then given the
official staff of office and declared prince of Wallachia. In return for this
great honor the emperor made one additional request: when established
on his new throne, though ruling an Orthodox country, Dracul must give
protection and free exercise of religion to those of the Catholic faith; the
Franciscan Minorites were specifically mentioned as deserving special

consideration and goodwill. Thus, Vlad Dracul was now tied to the empire by a threefold bond: as a Draconist, a vassal of Sigismund, and a fellow Catholic crusader.

The night of that memorable day was spent in festivities. Bonfires were lit, bunting adorned the small upper-floor openings of the tall wood-framed houses of the merchants along the narrow cobblestoned streets and covered bridges along the Pegnitz River, which winds its way tortuously through the city. There were fairs, public dancing, open-air plays with mimes and jugglers, hundreds of street performers. Dense crowds feasted in the public square facing the Gothic church of St. Sebald at the bottom of the Kaiserburg (the castle hill). It seemed as if the gaudily attired merchants — and even the populace at large in this imperial capital of all the Germanies — understood the importance of this feast day, even though they were only dimly aware of its true significance. The presence of the Wallachian boyars certainly did not pass unnoticed: the alien mode of dress, their rich furs and Byzantine garb, was stared at as an object of curiosity, raising quite a few hopes among the merchants who sought new avenues for trade with the German townships of Transylvania.

Additional evening festivities were witnessed only in seclusion by the mighty. With more bonfires lit, a mock tourney was organized late at night near the Tiergarten Gate on the outskirts of town in the presence of the emperor and the whole court. The most skilled knights of the empire, each bearing his family banner, were to display their prowess and equestrian style under their heavy armor. Among them was Vlad, riding an Arabian stallion, enrobed in his Dragon cape and also proudly exhibiting the Wallachian eagle, the emblem of his newly acquired throne. Following several sallies, lance in hand, Dracul displayed his unusual skills by unhorsing his well-armored opponent. An unnamed lady admirer watching from the imperial tribune hurled at the Romanian prince's feet a golden buckle marked with uncial characters. He cherished this trophy to the end of his life and bequeathed it to his son Dracula shortly before his death. In 1931 this trophy was identified among a few surviving objects found when Dracula's tomb was opened by two well-known archaeologists, Dinu Rosetti and the co-author's uncle George Florescu, who were able to trace the inscription to that memorable event. The buckle still bore the name of the well-known Nuremberg craftsman who had designed it.

CHAPTER 2
The Education of a Prince
1431–1448

V L A D ' S dreams of swiftly regaining the Wallachian throne were not immediately realized. The emperor Sigismund, as was his wont, practiced the politics of expediency and decided that despite the Dragon ceremonies, it was in his interest to continue to recognize Vlad's half-brother Alexandru Aldea, because the latter supported the prince of Moldavia, Alexandru the Good, an opponent of King Ladislas II Jagiello, who, in spite of his Dragon Order brotherhood was, as king of Poland, a rival of the emperor. Vlad's consolation was an appointment as military governor of Transylvania with the task of "watching the border area," since Aldea allowed his Wallachian territory to be used by the Turks as a base for inroads into Transylvania. The new governor decided in the spring of 1431 to establish his headquarters in the fortress of Sighişoara because of its central strategic location. The hillside fortress, with unusually thick defensive walls of stone and brick, three thousand feet long, had recently been rebuilt to withstand the most powerful artillery the Turks could muster. In addition, the fourteen battlement-capped donjons (massive inner towers), each named for the guild that bore its cost — the tailors, jewelers, furriers, butchers, goldsmiths, blacksmiths, barbers, ropemakers — made the fortress virtually impregnable. The old city is still dominated by the quaint Councilmen's Tower, where the local prison used to be located. To this day, both the chimes striking the hours of the day and the miniature figurines that strut out of their porticoes every hour are a tribute to the ingenuity of the Swiss clockmakers who originally designed it.

Given his new mission of protecting Catholicism, Vlad was well served in terms of the number of religious orders that had established houses in this partially German city: the Benedictines, Cistercians, Premonstratensians, Franciscans, and Dominicans. (Even today, as soon as the visitor emerges on the main square beyond the Councilmen's Tower, he can admire the elegant Renaissance lines of the principal Dominican monastery.) Among these church and monastic foundations, elaborate three-story homes, built of masonry and stone in a variety of gaudy colors, reflected the presence of a prosperous German mercantile community, which traded with Nuremberg and other western German cities. Like other Transylvanian cities such as Braşov and Sibiu, Sighişoara served as an entrepôt for goods moving from the German west to the Balkans and Constantinople and the Black Sea. In addition, it served western merchants taking the northeastern route to Poland and the Baltic Sea.

The house where Vlad took up his headquarters, in the main square near the Councilmen's Tower, was essentially not very different from the wealthy merchants' homes surrounding it. Today it is distinguished from similar neighboring houses only by a small plaque that indicates that Vlad Dracul lived there from 1431 to 1435. It is a massive three-story stone construction of dark yellowish hue, with a tiled roof and small window openings for defensive purposes, such as were customary in the Middle Ages, when street brawls were frequent. It probably dates back to the beginning of the fifteenth century. The three entrances are located on the western side of the building — one leading to the ground floor, presumably the headquarters of a small garrison assigned to Vlad's person, and the other two emerging via a narrow stairway at the upper levels, where Dracul held his mini-court.

The house was restored in 1976 on the occasion of the five hundredth anniversary of Dracula's death. In pulling down a partition, workers uncovered a fascinating mural, depicting three men and a woman, painted in neo-Renaissance style. The central figure was that of a somewhat rotund man with a double chin, long well-waxed mustaches, an olive complexion, oval-shaped eyes, arched eyebrows, and a finely chiseled nose. He wore a white Oriental turban and a loosely fitting gown of central European style, with wide sleeves fastened by a multitude of cruciform clasps. Significantly, he carried in his left hand a staff of office such as Vlad Dracul might have carried as governor, while his right clasped a golden cup, offered by a woman — possibly a reference to Dracul's unidentified lady admirer from Nuremberg, or else simply a boyar lady of his court. The uncanny similarity of the oval almond-colored eyes to those in the famous portrait we possess of Dracul's son Dracula suggests that the remains of that mural (now exhibited in the local-history museum of Sighişoara) may well represent the only surviving portrait of Dracul, even though it would have to have been painted posthumously from an original that no longer exists.

In the early history of Romania, chroniclers rarely mentioned women — partly because princes shared the "harem philosophy" of the Ottomans and made little distinction between concubines and legitimate wives. Insofar as the heir to the throne was concerned, the only thing that really mattered was, to use a local expression, to be "of the male royal bone." This fact explains the debates over who the real mother of Dracula was. Most historians believe that Dracul married Princess Cneajna, the eldest daughter of Alexandru the Good, Prince of Moldavia (1400–1431), a member of the Muşatin family. She was the sister of two succeeding Moldavian rulers, the princes Ilias and Bogdan II, father of the illustrious Stephen the Great. The marriage probably took place in 1425 after Vlad's return from Constantinople. Such a dynastic alliance with the sister Romanian principality made good sense, particularly in view of the Muşatins' close relations with the Polish king, an invaluable ally on the road to Vlad's ascension to the throne. This marriage bond also provides an explanation for the amity existing from this time onward between some members of the Moldavian and Wallachian ruling families. Both Prince Ilias and Prince Bogdan II were, after all, Dracul's brothers-in-law. Stephen the Great was Dracula's cousin, a relationship that forms an important part of our story.

The eldest legitimate son of Dracul was Prince Mircea, born in 1428; the second was Vlad Dracula, born in Sighişoara, under the sign of Sagittarius, in November or, more likely, December 1431. By far the most beautiful child of Dracul's was Radu, four years younger than Dracula, who was born in 1435.

In addition to his wife, Vlad Dracul, like his predecessors, had a number of mistresses; one of these was a Wallachian boyar lady known simply as Călţuna. She later took the veil and adopted the name of Mother Eupraxia when she became the abbess of a monastery. It was Călţuna who mothered Vlad the Monk, one of Dracula's half-brothers and later a bitter foe, who eventually became prince of the land. There were undoubtedly other illegitimate offspring, including yet another Prince Mircea of whom little is known. (Mircea was evidently a favorite name in the family, because of the illustrious grandfather.)

The early, impressionable years of Dracula's childhood at the exiguous court of Sighişoara were dominated by the women of the household, by lowly midwives, and by wet nurses. Princess Cneajna and the wives of a few exiled boyars were in charge of drilling into the minds of the young heirs the lesson that they were different from ordinary mortals and, depending upon fate, might someday be destined to hold an exalted station in life. As such, the heirs were the object of a great deal of adulation and love, the center of attention. Their rank also entailed that certain modes of behavior be instilled into them: how to dress correctly, mind basic manners, order about their child peers — lessons that were not soon forgotten in a very protocol-conscious society. The court ladies also taught the princes their native Romanian tongue (the language of command in the army).

From the tenderest age, a great deal of emphasis was placed on physical fitness — even at court, children were exposed to the elements on stormy days in true Spartan tradition; should they survive the chills and fevers of the accompanying colds, they were considered to have strong physical and moral character, essential traits of good warriors. For physical exercise, even a five-year-old tot had to be able to ride an unsaddled horse at a gallop to the local fountain or grazing field. Inevitably, since they lived in a trading center, the heirs were allowed to play truant with the sons of local merchants. There were, of course, the usual distractions that followed the feast days: puppet theaters, an old tradition of eastern Europe, with the manikins playing the roles of biblical or historical figures; ambulant artists, acrobats, minnesingers, and other street performers. In summer there were ball games, running and jumping contests, and games on quadrilateral swings made of red cloth and fastened in the form of a pyramid. In the winter they hunted eagles with slingshots, slid down the Sighişoara slopes on primitive double-runner sleds, trapped hares, and used the bow and arrow to sharpen the acuity of their eyes, all in preparation for the serious training in the handling of more sophisticated weapons that was to follow at a more mature age.

We are ignorant of the religious affiliations of Dracula and his brothers, but since both their parents were Catholics, it is more than likely that they were initially brought up in the teachings of the western church. Mircea, born in a German land, was almost certainly baptized a Roman Catholic. It is conceivable that Dracula and Radu, who spent their early years on Romanian territory, where Orthodox churches were handy, may have been secretly baptized in the Romanian church, though perhaps for diplomatic reasons they attended mass at first in the chapel of the Dominican monastery in the vicinity of their Sighişoara court. On the one hand, Dracul could hardly afford offending Emperor Sigismund, who had specifically requested that he support Catholic institutions in his country. On the other, he must have known that conversion to Orthodoxy was a necessity for a future prince, required by the fundamental laws of Wallachia.

There is an ominous sidelight that could easily have been dismissed as harmless child's curiosity, were it not for Vlad's awesome future reputation for impaling. Local tradition insists that the young boy showed, even at that early stage in life, a morbid curiosity in watching, from his first floor bedroom, criminals being led from the small jail in the Councilmen's Square to the Jewelers' Donjon, the usual place of execution by hanging.

The late medieval painters of the scions of the upper nobility and princely houses invariably depicted boys even as young as five or six as "little men" indistinguishable from their elders. In this respect, these painters showed remarkable acuity, since the children of fifteenth-century noblemen, even within the small confines of this Sighişoara court, were much more mature than their tender age would imply. They would occasionally escape from the women's quarters and eavesdrop on the more sophisticated conversation of the adults, even though the young princes were not able to understand the complexity of conversations that centered on immediate political objectives. Dracul's most pressing need was to consolidate his power in Transylvania, by forming alliances with and gaining the military support of neighboring German cities such as Braşov and Sibiu. "Know ye," he wrote to the head of the city council of Braşov, "that my Master the Emperor has entrusted me with the protection of this region, and pray do not without my consent make peace with my enemies in Wallachia." Again he wrote to the Braşovians: "I pray that like good brethren and friends you will follow me and give me your assistance." In addition, Dracul sought volunteers for his army from the two duchies of Făgăraş and Amlaş, traditional fiefs of the Wallachian princes, which had been placed under his jurisdiction by the emperor. He also obtained the right to mint coins (many of which have survived to the present day) in Sighişoara, bearing the effigy of the Dragon and the princely eagle of Wallachia, golden ducats that were legal tender all over Transylvania and Hungary and gradually replaced the currency that had been in circulation earlier. This was an enormous privilege, which contributed to Dracul's considerable personal fortune, money obviously needed not only for the luxuries entailed in court life but to raise armies and buy weapons with which to regain his throne.

Clearly Vlad's principal goal, from the very moment he set foot on

Transylvanian soil, was to regain what he considered was his legitimate throne, promised to him by the emperor at Nuremberg and a reward implicit in his act of vassalage. Mainly preoccupied by the Hussite problem in Bohemia, in spite of frequent Turkish inroads across the border, Sigismund continued to support Alexandru Aldea. From Vlad's perspective at Sighişoara, the emperor was certainly guilty of a breach of promise. It was only in 1434 that Sigismund, increasingly impatient with Aldea's closeness to the Turks, on the advice of Redvitz, the Grand Master of the Teutonic Order, instructed Dracul to buy from the Transylvanian townships the weaponry he needed and to gather an army composed of his boyar exiles, Romanians from the two duchies under his control, and whatever mercenaries he could afford. In buying weaponry, Dracul acknowledged the meaning and importance of the use of the cannon as a mobile offensive weapon. One of the cannons, engraved with the name of Master Leonardus, was so highly prized that Dracul gave this craftsman a bronze cup, still extant in the evangelical church at Sibiu.

Learning that his half-brother Alexandru Aldea lay on his deathbed, Dracul advanced toward Wallachia. In a number of skirmishes, he was able to repel the attack of various Turkish beys (leaders) on the Danube, who supported the dying cause of Aldea. Dracul and his army at last entered Tîrgovişte, the princely capital, in December 1436. Thus, during the winter of 1436–1437, Dracul finally realized his dream, sanctioned by the emperor since 1431: he became de facto prince of Wallachia and took up residence at the palace. His Moldavian wife and his three sons — Mircea, Dracula, and Radu — later joined him.

For Vlad Dracula, life at his father's court marked an altogether new experience, very dissimilar from provincial existence in Sighişoara, where he had been allowed at least sometimes to play truant. This new phase of his educational experience was to last six years. These years, even though he was only between the ages of five to eleven, seem to represent a formative stage in his upbringing. Both formal education and the accidents of politics were responsible for molding Dracula's complex personality. His apprenticeship for knighthood, patterned upon western precedent, began at Tîrgovişte. He was taught swimming, fencing, jousting, archery, court etiquette, and the more refined aspects of horsemanship, in which he had been roughly initiated as a small boy and in which the young prince excelled.

We know very little about the beginnings of his intellectual training. The first tutor engaged by his father was an elderly, highly educated boyar who had fought on the Christian side at the battle of Nicopolis. This man taught Dracula Italian and possibly a smattering of French and Hungarian, in addition to the rudiments of the humanities and world history. Monastic scribes also taught him the Cyrillic script and Old Church Slavonic, in use at the prince's chancellery, and Latin, the language of diplomatic correspondence. A new subject to which Dracula was almost certainly introduced and that was soon to be regularly taught to sons of princes was political science — in particular, the theory of the divine right of sovereigns and the politics of *raison d'état*. Both of these are reflected in the *Teachings of Neagoe Basarab,* political words of wisdom compiled in Wallachia between 1512 and 1521, after Dracula's time, but accurately reflecting the theory of government prevalent in fifteenth-century Wallachia. In essence these principles are not very different from the principles of Machiavelli's *Prince,* written in 1517. Some precepts in Machiavelli's text, such as "It is much better for you to be feared than to be loved," accurately reflected Dracula's future political philosophy, probably because he was taught them at this stage.

In addition to the influence of formal training, Dracula's personality inevitably bore the stamp of the uncertain and shifting fortune of his father's political career. When finally secure on his throne in 1436, Dracul, a wily politician, sensed that the tenuous balance of power was rapidly shifting to the advantage of the ambitious Turkish sultan Murad II. Having destroyed the independence of both Serbia and Bulgaria, Murad was contemplating the final blow against what was left of Byzantine independence. Thus, shortly after the death of his patron Sigismund, in 1437, Dracul signed an alliance with the Turks. Sultan Murad received Dracul and three hundred of his boyars in the city of Brusa (now Bursa) with great pomp as the Wallachian prince made his official act of submission and paid the ten-thousand-ducat tribute, a yearly custom (alliance or no) since Prince Mircea's time.

In 1438, the year following the great Transylvanian peasant revolt, Dracul accompanied Murad II on one of his frequent incursions into Transylvania, during which murdering, looting, and burning took place on a large scale. The councils of threatened cities and towns still believed that they could get better treatment from Dracul, a co-national, than from the Turks. This explains the eagerness of the mayor of the town of Sebeş to surrender specifically to Dracul, on condition that the lives of his townsmen be spared and that they not be carried into Turkish slavery. Dracul, according to his Dragon oath, was obligated to protect Christians against pagans, and on this occasion at least, he was able to save the town from complete destruction. Altogether 70,000 prisoners and much booty was captured during this first massive Turkish inroad into Transylvania. We know these details from a remarkable account written by a participant — the so called Student of Sebeş, simply identified as "Brother George," a prisoner who had fought with the courage born of despair, in the Tailors' Tower of Sebeş, which survives to this day and has been renamed in his honor the "Student's Tower." During his long period of Turkish captivity Brother George wrote his *Memoirs* in both German and Latin, providing a fascinating view of Turkish mores during the fifteenth century.

Dracul changed his pro-Turkish policies in the early 1440s in circumstances that can be explained only by a cursory glance at the general situation in southeastern Europe. One factor was certain: having put the affairs of the Roman Catholic church in some sort of order, Pope Eugenius IV had worked hard for the reunion of the Roman Catholic and Eastern Orthodox churches at the council held at Florence, a union that took place in the presence of the Byzantine Emperor John VIII on July 4, 1439. This was the essential precondition for a western crusade in defense of Constantinople. Another new element was the emergence of one of the most remarkable political and military leaders in Europe in the period before Dracula's reign. This man was John Hunyadi, and his life and career are deeply intertwined with those of both Dracul the father and Dracula the son. Claimed as a hero both by the Romanians and Hungarians, Hunyadi was not in the least hindered in his career by his lowly Romanian ethnic origins.

A portrait of Hunyadi reveals a man of medium height, with auburn hair and a reddish complexion, with a bull neck, brown penetrating eyes, and a well-proportioned body, a distinctive trait being his high forehead. He had very little formal education, though he spoke Hungarian, Romanian, Serb, Croatian, Italian, and a little Turkish. The ladies thought him no less agreeable because of his extraordinary charm and skill as a dancer. The guiding principle of his life was ambition, and all means were considered good to serve that end. A self-made adventurer, a shrewd businessman, and a banker of sorts, Hunyadi amassed a vast fortune and lent his money at interest to the Holy Roman Emperor. Hunyadi was a condottiere in the classical sense, with this one difference: He believed in the *crusading* ideal and wished to apply it in the Balkans in order to chase the Turks out of Europe and relieve the threat to Constantinople. In this sense Hunyadi was a good European, and Christianity was his "fatherland." This ideal notwithstanding, attaining political power, rather than making money, was his supreme goal. To that end, again, all means — money, titles, perhaps even crusading — were equally good instruments. Hunyadi wanted to achieve control of central and eastern Europe for himself and his sons by Erzsébet Szilágy, a member of the lower Hungarian nobility of Transylvania. In spite of changing political and military fortunes, Hunyadi was successful in the end in becoming viceroy of Hungary and governor of Transylvania, and he established his son Matthias, born in 1439, as one of Hungary's great Renaissance kings. (Matthias adopted the epithet Corvinus, from another family estate, recalling the Black Bird — *corvus* means ''crow'' — that, according to legend, had once saved him from death. Thus the Black Bird became the centerpiece of the new dynasty's coat of arms.)

To backtrack a bit, Emperor Sigismund, who had an eye for talent, recognized Hunyadi's courage and military potential and appointed him a page at his court. It was at Nuremberg during Dracul's investment in the Dragon Order that Hunyadi first met the future Wallachian prince, though the two men never became close. After a short time as a page at Nuremberg, Hunyadi was sent as a military apprentice to learn the latest techniques of war from a past master in that art, the condottiere Filippo Maria Visconti, who at the time was campaigning against the Venetians. The Transylvanian leader also studied the tactics used by Hussite Bohemians, whose armed battle wagons served as an offensive weapon and had the effectiveness of a modern tank; in defense, chained to each other, they had the staying power of a fortress.

When the emperor Sigismund died in 1437, Hunyadi thought it expedient to swear loyalty to the Habsburg archduke of Austria, who succeeded to the throne as Albert II. Albert had been handpicked as successor by Sigismund because he had married Sigismund's ambitious daughter Elizabeth. Albert was thus crowned the next king of Hungary with the traditional crown of St. Stephen in the ancient cathedral of Székesfehérvár (Alba Regia). An inexperienced but noble character, the young king had inherited a difficult situation: open revolt by the serfs in Transylvania, the lingering effects of Hussite rebellion in Bohemia, and defiance by the Hungarian nobility, which never had much fondness for the House of Habsburg. Despite these other problems, Albert decided to give priority to the danger posed by the Turkish inroads (like the raid Dracul joined) in Transylvania, which threatened both his capitals, Buda and Vienna. This is why he assigned John Hunyadi, now established as viceroy and governor general of Transylvania, the task of defending the southern portion of the kingdom. This initial modest defensive assignment was turned to good account in the following years by the ambitious

Transylvanian warlord dubbed the White Knight of the Wallachians. He operated upon the principle (later Napoleon's) that attack was the best means of defense. From this time until his death from the plague in 1456, Hunyadi was responsible for organizing no fewer than four major multinational crusades — in an endeavor to chase the Turks permanently out of their Balkan provinces and relieve pressure on the city of Constantinople.

Sultan Murad II, whose spies kept him accurately informed of events at the Hungarian court, such as Hunyadi's appointment, was determined to forestall Hungarian plans by striking first. He attacked Smederevo, the last free Serbian fortress outside of Belgrade, defended by George Branković, the despot of Serbia, and his sons Gregor and Stepan. In spite of heroic resistance, Smederevo was captured on August 27, 1439. The two boys, Gregor and Stepan, were taken hostage by the sultan in spite of the fact that the sultan had married Maria, Branković's daughter. Branković was able to flee across the Hungarian border, and one year later he decided to give to the crown of Hungary his capital city, Belgrade, which commanded an extraordinarily powerful position on the flank of the Hungarian kingdom, at the confluence of the Danube and the Sava rivers. Even before that "gift," Albert had little option other than to declare a crusade on the Turks. Unfortunately, before he could gather an army, he died of dysentery in Vienna on October 27, 1439, among the troops that he had assembled.

The succession to the Hungarian throne now hinged upon the actions of two powerful women. One was Albert's widow, Elizabeth, daughter of Emperor Sigismund, who was allied through her mother to one of the most influential German feudal families, the counts of Cilli. Estranged before his death from Albert, who had tried to exclude her from the succession, Elizabeth, an ambitious and domineering woman anxious to exercise power in her own right, spent little time mourning her husband. With the help of her mother, her relative and Branković's son-in-law Ulrich, head of the Cilli clan, as well as the newly elected Holy Roman Emperor Frederick III, a Habsburg cousin of Albert, she attempted to assert her own authority. Claiming that she was pregnant at the time of her husband's death, she said that she wished to secure the crown of Hungary for her unborn child. Idle gossip in Buda, however, had it that the child was not Albert's, but the fruit of an illicit affair with a Hungarian nobleman. This "child of miracle" was born on February 22, 1440, and, as we have seen, was appropriately nicknamed Ladislas Posthumus. In an attempt to ensure the legality of the succession, the scheming Elizabeth secretly sent her lady-in-waiting Helen Kottarenin to steal the crown of St. Stephen from the fortress of Visegrád where it was housed and had her infant boy crowned Ladislas V by the primate of Hungary, Denes Széchi, at Székesfehérvár, in accordance with the customs of the land. For safekeeping she appointed his uncle Frederick III as "guardian" and Enea Silvio de' Piccolomini (the future Pope Pius II) as tutor, while the Hussite Slovak mercenary Jan Jiskra of Brandýs formed her personal guard.

This clever coup was hardly in the interests of Hunyadi, the great White Knight of the Christians, who correctly foresaw a period of weakness and instability in Hungarian affairs. For that reason he, as well as a majority of the Hungarian nobility, favored the candidature of a young Polish king, the romantic and chivalrous Ladislas III, son of the great Jagiello. Eventually a compromise was worked out because Elizabeth did not have the power to oppose Hunyadi and the nobility: Elizabeth would recognize Ladislas III of Poland as king of Hungary during his lifetime but reserved the right of her son Ladislas Posthumus to succeed him if the Polish king had no heirs. The problem of the Hungarian succession was eventually resolved by the heroic death of the twenty-year-old Ladislas III on the battlefield at Varna, Bulgaria, in 1444, which left the throne of Hungary in the hands of Ladislas Posthumus.

Finally in control of the situation, John Hunyadi, governor general of Transylvania, came to Dracul at Tîrgovişte in 1441 on a mission from the newly elected Polish king of Hungary, demanding the renewal of the crusade against the Turks, which the Wallachians had forsaken during Albert's brief interlude as king. Persistent Turkish military pressure at Belgrade (now a Hungarian fortress) and the civil strife in Hungary made it imperative to secure Wallachian loyalties. The Hungarians further relied on the fact that as a member of the Order of the Dragon, Dracul would find it difficult not to renew his pledges of allegiance to the Christian cause. On the other hand, as a realist, particularly after the fall of Smederevo, Dracul was only too well aware of the overwhelmingly strong military position of the Ottomans: by 1442 they controlled the whole line of the Danube, and their garrisons occupied important fortresses such as Giurgiu and Turnu on the Wallachian side of the river. Added to these logistical factors, an argument that had some bearing on Dracul's decisions was the treacherous game played by Hunyadi, who, while appealing for his support, continued to give secret assurances to the son of Dan II, Basarab, the rival candidate for the Wallachian throne, who had made his headquarters in Transylvania. This last factor may have been decisive in Dracul's decision to preserve his neutrality between Turks and Hungarians, at least for a time. When the Turks entered Wallachia in March 1442, under their commander Şihabeddin, bey of Rumelia, Dracul remained neutral, simply allowing the Turkish troops free access into Transylvania. The Turks suffered a disastrous defeat and several of their leaders were slain.

Dracul's half-hearted fulfillment of his role as a vassal of the sultan planted the seeds of suspicion in the mind of Sultan Murad, who was an honorable man and believed in the sanctity of treaty obligations. The governor of Bulgaria, according to a Turkish historian, Mehmed Neşri, helped cast further doubt on Vlad's loyalties. "Gracious Lord," he told Sultan Murad, "Believe me, neither John Hunyadi nor George Branković [theoretically a vassal] is loyal to you. Nor should you believe that Vlad Dracul is a true friend — he is fickle." The sultan simply answered: "At springtime I will invite both of them to come to my court." Branković, with his suspicions of Turkish double-dealing, wisely stayed away in his fortress at Belgrade. The more trusting Dracul, taking with him his two youngest sons, Dracula and Radu, set out for Gallipoli to meet the sultan. As soon as he had reached the city gates, the prince was seized by a Turkish contingent, and bound in chains. His two young sons were taken away to the distant mountain fortress of Egrigöz in Asia Minor. Dracul was held in Turkish custody at Gallipoli and later, for just short of one year, in the Ottoman capital city, Adrianople, a "guest" of the sultan, while his eldest son, Mircea, undoubtedly Dracul's favorite, ruled in Wallachia (1442–1443). Dracul was eventually released upon the promise, sworn on both the Bible and the Koran, not to participate in any further action against his Turkish suzerain. He was to pay the usual tribute of 10,000 gold ducats, but to this was added the obligation of sending a contingent of young boys, five hundred strong, destined for the Turkish janissary corps — a new act of fealty. Given Dracul's previously unreliable record, one can sympathize with the Turkish concern with obtaining tangible guarantees that would obligate Dracul to keep promises that he had made and broken before. As a further guarantee of future loyalty, Dracul undertook to leave his two younger sons, Dracula, aged barely eleven or twelve, and Radu, not more than seven years old and "no taller than a bouquet of flowers." For the next six years Vlad Dracula, an adolescent, lived among the Turks without father or mother. He did not speak the language of his jailers. Their religion was strange to him. He must have felt abandoned by his father and other kin.

Contemporary Turkish chronicles tell us that Dracula and his brother Radu were held captive, at least for a time, at the fortress of Egrigöz ("crooked eyes") in the Kütahya district of the province of Karaman in western Anatolia. One of the co-authors visited Egrigöz, located almost three thousand feet above sea level. The town occupied a beautiful site on the southeastern slope of Mount Kocia. The whole region consists of small mountains and vast forests of oak, pine, and beech trees; it is similar to the sub-Carpathian region of Wallachia in which the two princes had been brought up. The two hostages were later transferred to Tokat, in the interior of Anatolia, and later to Adrianople. Dracula was held in Turkey until 1448. Radu stayed until 1462.

After their transfer to the capital city of Adrianople, the two boys traveled with the sultan's court in the company of other hostages to Bursa and the summer palace at Manisa. Indeed, the purpose of hostage taking was not merely to guarantee the good behavior of the parents, but also to influence mental attitudes, to instill in princes likely to succeed to the throne loyalty to the Ottoman Empire, without necessarily requiring that they convert to Islam. These youths were to be treated with kindness and civility so long as their elders maintained their pledge. These favorable terms would cease only if the original agreement were broken, or if the hostage misbehaved in an outrageous fashion. The story of the sons of the Serbian ruler Branković provides a good case in point: on May 8, 1441, the two young princes, Stepan and Gregor, having exploited the generous terms of their confinement by engaging in treasonable correspondence with their father, were punished by being blinded with red-hot irons — this in spite of the tears of their beautiful twenty-two-year-old sister Mara, the Sultan's wife.

One famous hostage at the court of Murad II was the nobleman George Castriota, from Kruja, also known as "Skanderbeg," the future hero of Albanian anti-Ottoman resistance. He was a much older man and an object of general admiration and awe, treated as an "uncle" and elder statesman by all the younger Balkan hostage princes. Another remarkable younger man, brought up at the same court and less than a year younger than Dracula (he was born on March 30, 1432) was none other than Murad's second son, Mehmed Çelebi, the future Mehmed II, who would become Dracula's protagonist. In such distinguished company both Dracula and Radu were brought up, tutored by the best minds and in the cultivated traditions of fifteenth-century Ottoman education. Among a stable of tutors and scholars was the famous Kurdish philosopher Ahmed Gürani, an imposing man with a beard who had the right to use the whip, even with the heir to the throne. Other reknowned teachers included the mullahs Sinan, Hamiduddin, and Iyas Effendi, a former Serbian prisoner of war. Beyond including the precepts of the Koran, Aristotelian logic, and applied and theoretical mathematics, Dracula's education was completed in fine Byzantine traditions inherited by the Turks. Dracula's knowledge of the Turkish language was soon close to perfect — a circumstance that was to stand him in good stead on future occasions.

Undoubtedly this six-year period of Turkish captivity, at an age when character is molded, constituted at least as significant a segment in Dracula's upbringing as his years at the Wallachian court. Thus the period is relevant in accounting for Dracula's cold and sadistic personality. On the whole, Dracula, a gaunt and rather ungainly youth, was a difficult pupil, prone to temper bouts; the whip and other forms of punishment were often resorted to in order to cow him into obedience. By way of contrast, there was Radu, whose unusual good looks and sensuality attracted the female members of the seraglio as well as the male "minions" in the Sultan's court. Because of their differences of character, temperament, and physique, the two brothers developed for each other an intense hatred, which was exacerbated by the associated differences in treatment they received.

Eventually the dark clouds of renewed warfare between the Turks and the Christian crusaders created difficult times for the two young hostages; their future became increasingly precarious. Encouraged by Hunyadi's victories in Transylvania in 1442, Pope Eugenius IV decided to proclaim the long-delayed crusade. It was calculated to liberate the people of the Balkan peninsula from Turkish oppression, effectively affirm the act of union proclaimed at Florence in 1439 between the eastern and western churches, and reassert the prestige of the papacy, still threatened by various antipopes and by the movement for constitutional government of the Roman curia. The chief architect of this new coalition of forces was the papal legate, Giuliano Cardinal Cesarini, though he had powerful allies in the papal legate at Venice, Cardinal Gondolfieri, and that clever young humanist from Siena, Enea Silvio de' Piccolomini, not yet Pope Pius II. The pope's proclamation and Cesarini's efforts resulted in the so-called long campaign of 1443, led by John Hunyadi, Branković of Serbia, and Cardinal Cesarini himself, all under the command of King Ladislas III of Poland and Hungary. It was "long," because it lasted more than six months, well into the winter season (at a time when wars were usually fought only in the summer months).

Having surrendered his two sons as hostages to the sultan, Dracul dared do no better than send a small contingent under his eldest son, Mircea, to collaborate with the Christian force.

The Christian army of 25,000 men, including Poles, Romanians, Serbs, Germans, and Austrians, which had left Belgrade in the fall, won a splendid victory against the Turks at Niš, captured Sofia, the capital of modern Bulgaria, and seemed on the verge of liberating the whole Balkan peninsula amid the enthusiasm of the local Bulgarian population. Enea Silvio de' Piccolomini, then secretary to the Holy Roman Emperor Frederick III, was, according to his memoirs, sanguine in believing that the moment had come for the Turks to be chased out of Europe. Unfortunately, by Christmastime, winter had set in in the passes leading through the Balkan mountains of Bulgaria, and the crusaders became victims of the first frost and snows in treacherous terrain while provisions were beginning to fail. Hunyadi gave the orders to retreat to Belgrade, where Christmas was spent in celebrations.

The long campaign of 1443 confirmed the fact that the Turks could be defeated by the people of central and eastern Europe, even without western aid. The truce proclaimed at Szégedin at the end of the year by the Polish king, and at Adrianople by Murad, offered the Christians remarkably generous terms that would include returning some captured forts to the Serbs and the Hungarians and liberating all the hostages, including Dracula and Radu and the blinded sons of Branković. It was signed by the protagonists, who swore on the Koran and the Bible respectively, and extended a five-year armistice needed by Murad to confront his enemies in Asia. Only the Serbian despot Branković, however, remained true to his word, so that his two sons were actually returned.

In the autumn of 1444, the Polish king, on the entreaties of the papal legate Cesarini, broke the treaty and started a new crusade against the Turks. This breach of contract enraged the sultan and brought ill fortune to the Christian armies, at the notorious battle of Varna. The pope had absolved the Christian crusaders of their oath on the grounds that the sultan was an "infidel." This time the cardinal planned a more ambitious undertaking, which would involve the collaboration of a crusading army with the Venetian fleet, whose task it was to prevent the Ottoman army from crossing the Bosporus from Asia Minor to Europe.

When the crusade, led by Hunyadi, Cardinal Cesarini, and the young king of Poland, set out on the Varna campaign, a special appeal was made to Dracul. He had, as noted, sent a token contingent under his son Mircea to help the crusaders during the long campaign of 1443. This time, the

Christian army was to advance along the Danube, rather than to penetrate deep into Balkan territory as they had done before. Dracul met Hunyadi personally at Nicopolis to discuss his eventual participation and the strategy to be followed. As he caught sight of the Christian army, the experienced Wallachian prince noticed the small number of tents that housed the army of 15,000. During a council of war he told the assembled commanders, "The Sultan goes on a mere hunting expedition with more troops than the Christians are bringing into this battle," and he urged the king of Poland to turn back. Dracul also had moral scruples, given the fact that the Christians had violated the sanctity of a treaty that had just been signed. In addition, being superstitious, Dracul believed in an old Bulgarian soothsayer who had forewarned him that nothing good would come of the Christian venture. Even though the papal legate attempted to quiet his conscience by absolving him of his Turkish oath, Dracul finally chose once again to steer a safe middle course, by sending only a small contingent of 4,000 cavalrymen under his son Mircea to assist the Polish and Hungarian armies in the operations along the Danube.

Mircea fought with a great deal of courage, according to Michael Beheim the meistersinger, who has left us an interesting poem on the Varna crusade based on testimony from a German veteran called Hans Mägest. At the siege of Petretz in Bulgaria, Mircea made use of cannon fire for the first time in Romanian military history, to destroy the walls of the city, and then led his troops to attack the Turkish garrison through the gap created. He succeeded in entering the city and finally captured the fortress, hurling some fifty surviving Turks to their deaths into the water-filled moats some fifty feet below. The Wallachians, however, were unable to save their allies from their tragic fate on the hills outside the Bulgarian port of Varna.

From their camp in a strategic location, the Christian forces were surprised to see Murad II's vastly superior forces camped on the outskirts of the city. The Turks outnumbered the Christians three to one. The Burgundian boats and those of the Venetians had failed to stop the sultan's army from crossing over from Asia Minor into Europe. The battle of Varna turned into a disastrous defeat for the Christian cause. During the encounter, the horse of the Polish king was pierced by a Turkish spear; young King Ladislas fell to the ground to face hand-to-hand combat with the elite Turkish troops. They chopped off his head and placed it on a pike for all to see. Seeing that the king was dead, John Hunyadi rushed forward with the faithful Wallachian troops in an attempt to snatch the young king's body from the clutches of the infidels. But his energies were fruitless. Hunyadi and his Wallachians could not even get near. All around him, Hunyadi saw his troops fleeing; he barely managed to escape. It was a calamity from which he never recovered. Giuliano Cardinal Cesarini, the military hero of the Hussite wars, was found dead, lying naked, stripped of all his belongings, on a desolate mountain pass just outside the city of Varna.

Another eyewitness to the campaign, Andrea de Palatio of Parma, accused Mircea's Wallachian contingent of having betrayed Hunyadi in the heat of battle. This accusation seems hardly warranted, given Beheim's account; it was more likely thanks to the Wallachians, who knew the terrain of the Varna region well, that the few escapees, who included Hunyadi himself, managed to extricate themselves from an extremely difficult situation.

By allowing his son Mircea to cooperate with the Christian forces at Varna, Dracul had broken his promise to the sultan and consequently risked the lives of his two sons. Vlad Dracula, of course, learned that his father had violated the oath and put his life in jeopardy. The boy must have come to think then that life was cheap, when one could not even trust one's own father. Henceforth, to all appearances, Vlad Dracula depended less upon human relationships. Dracula's father, after all, was conscious of what he was doing; in a letter to the city fathers of Braşov, Dracul indicated that he knew that he was risking the lives of his sons. He complained about how any of the citizens of Braşov could possibly doubt the depth of his loyalty to their cause. "Please understand," he wrote, "that I have allowed my children to be butchered for the sake of the Christian peace, in order that both I and my country might continue to be vassals to the Holy Roman Emperor." The two children were neither butchered nor blinded, as the father believed they would be. Nor were they executed in the following year, 1445, when Burgundian galleys under Walerand de Wavrin sailed up the Danube, attacking the Turkish fortress of Turtucaia and capturing Giurgiu with the collaboration of Mircea and, this time, of Dracul himself. The purpose of that expedition was to avenge the Varna tragedy and find the bodies of the Polish king and the cardinal.

Although Dracul's two boys were not killed, their lives were certainly in danger, and the terms of their imprisonment were made harsher. A Turkish document states that Radu, the handsomer of the two, had to defend his honor against the sexual advances of no less a person than young Mehmed himself, the heir to the throne. The Byzantine chronicler Laonicus Chalcondyles described Radu's beauty and voluptuousness, which had won him the favor of the future Mehmed II. He gives us a vivid account of the manner in which Radu defended his honor against advances of the drunken prince, who did not follow the prescription of the Koran, by using his sword to wound his would-be lover. Fearing for his life, Radu spent the night hidden in a tree outside the seraglio for fear of Mehmed's vengeance. Being weak-natured, though, he eventually succumbed to sensual pleasures and became Mehmed's minion. He also became Mehmed's protégé and chosen candidate for the Wallachian throne, not leaving Turkey until 1462. Submission was also the price paid by Radu for his becoming a full-fledged officer at the sultan's court, which probably took place in 1447, under Murad II.

Dracula, as noted, proved a more difficult prisoner, and whatever duress he had to suffer toughened his character to a diamondlike hardness. Being perpetually aware of the danger of assassination and, consequently, of the expendability of life, Dracula became a cynic. He also gained invaluable insights into the torturous workings of the impressionable Turkish mind and learned the effectiveness of the Ottomans' use of terror tactics. He was to employ this knowledge to great advantage in his subsequent career.

In essence, the two boys had been spared because Sultan Murad preferred to use them as pawns who might yet contribute to Dracul's defection, even after the campaign of 1445. In the long run, this presumption turned out to be correct. The temporary incursion of the papal Burgundian fleet on the Danube under Walerand de Wavrin, though a fascinating military episode, cannot be looked on in any other light than as a mere epilogue, which in no way altered the balance of forces after the great Christian disaster at Varna. The Turks remained in a position to resume their offensive on the Danube in the summer of 1446. In that year Dracul was officially informed that his sons had been spared, and the Turks offered to renew peace negotiations, under terms that Dracul accepted; a new treaty was signed in the summer of 1447. In addition to the stipulations previously assented to, there was an obligation to expel the 4,000 Bulgarians who had taken refuge on Romanian soil during the 1443 campaign, and to abandon the fortress of Giurgiu and other townships Dracul had conquered on the Danube. Wallachia, however, was allowed to remain an autonomous land.

In spite of their temporary rapprochement in 1445, relations between Hunyadi and Dracul had never been close. Initial mistrust was compounded by Dracul's ambivalent Turkish policies, though the basic reasons for Hunyadi's decision to eliminate Dracul rose from the circumstances that followed the debacle at Varna. In a council of war held somewhere in Dobruja, in what was Turkish-occupied Bulgaria at the time, both Dracul and Mircea held Hunyadi personally responsible for the magnitude of the Christian disaster, because of Hunyadi's having refused to take Dracul's advice at Nicopolis. Young Mircea, aware of the fact that the shoddy Burgundian and Venetian fleet had been incapable of coordinating efforts to prevent the Turkish landing on the Danube, argued for the arrest, trial, and execution of Hunyadi, who was temporarily Dracul's prisoner. The "White Knight's" generous past services on behalf of the Christian cause and his international reputation undoubtedly saved his life. Dracul eventually ensured Hunyadi's safe passage to his Transylvanian homeland. But, if nothing else, the humiliation Hunyadi endured gave him the pretext to lead a punitive expedition against Dracul in November 1447.

Given the anarchy that attended the death of the Polish king, Hunyadi clearly nurtured ambitions of his own, extending not only to seeking the Hungarian and perhaps even the Polish crown but also to securing the principality of Wallachia for himself. At the very least, he wished to ensure the succession of a safe and loyal ally in Wallachia. He found one, in the person of Vladislav II, a member of the rival Dăneşti clan, who had been residing at Braşov. Hunyadi thus launched a deliberate propaganda campaign against Dracul, portraying him as a "fickle ally" who had always secretly supported the interests of the Sultan. During the month of November 1447 he came in person to meet Vladislav in Braşov, then crossed the Carpathians heading towards Tîrgovişte, in the company of his new candidate. Forewarned, Dracul and Mircea ordered the city to close its gates, but a boyar revolt took place, hatched by the partisans of the Dăneştis. In the end father and son were forced to defend themselves, to little avail, with a small number of loyal boyars within their own city. Mircea was captured by the citizenry of Tîrgovişte, tortured, and killed in the most horrible fashion, being buried alive.

Vlad Dracul succeeded in fleeing the city during the night, hoping to reach friendly Turkish troops on the Danube. He never got that far, being caught and assassinated in the marshes of the village of Bălteni close to Bucharest, where a small chapel still stands in his memory at the very place where he was felled by his Dăneşti enemies. A few faithful followers took his body and buried him in a small wooden chapel, at the site of the present Monastery of Dealul near Tîrgovişte. Dracul's tomb and that of Cneajna, his wife, have never been found, nor have any paintings of them survived beyond the fresco recently uncovered at

Sighişoara. After his death, however, Dracula's father was fondly remembered by some of his contemporaries. The official court historian at Budapest, the Italian humanist Antonio Bonfini, wrote that Dracula's father had been "a righteous and unconquerable man, the mightiest and bravest in battle, since with only a few men at his disposal and due solely to his own heart and wisdom, he waged a long war with the Turks, supported by his soldiers, who proved to be valiant beyond belief and without any foreign help, and the war was such that even all the Christians put together could hardly have faced." Walerand de Wavrin, who had become personally acquainted with Dracul during the joint attack on the fortress of Giurgiu in the late fall expedition on the Danube in 1445, declared that he had been "very famous for his bravery and for his wisdom."

When tidings of the precise circumstances of the brutal slayings of his father and brother Mircea, whose heroic exploits he had followed from afar, reached Dracula at Adrianople, there must have been anguish in his heart — but above all, he must have felt an intense desire for vengeance against his family's murderers, in accordance with the "eye for eye and tooth for tooth" principle. He had to wait almost ten years though, for an opportunity.

CHAPTER 3

The Thorny Road to Power

THE impact of Vlad Dracul's death was like that of a thunderbolt out of a clear blue sky. He had, after all, been one of the mainstays of the Christian resistance, a most effective crusader and the only representative of the Dragon Order who remained loyal to his oath, at least in fighting the Turks. Dracula was officially informed of his father's death by Sultan Murad II at the end of the year 1447, since news traveled slowly from Wallachia to Adrianople. He was now completely free. Dracula was made an officer in the Turkish army; he was also given to understand by his Turkish masters that they considered him as a candidate for his father's throne — his stern character and leadership qualities had evidently impressed Murad. (Only later did Radu, as noted, gain this favored position.) The actual assumption of the Wallachian throne was to await the first favorable political circumstances.

At a more personal level, there exists an oral Romanian peasant tradition, a most poignant story that still survives in the regions where the indirect descendants of a certain boyar Cazan survive to this day and that may well contain a grain of truth. Sensing that his end was near, fleeing Tîrgoviște for the Danube, Dracul turned to Cazan, his former chancellor, and asked that he remit to his son and heir, Vlad Dracula, two precious relics: the Toledo blade granted to him by Emperor Sigismund at Nuremberg in 1431, and the gold collar with the dragon insignia engraved upon it. Riding day and night from his estates in Oltenia, Cazan undertook this perilous journey, crossing the Danube in Dobruja, and reached Adrianople within five days at gallop speed. Cazan then handed

Vlad Dracula the precious relics and gave him a detailed account of his father's and brother's brutal slayings. According to the story, Vlad Dracula then took an oath, witnessed only by the boyar, that henceforth he would not rest until he had avenged this crime and killed Vladislav II in person.

A first opportunity presented itself to the seventeen-year-old Vlad Dracula in 1448, as John Hunyadi was trying to rebuild an anti-Ottoman front along the Danube River. The Transylvanian governor crossed the Danube into Serbia during the month of September, and penetrated deep into Turkish territory, where he hoped to make a juncture with the army of the Albanian leader, a renegade Muslim and Dracula's former companion as a hostage, George Castriota. The sultan had been so impressed with Castriota's prowess that during his hostage years he named him Alexander (Iskander in Turkish) for Alexander the Great. To the name Iskander the sultan added the honorific title of "bey" (chieftain). When Castriota fled the Turkish court for Albania, his compatriots heard the words "Iskander bey" as "Skanderbeg," and the name stuck. Skanderbeg, like Vlad Dracula in Wallachia, turned into one of the most ardent fighters for independence against the Turks.

During the first half of October, Hunyadi's Christian army reached the Serbian plateau known as Kosovo Polje, where the Serbs had suffered their historic defeat at the hands of Sultan Bayezid in 1389. While Hunyadi had advanced with his troops, Turkish spies and scouts, who functioned much better than those of Hunyadi, had informed the sultan's army of the exact position of the Christian troops. During three days (October 17, 18, and 19), the second battle of "the field of the Black Birds" took place. It resulted in a serious defeat for the Hungarian-led army and for the eight or nine thousand Wallachian soldiers under the command of Hunyadi's puppet, Vladislav II Dăneşti. The historian Chalcondyles referred to this when he wrote, "On the left wing was Dan [Vladislav II], who was his [John Hunyadi's] great friend, the one whom he had brought to the Dacian land because of his hatred toward Dracula." As happened following the battle of Varna, Hunyadi was barely able to escape from the defeat at Kosovo; the rear guard of Skanderbeg's Albanians saved the remains of the army from total annihilation. As he tried to flee northward on foot, Skanderbeg was taken captive by the Serbian despot George Branković, who wanted to avenge himself because his principality had been looted during the southward passage of the Christian crusaders. Hunyadi was temporarily imprisoned by Branković in the Serbian fortress of Smederevo. He was freed only after promising to negotiate a marriage between his son Matthias and Elizabeth Cilli, the daughter-in-law of Branković.

Given the decline in Hunyadi's power and prestige following two major defeats, Vlad Dracula was able to make his first major move toward seizing the Wallachian throne. Supported by a force of Turkish cavalry and a contingent of troops lent to him by the neighboring Danubian pasha Mustafa Hassan, Dracula led a bold and successful coup, though it was bound to invite severe reprisals from the Hungarian side. The vice-governor of Transylvania, Nicolae of Ocna, immediately asked Vlad Dracula to come and justify his usurpation of power. He was also asked to give information on the whereabouts of John Hunyadi, who had simply "disappeared" after the battle of Kosovo, in the eyes of the uninformed Hungarian authorities. In a letter still extant in the Braşov archives, Vlad Dracula responded that he could not attend the proposed meeting with the Transylvanian vice-governor, since this would only arouse suspicions from the Turks, who would immediately kill him. He also answered that he was unaware of Hunyadi's exact whereabouts but thought that he had perished in battle. Being cautious, however, he declared that should Hunyadi succeed in returning to Transylvania, he, Dracula, would seek to establish peaceful relations with the Transylvanian governor.

Vlad Dracula realized that he could stay on the throne only so long as the Turks were in control of the situation. But after achieving victory at high cost at Kosovo, Sultan Murad II neglected to pursue the retreating Hungarian army. In fact, during three days and three nights Murad remained on the field of battle in order to bury the numerous Turkish dead. He lost valuable time by not advancing against his enemies at once.

Vladislav II, who thus escaped capture, with the assistance of the prince of Moldavia, Petru II, his relative by marriage, who had ascended the throne in March, managed to remove Vlad Dracula from the throne. Vladislav II won over the remnants of the Hungarian army to his side, crossed the Danube River into Wallachia, engaged Vlad Dracula's army, and defeated it by Christmastime. Dracula was forced to flee southward and once again found refuge at Adrianople with his Turkish protectors. His first period of rule had lasted barely two months. His victorious opponent Vladislav II reoccupied the throne, but this time began to make overtures to the Turks, sensing that the balance of power was beginning to shift to their side.

What happened to Dracula after that date? After some time spent at the court of Murad II, the "son of the dragon" fled to Moldavia, where

Bogdan II, the father of the future Stephen the Great, Moldavia's most famous ruler, was prince. Since Dracul had taken as his wife a sister of Bogdan II, the reigning Moldavian prince was Dracula's uncle. The Moldavian-Wallachian connection had been cemented even closer by political fate, which had compelled Bogdan some years before to seek refuge at Dracul's court in Tîrgovişte. In addition, Bogdan's wife, Princess Oltea, was of Wallachian origin, almost certainly related to the Draculas. These family ties themselves sufficiently account for the good reception Dracula received at the Moldavian court. Dracula lived at Suceava, the capital city, or in its vicinity from December 1449 until October 1451 in the company of his cousin Stephen, who was a few years younger than he. The two cousins were likely educated together by learned monks from neighboring monasteries and by chancellery scribes. Thus, Dracula was able to complete his interrupted Romanian education at a time when Moldavia was beginning to experience the initial impact of Renaissance culture coming from Italy by way of Poland and Hungary. These princes' sons also became close friends and may have taken a formal oath obligating them to assist one another in securing their respective thrones. In June 1450 the princes fought side by side under the banner of Prince Bogdan, defeating an invading Polish army at Crasna, and thus gained valuable military experience. These bonds formed during Dracula's period of Moldavian exile lasted throughout his lifetime, the only shadow (albeit a significant one) being Stephen's betrayal in the summer of 1462.

Dracula's stay in Moldavia was suddenly terminated by the brutal assassination of Prince Bogdan II by Petru Aaron, his brother, the leader of yet another rival faction, in October 1451, not far from Suceava. In those circumstances, perhaps because of lack of alternatives, both Dracula and Stephen escaped to Transylvania via the famous Borgo Pass (the scene that provides the awesome gothic setting in the first few chapters of Stoker's novel), though this route put them at the mercy of none other than Hunyadi, the man who was at least morally responsible for the assassination of Dracula's father and brother.

Because of two successive defeats at Varna and Kosovo, Hunyadi had, as noted, lost much of his prestige and power, and both the title of "viceroy of Hungary" and "governor of Transylvania" had been taken away from him in the name of Ladislas V Posthumus, ruler of Hungary (even though not yet crowned), and the powerful Hungarian diet, which had always distrusted him. But he still preserved the humbler title of "count of Bistriţa, Severin and Timişoara" and retained his vast estates in Transylvania. Above all he was supreme military commander on the eastern front and had an important army of mercenaries under his command at his headquarters at Castle Hunedoara. For Vlad Dracula to seek refuge on territory thus still under the control of his family's enemy, "the White Knight," was, to say the least, foolhardy.

In entering Transylvania, the two sons of princes had for this reason carefully bypassed the fortified town of Bistriţa, where Hunyadi's mercenaries were in control and headed southward toward Braşov, by way of Sighişoara. Encouraged by an exchange of letters he had had with the city fathers preceding his brief rule in 1448 and by the support of a small number of exiled boyars there who were the enemies of Vladislav II, Vlad Dracula was planning to use that city as a base of operations for a campaign to regain his throne. Hunyadi, however, was equally determined to thwart any such effort. When the envoy of the former governor first reported Dracula's presence in Braşov in February 1452, Hunyadi lost no time in writing a stern note to the mayor and the city council, asking that the authorities apprehend the Wallachian refugee and chase him out of the country. Hunyadi was still loyal to his protégé, Vladislav II. It is conceivable that Dracula, in response, may have fled to Moldavia once again for a period of time, since Bogdan's murderer had been replaced by a friendlier candidate. In all likelihood, however, Dracula stayed in the vicinity of Braşov, kept in hiding on the estates of some friendly boyar. On September 24, 1452, he was still reported to be in the vicinity of that city, since Vladislav II sent an official letter of protest to the mayor of Braşov. Finally, Dracula decided to flee to the neighboring city of Sibiu. The authorities there were apprised of his presence. The vice-governor, Nicolae of Ocna, followed Hunyadi's instructions and took immediate action: he hired an assassin, who planned an ambush in the village of Gioagiu. Somehow forewarned, as on so many occasions, Dracula managed to escape.

At what point could Dracula afford to come out of hiding and what were the circumstances that led to his making peace with Hunyadi? The principal factor that brought the two men together was a cooling in the relationship between Hunyadi and his protégé Vladislav II. One reason for this was Hunyadi's unilateral seizure of the duchies of Făgăraş and Amlaş, traditional fiefs of the Wallachian prince. Amlaş was given to the citizens of Sibiu, while the fortress of Făgăraş and the surrounding territory was taken over by Hunyadi himself. This led to open hostilities with Vladislav II, who sought to regain control over land that he considered his own. Another factor was Vladislav II's aforementioned decision to improve his relationship with the Turks, a persistent desire of the boyar council. In January 1451 Vladislav had sent a delegation of boyars to congratulate the new sultan, Mehmed II, upon his accession to the throne — thus in a sense reverting to the traditional Wallachian policy of double allegiance to the king of Hungary and to the Turkish sultan, which had been followed by his enemy Dracul.

On Hunyadi's side, advance knowledge from his envoys posted in Constantinople on Mehmed's preparations for the conquest of that city brought the Transylvanian commander-in-chief to the realization that he needed all the talent he could muster to challenge the unlimited territorial appetites of the new sultan. At the time, his own diplomats were still negotiating with Constantine XI, the last Byzantine emperor, to determine last-minute contingencies to save the city. Upon reflection, Hunyadi became convinced that this young Wallachian warlord, whom fate had thrust upon his soil, had intimate knowledge of the workings of Mehmed's mind, and, having served five times in the Turkish army, knew their tactics and military organization. The presence of Vlad Dracula's brother in the Turkish camp might prove an additional asset. On Dracula's side there was the thornier moral problem of forgiving the double crime of 1447 — his father's and older brother's assassinations. If conscience he had, Dracula must have placed it in his slipper.

This about-face on the part of both men was hardly unexpected in this age of self-serving politics. It is certain that personal ambition was uppermost in the minds of both the older crusader and the younger man when they first met in Hunyadi's lofty Gothic palace, still in existence, located on a mighty rock on the western suburb of the north-central Transylvanian city of Hunedoara. The meeting took place in the knight's room, where among a gallery of family portraits hung an imposing painting of the former viceroy and his wife, Erzsébet Szilágy. There is no record of the precise words exchanged between the two men, but obviously a deal was struck. Vlad Dracula was offered a military appointment in Hunyadi's army and a minor function at his court, with residence at Sibiu; the Saxon authorities there were instructed to tolerate his presence. Dracula could not have found a more experienced tutor in the tactics and strategy of eastern wars — Hunyadi was still internationally held to be among the foremost military commanders of the day.

Hunyadi must have valued having Vlad Dracula in his service, for he gave him the maximum exposure. He took Dracula with him for the opening of the Hungarian diet at Györ and formally presented him to King Ladislas Posthumus, who had finally been declared of age by his guardian, the emperor, and anointed king of Hungary in 1453. Dracula, who was present at the coronation, swore allegiance to Ladislas Posthumus and was also present at the formal banquet and celebrations that followed, held at the royal palace in Buda. (In the course of this jubilant atmosphere Hunyadi also made his peace with the powerful relative of the former Emperor Sigismund, Count Ulrich Cilli, a devoted partisan of the new Holy Roman Emperor, Frederick III.) It was with the full consent of the Hungarian king and the Transylvanian diet that Dracula, at Hunyadi's suggestion, accepted responsibility for the defense of the Transylvanian frontier against Turkish attack. In essence, he was assigned very much the same role that his father Dracul had played from 1431 to 1436. His headquarters were to remain at Sibiu. It was in this German Saxon city that he learned of the fall of Constantinople to the Turks, an event that had been anticipated since Sultan Murad II's death by a stroke at the age of forty-seven on February 3, 1451, and his ambitious son's succession.

The new heir was Murad's nineteen-year-old second son, Prince Mehmed, who had ruled during two earlier years (1444–1446), following his father's temporary resignation, but had made himself thoroughly unpopular through his high-handedness and debauched living. As soon as he assumed the throne for the second time, Mehmed confirmed the negative image earlier formed of him by putting to death his half-brother, only a child, but a potential rival. In fact, the child's own mother was busy honoring the new sultan, Mehmed, at the very moment when her son was being drowned in his bathtub.

Mehmed's extravagant living, his ruthlessness and inordinate ambitions, coupled with the fact that his mother was a humble slave, had alienated him from his father, who was a gentleman in matters of international politics, always preferring peace to the uncertainties of war and retaliating only when attacked. Western diplomatic observers who rejoiced at the death of Murad II had underestimated the character and determination of the young sultan, who turned out to be a more formidable foe than his father. The first warning came from the Turkish grand vizier Halil Pasha, who believed in coexistence between the Turkish and Byzantine world (it was said by some that he had sold himself to the Byzantines for a high price). Halil had earlier cautioned the emperor Constantine about his unruly ward, drawing his attention to Mehmed's desire to conquer the Imperial City for reasons of prestige: "O you foolish Greeks!" he exclaimed. "My master Mohammed is not like his father, Sultan Murad. You are mistaken in your threats. Mohammed is not a child to be frightened. If you wish to call on the Hungarian

[Hunyadi], do it! If you wish to recover your territories, you may try! I promise you, you will only lose the little you have left!''

An incident that later took place in the imperial palace between Halil and the sultan left little further doubt as to the sultan's intentions. Roaming restlessly at night through the streets of Adrianople, the new sultan seemed haunted by the idea of conquest, but before embarking upon such an ambitious project as the siege of Constantinople, he wished to ascertain the thoughts of his subjects. One sleepless night in 1452, the sultan got up and sent his eunuch to summon Halil Pasha. The latter, knowing Mehmed's cupidity, took the precaution of taking a bowl of gold with him to this meeting. When he arrived he found the sultan fully dressed, sitting on the edge of his bed. The sultan, eyeing the gold, exclaimed, ''What is the meaning of this?'' The grand vizier meekly replied, ''It is customary when a noble is summoned to his master that he not appear with empty hands.'' Mehmed then revealed his thoughts to Halil: ''It is not gold that I need; I want but one thing, your help in seizing Constantinople!'' The vizier bowed to the sultan's will, and the sultan shouted, ''Relying on the support of Allah and his Prophet, we will take the city!''

Against Mehmed stood the youthful emperor, Constantine XI Dragases, of the Paleologus dynasty. He had succeeded to the imperial purple following the death of his brother John VIII in January 1449. The last emperor struck an imposing figure: he was tall, with strong regular features, a man known for his valor, integrity, and personal courage rather than concerns for ceremony or ritual. He habitually was clothed in either the white garb of a penitent or else, to attract attention to his potential military role, he wore plated armor and a steel helmet. He had married twice, but, as was the case with his brothers, he was destined to die without heirs. On the whole, he had given up the idea of obtaining military help from the west; unlike his brother, he was not prepared to beg for such aid. As a realist he was fully aware of the desperate nature of the situation. He had conceived of a few hopeless initiatives such as marrying Sultan Murad's widow, the Serbian sultana Mara, but the lady preferred to remain in the relative safety of the Serbian monastery to which she had retired. The emperor had accepted the union of the Roman Catholic and Orthodox churches proclaimed at Florence in 1439, and joint services had been held at the church of St. Sophia. The populace, however, had shunned such events, refusing to concelebrate, and eventually the great cathedral built by Emperor Justinian was closed down. The only real hope of the Byzantines was pinned on John Hunyadi, who had sent a delegation to Constantinople as soon as he realized that the spoken intentions of Mehmed to capture the city were no idle threat. However, Hunyadi's ambassadors were withdrawn before the Turks began action to isolate the city. Ever practical, the Transylvanian warlord, now counseled by Vlad Dracula, decided that he must concentrate his diminished resources on defending his own borders, both in Transylvania, where Dracula was in command, and at his southern flank, which centered on the fortress of Belgrade, of far greater strategic significance than the imperial Byzantine city.

It is easy to overdramatize the atmosphere of pessimism and gloom that permeated the beleaguered city once the intentions of the sultan were made clear. But such an atmosphere did prevail. It was compounded by a series of ill omens, many of which are mentioned in Chalcondyles' account of the siege that undermined the morale of a superstitious populace. A few days before the final assault on May 24, 1453, the dome of the cathedral of St. Sophia came alive with a red glow, which rose slowly up from the base to the top of the dome. The light reportedly stayed there, suspended, for some time, then mysteriously flickered out. Some thought that this light came from the Turkish campfires around the city, but this was not so, since these rays shone from the distant countryside far behind the Turkish camp. The optimists believed that they were the bonfires of the great Christian warrior John Hunyadi on his way to save the city. Sultan Mehmed II himself was frightened by the lights, though his seers consoled him with the thought that they were a sign from heaven that the true religion of Islam would finally prevail to enlighten the ancient city. There was also an eclipse of the sun. Prophets had long proclaimed that the city would never fall while the moon was glowing in the heavens! Another incident defied rational explanation. During a solemn procession led by the emperor through the city on the way to the cathedral of St. Sophia, to invoke God's blessings, the heavy ikon of the Blessed Virgin, said to have been painted by Saint Luke himself, slipped from the hands of its bearers and fell to the ground. For a while the bearers were unable to raise it up again. Only after fervent prayers was the task accomplished. As the procession continued, a violent storm accompanied by thunder and lightning broke out, followed by torrential rain, which caused widespread flooding. Then a thick fog settled over the city; no one had ever seen such dense fog in May. It seemed to many that God had brought in the fog in order to conceal His departure from the city. The historians at the time also remembered an ancient prophecy to the effect that the *last* emperor would have the same name as the first,

Constantine, the original founder of the city, yet another sign of doom. Cynics responded with the words attributed by some to Grand Duke Lukas Notaras, who acted as a kind of prime minister and was grand admiral of the fleet: "I would rather see the turban of the Turk in Constantinople than the red hat of any Roman Catholic cardinal!" So great and so widespread was the hatred of the Latin "heretics" even at this hour of need.

Stargazing and defeatist oracles had less to do with the pessimism of those who were in the know than the statistical fact the Constantinople simply did not have enough able-bodied men to cover fourteen miles (nine miles facing the sea and five miles facing land) of walls and towers originally built by Emperor Heraclius in the seventh century. The total population of the city had shrunk from over a million in its heyday to about 50,000 to 60,000, many of whom were members of the clergy, in 1453. When the Turks began their operations against the city during that spring, a multinational army of at most 18,000 or 20,000 poorly equipped men (Greeks, Genoese, Florentines, Catalans, Venetians, a papal contingent, and other small groups from many states) was all that the emperor could muster. The army was supported by a small fleet of sixteen fighting ships (five Venetian, five Genoese, three from Crete, a colony of Venice, one from Ancona, one from Catalonia, one from Provence) — altogether a force totally inadequate to protect the straits and the coast. The best that could be improvised was a boom composed of chains that stretched from the seaward wall facing the Sea of Marmora to the Genoese colony of Galata to the north of the city. The only secret weapon still used by the Byzantines was a mysterious explosive combustible compound known as "Greek fire," which was placed in a tube and flung by hand to the decks of the defensive fleet, to set the attacking Turkish galleys on fire.

Sultan Mehmed was very boldly determined to challenge the alleged supremacy of the Greco-Venetian defensive fleet by means of a gamble he was not quite certain of being able to carry out. He went to war de facto by declaring the Bosporus — the narrow neck of water that separates the Black Sea from the Sea of Marmora — closed to those ships of all nations who refused to pay a fee. In order to enforce this decree, the sultan decided to build a formidable fortress on the European side of the Bosporus (a smaller one had already been constructed on the Asiatic side a few years before). Completed at breakneck speed within five months, it soon became known as "Cutthroat Castle," because it stood at the narrowest point of the Bosporus and could thus bombard any vessels trying to sail through to Constantinople. The noose around the neck of Constantinople thus began in advance to tighten; the process of cutting off the imperial city from the west had begun early. To counter whatever strategic and technological advantages the Greek fleet and its allies may have possessed, Mehmed was determined to experiment with a revolutionary use of military hardware to launch his offensive.

The invention of gunpowder and the destructive capacities of the cannon had always fascinated him. He learned from his father that cannon fire had been used with remarkable success by Prince Mircea, Dracula's brother, during the Varna campaign, at the siege of Petretz in Bulgaria and later by Vlad Dracul at the siege of Giurgiu in 1445. Intrigued by the success of the Wallachians and others, Mehmed had also learned that some of these mobile guns had been manufactured in the cannon foundries at Braşov by craftsmen who would sell their services to whoever paid them most. Among such cannon forgers was a certain Urban, who had offered to build a cannon foundry at Constantinople for Emperor Constantine XI. The bid was rejected by the emperor, who could not meet Urban's steep price. The circumstances that brought Urban's name to the attention of Sultan Mehmed are unknown, but when Urban met the sultan, a deal was quickly struck. Mehmed asked Urban a simple question: "What is the largest cannon that you can construct that would be capable of battering down the huge walls that Emperor Heraclius built?" Upon being given the specifics, the sultan told Urban he could name his price. As in the case of "Cutthroat Castle," a monstrous cannon nicknamed the "Basilica" (a play on words with the Greek imperial title Basileus) was built at record speed. The cannon was 27 feet long, had a 48-inch bore, and was capable of firing projectiles weighting 600 pounds, propelled by 150 pounds of gunpowder. The weight of Basilica was such that it required 700 men and 15 pair of oxen to pull it for its initial test shot in the vicinity of Adrianople. It is said that the shot left a crater six feet deep and that the attending noise and smoke was so intense that it created panic among the villagers nearby. This cannon had limited value because of the effort required to move it into place, the need for trained western experts to man it, and the fact that it could be fired only seven times in twenty-four hours because of the danger of exploding due to overheating. However, in the long run the Sultan's faith in the effectiveness of cannon fire was justified, since it helped soften the defenses of Constantinople and created irreparable breaches in both the walls and the outer fortifications.

The disparity between the Ottoman and Byzantine forces has been overplayed by all the Greek historians of the period in order to capture the attention of potential western leaders. In actual fact, the regular Turkish army was composed of no more than 100,000 men — roughly divided into 60,000 Asiatic cavalrymen, 10,000 janissaries, and 20,000 camp followers. In addition, there were various vassal contingents, numbering about 10,000. The fleet included one hundred triremes (three oarsmen to a bench) and some long sailing ships used for attack in the manner of a modern torpedo boat. Since the Turks were never particularly famous for their seamanship, their fleet was manned by Christian recruits. The grand admiral of the Turkish navy happened to be of Bulgarian origin. By a clever ploy, the latter circumvented the iron chain that the Byzantines had laid to close the entry of the golden gate, by transporting most of the fleet overland, beyond the Genoese-inhabited suburb of Pera, thus enabling it to bombard the seaward walls of the city effectively.

So, on Monday, May 28, 1453, an ominous silence settled on the beleaguered city, where hopes of relief were rapidly dwindling away. Some citizens foolishly entertained the thought of a miracle such as that Mehmed and his troops might suddenly melt away and abandon the siege. In fact, the sultan had declared that last Monday before the final attack to be a day of rest. Thus, the loud sounds of the Turkish siege had stopped, not because it had failed, but precisely because the siege had been successful to that point. In Mehmed's view, the city walls had been sufficiently weakened by earlier cannonshot to allow for the final assault. To counteract this Turkish quietness, the emperor ordered the church bells rung and the liturgy to be celebrated in both Latin and Greek in the Cathedral of St. Sophia. For the previous five months, no pious Orthodox Christian had set foot in that church, ever since the hated union had been proclaimed there on December 12, 1452. But now, on that Monday, May 28, past differences and hatred were forgotten. Together Italians and Greeks, Roman Catholics and Eastern Orthodox Christians went to confession, took communion, and sang the Kyrie Eleison, "Lord, have mercy!" For one brief moment the union of churches became a reality.

At half past one in the morning on Tuesday, May 29, the sultan himself ordered the final assault. As predicted, a waning moon hung in the sky First the sultan's European mercenaries charged the walls. There followed the assault of the sultan's bodyguards, who had their weapons raised to kill any of the mercenaries who might become cowardly. Behind them marched the elite troops, the janissaries, with their military band blaring tunes to a rapid marching beat. After them the regular Turkish soldiers stormed the walls. For a while it seemed as if the walls just might hold.

Woodcut frontispiece of Dracole Waida, Nuremberg, c. 1488, a manuscript that begins "In the year of our Lord 1456 Dracula did many dreadful and curious things . . ."

Portrait presumed to be of Vlad Dracul, Dracula's father. It was discovered during the restoration of the Dracula homestead in Sighişoara in 1976 and is evidently a seventeenth-century copy of an earlier portrait. At present it is located in the Sighişoara Historical Museum. A copy of the Ambras portrait of Dracula in the upper right corner reveals the likeness to Dracula.

The "Knight's Hall" where Vlad Dracul was given the insignia of prince of Wallachia by the Holy Roman Emperor, in the presence of a few dissident boyars, on February 8, 1431.

Seventeenth-century print of Sighişoara showing the fortress and the clock tower at the top of the hill where Dracula's homestead is located. From an *Album of Sighişoara* published in Bucharest in 1965.

John Hunyadi (1387–1456), ban of Severin (1438–1441), prince of Transylvania, hereditary count of Timisoara and Bistriţa, governor-general and regent of Hungary (1444–1453). Father of King Matthias Corvinus, he was known as the ''White Knight'' of the Christian crusaders. Nineteenth-century print by Sebastian Langer.

Ladislas V, nicknamed ''Posthumus,'' king of Hungary (1444–1457). Anonymous contemporary painting of the Austrian school.

Castle Hunedoara,
Hunyadi's headquarters in
Transylvania.

Seventeenth-century
engraving of the fortress
of Belgrade on the
Danube, showing the
upper and lower castle by
the artist Milos Crnjanski.

Main entrance over what
was formerly a
drawbridge to the fortress
of Belgrade.

The best known of Dracula's portraits, located at the "Monster Gallery" at Castle Ambras (near Innsbruck). It is a copy, painted anonymously during the second half of the sixteenth century, of an unknown original. The original portrait was probably painted during Dracula's imprisonment at Buda or Visegrád after 1462. First listed in the Ambras collection in 1621.

Chindia Watchtower, the only nineteenth-century reconstruction of Dracula's original palace at Tîrgovişte, now largely in ruins. Apart from its role as an observation post, it also enabled Dracula to watch the impalements going on in the courtyard below.

Eerie remaining wall of
Dracula's famous castle
on the Argeş, before
restoration.

CRONSTAD.

Seventeenth-century engraving of Braşov (Kronstadt or Cronstad in German) as it existed in Dracula's time, showing the city walls and defensive towers as well as Tîmpa Hill where many of Dracula's atrocities were committed.

Castle Bran. Originally a fortress of the Teutonic Order founded in 1212 and known as Dietrichstein, it was taken over by the German Saxons to protect Braşov at the end of the thirteenth century. Briefly under the rule of Prince Mircea, it was given by Emperor Sigismund to the princes of Transylvania and eventually to the city of Braşov. It is often mistaken for Castle Dracula.

But the sultan ordered the elite troops to renew the attack. At the Saint Romanus gate a giant named Hassan breached the walls first and was killed. But other janissaries followed. The Byzantine emperor himself, Constantine XI, was last seen at that very Saint Romanus gate, having thrown away his royal robe, fighting like a common foot soldier. He died a martyr, like a captain who would not desert his sinking ship.

When the Turks finally overran the city, they ripped people's clothing off to use as ropes to bind captives together. In the great cathedral of St. Sophia the priests were still celebrating the morning mass when the Turkish invaders arrived. According to legend, the celebrants were seen to disappear into the southern interior wall of the cathedral with their chalices still in hand; the walls closed behind them. Prophets predicted that these walls would reopen only on the day when Constantinople became a Christian city again, which has not happened thus far.

Sultan Mehmed II waited until the traditional three days of looting had passed (about 4,000 people were killed and 50,000 men, women and children enslaved) and then entered the city. He rode straight to the cathedral of St. Sophia, went to the altar, and intoned the Muslim prayer, "There is no God but Allah, and Mohammed is His Prophet." The capture of Constantinople had been a Muslim goal almost as old as that religion itself. It was believed that the Prophet Mohammed had said, "Blessed be he who conquers Constantinople." Henceforth Mehmed II became known by the Turkish epithet *Fatih,* meaning "Conqueror." The Ottoman Empire was now geographically part of Europe, though Europeans still could not accept that fact, because the Turks were not Christians.

The fall of Constantinople, a metropolis that had been isolated by the Turks ever since their conquest of most of the Balkans, was one of the great turning points of history, equal to the later fall of the monarchy in France in 1789 or the Bolshevik revolution of 1917, which marked the birth of a new era. Certainly, Pope Nicholas V, who had done little more than equip three Genoese galleys loaded with weapons and food for the beleaguered city, thought of the "fall" as one of the world's major calamities when he wrote, "The light of Christianity had suddenly gone out. We shall not see it again in our lifetime." This sense of personal guilt undoubtedly shortened the pope's life. Equally perturbed was the humanist Enea Silvio de' Piccolomini, who also lamented the massacre of his fellow Christians. The future Pope Pius II, however, laid emphasis on another aspect of the tragedy, calling it "the second death of Homer and Plato," since it was Greek-speaking civilization that had fallen. When news reached Paris and London of this calamitous event, King Charles VII of France and Henry VI of England ordered their respective courts to go into mourning. Even in distant Moscow, the bells of the church at the Kremlin tolled, as requiem masses were held in memory of fellow Orthodox martyrs.

Most immediately affected, though, by the Turkish conquest were the neighboring states, Vladislav II's Wallachia in the first instance, Transylvania, under the watch of Vlad Dracula and Hunyadi, and, of course, Hungary, under its inexperienced Ladislas V Posthumus. More distant in a geographic sense, though by virtue of traditions and status deeply committed to the defense of the Christian world against the Ottoman, was the newly crowned (in 1452) Holy Roman Emperor of the German states, Frederick III, who had just returned from Rome with his young Portuguese bride Eleanor, fortified by the prestige of a papal coronation. However, Frederick III, though he expressed pious words of sympathy, was far more concerned with the consolidation of his power in Europe, preserving his ascendency over Ladislas V Posthumus and launching a crusade against the heretic king of Bohemia, George Poděbrady, a closer threat than that presented by Mehmed II.

While details about the fall of Constantinople reached western Europe only after months of delay, news about the extent and horror of the catastrophe was brought to all the Romanian provinces from the beginning of the siege by a steady flow of refugees who inevitably had to pass through these frontier lands. Among the first were a number of Venetian sailors who had survived the sinking of their galley in the Sea of Marmora by swimming ashore to the Thracian coast. They had made their way through Bulgaria, being given food and shelter by the native population, crossed the Danube through Wallachia, and headed toward their homeland through the Transylvania pass at Turnu Roşu after passing through Sibiu, Dracula's command post. Among countless stories of sufferings and atrocities, they related how those of their shipmates who were captured by the Turks were impaled by order of the Sultan on stakes planted in full view of the beleaguered city. This act was aimed at persuading the citizens to surrender without a struggle; then, in accordance with custom, the Turks could show leniency toward the population. The description of this gruesome scenario raised a few eyebrows, though impalement was known to and used by the German Saxons as a form of punishment for capital offenses.

One ruler who was kept precisely informed of events in Constantinople was Vladislav II in Tîrgovişte, because he had had a boyar observer permanently attached to the sultan's court since Mehmed's accession in 1451. An invaluable informant in Tîrgovişte was a Romanian bishop called Samuil, who managed to escape from Constantinople after its conquest, reaching the Wallachian capital toward the end of June 1453. He was received in audience by the prince, and one can assume that Vladislav's increasingly pro-Turkish stance was a result of this meeting, since the bishop described in vivid details the kind of punishment inflicted by the sultan on his enemies. Bishop Samuil also sent one of Vladislav's boyars with a letter addressed to the mayor of Sibiu, to inform the Saxons of the ultimate aims of Mehmed. Bishop Samuil warned the mayor, Oswald Wenzel, that "the Turks will eventually subdue all of Christianity if God will allow it. . . . They will next conquer the lands [meaning Belgrade] of the despot George Branković of Serbia. . . . They also say that the city of Sibiu, which lies on their path, must be destroyed." Since his own city was specifically mentioned, the mayor of Sibiu became very alarmed: "Sibiu, Sibiu," he wrote in desperation, "why, this is Hermannstadt [the German name of the town]! . . . Turkish conquest of our fortress will mean not only the conquest of Hungary but that of all of Christianity." He appealed to Hunyadi, commander-in-chief of the region, to Ladislas V Posthumus, the king of Hungary, to Vlad Dracula, who had made his headquarters in the town, to the mayor and city council of Vienna, and to the Holy Roman Emperor himself for help.

Hunyadi did not need the advice of Oswald Wenzel. He was sufficiently conversant with the sultan's state of mind and ambitions to realize that the conquest of Constantinople represented but a first step, which would lead to attempts at further annexations. (In this respect he was kept remarkably well informed by his personal envoy and confidant, János Vitéz, a remarkably acute statesman and diplomat, who was to become the future bishop of Oradea and primate of Hungary.) He knew he must defend his realm at certain strategic points: in the first instance, the fortress of Belgrade, which protected the southern flank of Hungary, must be consolidated. Fully aware also that the Turks were virtually in control of Wallachia (their merchants and spies were swarming in the capital and other major cities), Hunyadi further decided to punish his former protégé Vladislav II by consolidating his control over the duchies of Făgăraş and Amlaş (Wallachian enclaves within Transylvania). He next appealed to the German townships to provide him and Vlad Dracula with the weapons and finances to equip and pay for the new army of mercenaries that was needed to reinforce the local garrisons at Sibiu and Braşov. Finally, it was important to raise this new army from among Romanians, Germans,

Slavs, and members of the lower nobility of Transylvania, traditional components of his earlier crusading armies. He knew he could not count on the upper nobility of Hungary, who preferred the security and comfort of their estates; nor could he persuade his inexperienced liege King Ladislas Posthumus to take formal command — the boy king preferred the distractions of the courts at Buda or Vienna over campaigning. The Transylvanian leader confirmed the appointment of his eldest son, Ladislas, as military head of the southwestern flank to lead an offensive in Croatia, while Dracula, as commander-in-chief in Transylvania, was given the role of forestalling an attack by Vladislav II — now the sultan's ally.

János Vitéz, Hunyadi's confidant, guessed correctly that Mehmed's next blow would not be delivered against Transylvania, where his flank was sufficiently protected by the loyalty of Vladislav II and his Moldavian counterpart Petru III Aaron, equally won over to the sultan's cause. The main Turkish offensive was to be against the powerful strategic fortress of Belgrade, which commanded an impressive location on a hill at the confluence of the Sava and Danube rivers. Together with its string of tripled walls, outer fortifications, towers, and battlements, it is still, notwithstanding the destruction wrought by time and innumerable sieges, one of the most impressive sights in the present day capital of the Socialist Republic of Yugoslavia. The garrison of Belgrade, under the command of Mihály Szilágy, Hunyadi's brother-in-law, was small, comprising no more than 5,000 or 6,000 men, but they could rely on the help of the local Serbian population, which had chosen to live within the city walls after the despot Branković had handed Belgrade over to the Hungarians in 1420.

There was no question that from Hunyadi's point of view the fall of Belgrade would represent a catastrophe of incalculable proportions. It would open up the Danube to a Turkish fleet, which hence would be free to attack Buda or even Vienna. Thus it would threaten the security of Hungary and the Holy Roman Empire. For Hunyadi personally, the loss of Belgrade would spell the end of all his ambitions and the even greater hopes he nurtured for his sons László and Matthias.

The intention of Sultan Mehmed to attack Hungary by way of Belgrade first became apparent during the winter of 1455–1456, when he assembled a large army of perhaps 90,000 men in the vicinity of Adrianople, while a fleet conservatively estimated at some 60 ships was being fitted on the Danube delta. The worst suspicions were confirmed when German and other gunsmiths took up residence in Kruševac in central Serbia, with instructions to build mortars and cannon.

There was, however, a response from a totally unexpected quarter. It came in the person of a seventy-year-old Minorite Franciscan monk who has since been canonized by the Roman Catholic church: Saint John of Capistrano. He was an extraordinary survivor of an earlier period of Medieval crusading (the likes of which was not seen again in Europe until the siege of Vienna in 1683). John of Capistrano, whose imposing bust still adorns the main facade of Saint Stephen's Dom in Vienna, certainly looked the part of a Peter the Hermit, the crusading leader of the eleventh century. Small of stature, with an emaciated frame, hollow cheeks, deep-set eyes, and parched skin, he had the countenance and stature of a mystic as he gathered the faithful around him in the city of Győr in Hungary and preached the crusade to the common man in Latin. No one understood his exact words, but the tone of the message was unmistakable as he thundered: "God wills it that we chase the Turks out of Europe and for whosoever follows me, I will obtain plenary indulgence for him and his family." It was more a matter of heart than rational thinking that induced a ragtag army of some 8,000 inexperienced and poorly equipped peasants, lower burghers, students, and clergymen to follow John on his southeastward march. They had gathered all the crude weapons they could assemble: slings, cudgels, scythes, pitchforks, stakes, and other farm implements. It was, however, their determination and fanaticism that proved more than a match for the holy war proclaimed by the sultan and the tried military talent of the Turks and janissaries. The generals and the diplomats who attended John's demagogic harangue at Győr — Hunyadi, his son László, János Vitéz, Vlad Dracula, even Pope Calixtus III's legate, Juan Cardinal de Carvajal — were not impressed by what they regarded as a "mob." In the end, though, these leaders found they had underestimated the power of faith to move men.

At a meeting summoned by Hunyadi at Hunedoara on January 13, 1456, basic strategies for the impending campaign were laid out and assignments to the military leaders given with little reference to John of Capistrano's crusaders, who worked essentially as an independent force. Dracula, with an army composed mostly of Romanian mercenaries, was instructed by Hunyadi to stay at Sibiu and watch the Transylvanian passes. In addition, his young protégé was given to understand that he could proceed with the offensive against Vladislav II at whatever time he would deem appropriate, thus to relieve pressure at Belgrade by compelling the Turks to keep a body of troops on the Danube. In essence, Dracula's mission was part of the overall strategy in protecting the eastern flank of the Belgrade defensive operation. In turn, Dracula's cousin

Stephen of Moldavia, also in Hunyadi's entourage, was waiting for an opportunity to overthrow the other Turkish vassal, Petru III Aaron. By June 1456, in the words of the historian János Thuróczi "as the grain began to ripen," a vast army, accompanied by 300 siege guns and 27 enormous cannons, followed by the fleet on the Danube, moved northward, capturing on the way a number of Serbian cities that had maintained a precarious autonomy under Turkish rule. Hunyadi sent the customary diplomatic appeals to the west by means of his intermediary János Vitéz; as usual, there was no response.

The greatest achievement of John Hunyadi and John of Capistrano, unlikely allies that they were, was breaking through the ring of Turkish land forces, as well as the chains of Turkish flotillas that blocked access to the city, to effect a juncture with the city's defenders. On July 21, having finally penetrated the outer defenses and moats, Mehmed gave orders for a final assault. In desperation, the sultan tried to arouse enthusiasm in his troops by joining the melee in person, only to be wounded in the thigh for his pains. Though the Turkish army had penetrated the city, it was unable to capture the fortress on the hill, defended by 16,000 men evenly divided between John of Capistrano's crusaders and Hunyadi's professionals. For Mehmed, who lost as many as 24,000 of his best soldiers and whose sailors colored the blue Danube red, it was a disastrous defeat. The relief of Belgrade was described as a "miracle" by Bernhard von Kraiburg, chancellor of the archbishop of Salzburg, in which "8,000 simple people" had defeated a vastly overwhelming Turkish force. In retreating toward Sofia, the ailing sultan was so angry that he wounded a number of his generals with his own sword and later had them executed. When the successful defense of Belgrade was reported to Rome, Eugenius IV called it "the happiest event of my life"; believing that a miracle had truly occurred, the pope made preparations for the beatification of John of Capistrano.

Typically, one reason why the upper nobility of Hungary had refused to leave their Transylvanian estates to join the crusade was rumors to the effect that during the summer, the plague had flared up once again in the Danubian plain, infected rats accompanying the Turkish forces from Anatolia, where the disease was endemic. As news of an actual outbreak spread, the more affluent people, who included members of the courts at Tîrgoviște and Suceava in Moldavia, scurried for shelter in the mountainous regions, which were considered relatively safe havens. During the summer of 1456 the plague struck Hungary, Croatia, and Slovenia, sparing neither young nor old, poor nor rich. Among its early victims of note was Elizabeth Cilli, the beautiful young lady destined for Hunyadi's youngest son, Matthias; she died at Buda. On August 11, amid the festive atmosphere that followed the Christian relief of Belgrade, Hunyadi, well into his sixties, his health undermined by fatigue and exhaustion, also succumbed to the disease at Zenum in Serbia, only a few miles from the site of his triumph. The even more aged John of Capistrano, whose crucial role is commemorated on a small stone plaque located at the precise point where the crusaders entered the fortress, was also felled by the dread disease a few months later, on October 23, at Ujlak, in Hungary. The death of Hunyadi prompted his son László to take official command of Belgrade during the winter of 1456–1457.

As Hunyadi and John of Capistrano had been marching with their motley force toward Belgrade, Dracula had lost little time in planning his own diversionary offensive, aimed at paralyzing any action that Vladislav II might have planned to help Mehmed's offensive. Vlad Dracula's pledge of allegiance to the crown of Hungary and to the Christian cause, a pledge also implicit in his Dragon oath, had signified a permanent rupture with his former Turkish protectors and now legalized this action. He set out in mid-June through the Carpathian pass at Bran with a small motley force composed of a few exiled boyars, Hungarians, and Romanian mercenaries, and the moral and material support of the German cities of Transylvania. By mid-July, at the very time when the Turks and Hunyadi's forces were locked in combat at Belgrade, Dracula engaged Vladislav II in combat somewhere near Tîrgovişte. He had the satisfaction of killing his mortal enemy and his father's assassin in hand-to-hand combat. The far more cruel circumstances of avenging Mircea's death — buried alive at Tîrgovişte — lay ahead. Vladislav II's tomb can still be seen at the Monastery of Dealul near Tîrgovişte, with a brief inscription that was placed on it a century later through the intervention of the heirs to the Dănesti line. The date of his death is still marked: August 22, 1456. At a century's distance, the Dănesti heirs were guilty of a pardonable dating error of one month. We know from other sources that Vladislav's death had actually occurred in July. By August 22 Dracula was already prince of Wallachia.

CHAPTER 4
A Machiavellian Ruler at Home

T H E future court historian of King Matthias, Antonio Bonfini, was among the first to make mention of an unusual comet that appeared during the month of June 1456, noticed earlier by Chinese astronomers: "as long as half the sky with two tails, one pointing west and the other east, colored gold and looking like an undulating flame in the distant horizon." It became the object of study by one of the leading astronomers of the period, the Florentine Toscanelli, during the seven weeks and four days of sighting in central and eastern Europe, and was also brought to the attention of Sultan Mehmed shortly after the disaster at Belgrade. An exact description of the cyclical character of the trajectory and precise calculation of orbit of what turned out to be the most famous comet in history had to await the astronomer Edmund Halley (1636–1742).

In Dracula's time some astrologers, on the basis of previous sightings, viewed the comet simply as an omen of bad luck: the prelude to earthquakes, plagues, wars, and other natural catastrophes. In southeastern Europe the appearance was thus at first linked with the military offensive of the new sultan Mehmed II, and later with the deaths of John Hunyadi and John of Capistrano at Belgrade. Antonio Bonfini had foretold the death of the great Transylvanian military leader thirty days before the "appearance of a star with a tail during the month of June" — a prophecy that turned out to be accurate.

On the other hand, other seers looked upon comets as good auguries. After all, such a star had shone in the sky at the time when Attila's Huns had been defeated on the plains of Catalonia. In June 1066 another sighting had closely coincided with the victory of William the Conqueror over the Saxons. For the pro-Norman, it was surely a good augury then. As for the appearance of a comet in 1456, it could also be alleged that, in spite of the deaths of the two great crusaders Hunyadi and Capistrano, since the city of Belgrade had actually been saved from Turkish conquest, a comet might again be a good omen.

Dracula and his astrologers must have considered its appearance in a positive vein, since during the period of its sighting he achieved his dream of securing his ancestral throne. This positive view is further suggested by the fact that the only Dracula coin discovered so far is one that depicts on one side the profile of the Wallachian eagle with its wings extended and a cross in its beak, and on the other, a crescent mounted on a star trailing six undulating rays in its wake. The coin, bearing the hallmark of a Braşov goldsmith, was of very high quality and obviously meant to replace those of Dracula's father, which bore the Dragon symbol. This particular coin has additional interest in being the only instance of Halley's comet being used in the heraldry of coins.

Barely aged twenty-five, Dracula began his most important reign in August 1456, elected by a small rump boyar council, in accordance with the fundamental laws of the land. He was subsequently anointed by the metropolitan of the land in the cathedral of Tîrgovişte (Biserica Domnească), with all the usual regalia attending such an event. Like his predecessors, he adopted the pompous title of ''Prince Vlad, son of Vlad the Great, sovereign and ruler of Ungro-Wallachia and of the duchies of Amlaş and Făgăraş,'' which he had recently acquired from the Hungarian king Ladislas V in return for his allegiance. As soon as he was established on the throne, Dracula began correspondence in September 1456 with the mayors of Braşov and Sibiu, as well as Hunyadi's son László, the new governor of the fortress of Belgrade and commander-in-chief of the Transylvanian territory. To secure his northern frontier with Moldavia, Dracula attempted to stir a revolt among dissident boyars of that country against the rule of Petru Aaron, his enemy, and thus to pave the way for the restoration of his ally and cousin Stephen (subsequently Stephen the Great), who was to be established on the throne of Suceava the following year (1457), with the help of a contingent of 6,000 Wallachians. By taking such actions, all of which emphasized his loyalty to the Christian cause, barely a month after his election, Dracula aroused the suspicion of the Turks. Hence a delegation from Sultan Mehmed was officially received at his palace in Tîrgovişte. Adroitly playing on old loyalties, the

Turkish emissaries demanded a yearly tribute (2,000 gold ducats), and the right of free passage for the Turkish army through Wallachia (for possible raids into Transylvania) as the price of Turkish recognition. Dracula assented to these terms, though with his father's experience of 1442 in mind, he refused the customary humiliation of traveling to Constantinople to pay his official homage in person.

Dracula's unusual appearance had attracted general attention ever since he was introduced at the Hungarian court at Buda in 1452. We know what he looked like, because of a copy of his portrait, the first life-size portrait of a Romanian prince, which presently hangs in the so-called monster portrait gallery of the Ambras Museum near Innsbruck. A miniature version of this truly extraordinary painting, painted by an artist of the Nuremberg school, is presently located at the Kunsthistorisches Museum in Vienna.

A careful analysis of the Ambras portrait reveals a strong, cruel, and somehow tortured man. One is immediately struck by his large, deep-set, dark green, and penetrating eyes. They appear doubly framed by deep shadows below and long eyelashes and arched brows above. The artist has captured a gaze that is distant and without real focus, though the expression as a whole is disdainful and imperious. Dracula's face is emaciated, with high cheekbones; his complexion is sallow and sickly. His nose is long and a little bent. The tightly sealed lower lip, which alone is visible, is red and disproportionately thick, suggesting sensuality. The Romanian historian Ion Bogdan, who in 1896 wrote the first monograph on Dracula, thought that the peculiar formation of the lower lip revealed an uncontrollable nervous twitch that may well have affected Dracula's whole face, in the manner of Peter the Great's, throwing it temporarily out of line. By the standards of the day, Dracula might be considered a handsome man, with his jutting chin bespeaking strength of character. The mustache entirely covering his upper lip (he was otherwise cleanshaven), though, is peculiarly elongated, straight, and meticulously curled at the ends, unlike the drooping mustaches popular among most princes of the period. Given the graying auburn reflection on his mustache, one might guess that he was fair-haired. His locks are, at any rate, long and curled, and fall far below his shoulders. From a pronounced bulge below his chest, one might surmise that Dracula was far from gaunt and probably not very tall.

Dracula's costume is that of the Hungarian nobleman of the period. It is in no way Oriental or Turkish, emphasizing his predilections for the west. Covering his mantle, and topped by gold brocade, is a wide collar of sable, an expensive fur rarely seen on the shoulders of Romanian princes. According to the Vienna miniature, the mantle was closed with three large golden buttons interlaced with red filaments. His close-fitting headgear was made of red silk with nine rows of pearls at the brim, very different from the tall ugly turbans worn by Turks and Greeks. A large clasp or brooch in the form of a star, at the forehead, in the center of which was a topaz, seemed to hold together a cluster of large pearls. The topaz held a cluster of feathers, presumably ostrich, tipped with additional precious jewels.

It seems likely that the portrait was taken from life, since it closely matches the only known detailed written description of Dracula, which came from the pen of the man who was soon to be papal legate to Buda, Niccolò Modrussa (Modrŭs), who knew the prince during his Hungarian captivity. His description reads:

> He was not very tall, but very stocky and strong, with a cold and terrible appearance, a strong and aquiline nose, swollen nostrils, a thin and reddish face in which the very long eyelashes framed large wide-open green eyes; the bushy black eyebrows made them appear threatening. His face and chin were shaven, but for a moustache. The swollen temples increased the bulk of his head. A bull's neck connected [with] his head from which black curly locks hung on his wide-shouldered person.

This disagrees with the portrait only concerning Dracula's complexion and the color of his hair. The overall impression derived from both views is that of a sensitive man with a keen and lively intelligence. His looks also suggest an overpowering, haughty, authoritarian personality with cruel instincts.

Such was the man destined to become the absolute autocrat of Wallachia and the two Transylvanian duchies of Făgăraş and Amlaş during the next six years. Although, as we have noticed, the total size of his country was not large, Dracula preferred to center his authority in the northern part of the country, where his ancestors had established their capitals, because of the protection afforded by the Carpathian mountains and proximity to his Transylvanian possessions. Although the internal documents of the period are not ample, they at least provide us information on the various locations where Dracula chose to establish his headquarters for varying periods of time. An interesting trait in terms of preference was his love of inner spiritual peace, solitude, and tranquillity afforded by the monasteries of Wallachia such as Tismana, located in the eastern part of the country; Cozia, where his grandfather was buried, in the valley of the river Olt; and the island monastery of Snagov, all of which, given his evil reputation, will require much more extensive comment. Like his grandfather Mircea, Dracula also wished to make a point of spending more of his time in the Danubian plain. In this respect, Dracula founded the fortress of Bucharest, hitherto a series of connected villages, the present-day capital of Romania. He accordingly strengthened the city and built its outer walls. The initial Dracula document commemorating this site refers to its location near the Dîmboviţa River and is dated June 13, 1458. It became a fortress only the following year, when Dracula signed and dated a letter on September 20, from the Castle of the Dîmboviţa River.

Most of Dracula's internal documents, founding monasteries, granting land to boyars, et cetera, were issued from Tîrgovişte, which had been the capital of the country since his grandfather Mircea's time. In Dracula's day, the capital city and ecclesiastical see of Tîrgovişte was a sprawling town, with outskirts spreading beyond the limits of the city walls. Like Louis XIV's Versailles, Tîrgovişte was not only the seat of power but the center of the nation's social and cultural life. Its general location is in the foothills of the Carpathian mountains, a fertile wine-producing area of northern Wallachia known as the *podgorie*. Surrounding the city, as far as the eye could see, there was a network of interconnecting lakes called *eleşteile,* richly stocked with trout and other fish, which provided sporting activities for the rich. It is conceivable that on these hills to the north of the city there already existed in Dracula's time a small wooden monastery called Saint Nicholas of the Wines, long since gone — at the site of which the renowned Monastery of Dealul was later built — where many members of Dracula's family, including his father (whose tomb has totally disappeared), were buried. As one crosses the moat and the city walls, which, judging by contemporary prints, were never heavily fortified, one is able to catch a glimpse of the city itself, dominated by various churches, the first of which was once the cathedral, of which we have lost all traces, where princes were invested by the metropolitan. The ruins of a fourteenth-century Franciscan church, built on a knoll on the outskirts of the city, which Dracula occasionally visited — an important landmark for our story — still exist. Sprawled throughout the city were the Byzantine-style houses of the boyars, containing more diminutive chapels, of which not a trace remains. Within the comparative security of walled palaces, the upper class, which included the prince, attempted to imitate the Constantinople-inspired etiquette of a royal court. Beyond the boyars' houses and interspaced among gardens with lavish floral layouts were located the more modest houses of the merchants, the artisans, and other dependents of the princely and boyar courts.

The principal surviving monument of Dracula's Tîrgovişte is the ruined princely palace, destroyed several times by the Turks and rebuilt many times. The ruins of Dracula's palace can still be distinguished from the more massive remains of subsequent additions, but little is left of his palace except for the Chindia Tower, which was poorly restored during the nineteenth century; the ruins of the cellar, where the partitions of the cells can still be noticed; and the remains of the foundation, indicating the general plan of the palace. The old palace complex was undoubtedly built by Prince Mircea at the close of the fourteenth century. We can only speculate on its architecture, which was probably Byzantine. The materials used were brick and river stone. The north wing was bordered by the Chindia watchtower, which was built by Dracula himself. Its principal function was to allow the garrison to keep a vigil on the countryside for an impending attack on the city. In addition, it provided a suitable platform for Dracula to watch the punishments that were meted out in the courtyard below.

The princely chapel of the Holy Paraclete, closest to the palace, was connected by an underground passage to Dracula's living quarters. To the west there lay the prince's gardens, extending even beyond the palace walls. The whole area was surrounded by tall and thick battlements, which coincided with a portion of the city walls in the fifteenth century. Under the bell tower to the southeast was the chief entrance to the courtyard.

Study of the foundations suggests that the principal building had only one floor above the foundation, was rectangular in shape, and of modest proportions. Even the main hall, presumably the notorious throne room or banqueting hall, was no longer than about forty feet. This was the room where Dracula held boyar councils, received diplomats, and entertained foreign visitors, and where some of his famous massacres took place. The only serious problem raised by its small size concerned the number of victims who may have perished at one time — for the room could hardly encompass more than a few hundred. We know next to nothing of the prince's private or working quarters and those of his wife and children, beyond the fact that they were probably located nearby. The deep and roomy cellars built of stone — with walls over twelve inches thick — have been preserved best. They contained the princely kitchens, the baths, the wine cellars, and also torture chambers for prisoners. The governor, palace officials, guards (*sluji*), and courtiers (*curteni*) undoubtedly lived in other buildings.

All in all, the importance of Tîrgovişte as a political and diplomatic center cannot be overemphasized: judicial and chancellery enactments, decisions affecting peace and war, massacres and impalements, and most of the surviving Dracula correspondence emanate from this palace.

Even though Tîrgovişte continued to remain Dracula's official capital, the prince showed increasing preference for Bucharest, and during his brief third reign, he did not consider his campaign finished until he had recaptured Bucharest in the late fall of 1476. We presume, in fact, that during his third reign Bucharest had become de facto the official capital of the land, as the fortress had been greatly reinforced by Dracula's brother Radu, who had secured the throne in 1462. At that time Matthias Corvinus, John Hunyadi's son, described the city to Pope Sixtus IV as the most powerful fortress of the land. The reason for this preference for Bucharest over Tîrgovişte is easily apparent: as a new town, it was immune from the spirit of intrigue and anarchy rampant in the old capital, which Dracula had never really trusted; economically, too, it was a sound location between Tîrgsor, an important commercial center, and the Danube. Strategically, it lay closer to the Turkish border, and thus represented a first line of defense preventing Turkish penetration of the country.

All that is left of Dracula's Bucharest are the remains of his palace (Curtea Domnească) in the heart of the city. The visitor can still distinguish a large hallway where Dracula and his boyars held court and the location of his private quarters. Given the thickness of the surviving walls, one can presume that the fortress was constructed with the help of Saxon builders from Braşov and Sibiu, masters in the art of defensive construction. However, the fact that, at least during Dracula's first reign, Bucharest was merely referred to as a *castro* (minor fort) indicates it was not then designed to serve as a powerful fortress, such as Giurgiu on the Danube, or, for that matter, Castle Dracula on the Argeş River. It was no more than a fortified palace surrounded by a powerful wood palisade on one side and the Dîmboviţa River on the other.

Dracula had an obsession for building walls. He built the walls of Bucharest; he may also have fortified the monastery of Snagov nearby, used as a princely treasury for some years. He built small mountain fortresses at various strategic frontier points, some of which have totally disappeared, surviving only in local folklore. Of course by far the most notorious fortress was Castle Dracula, even though Stoker centered his plot on another castle connected with Dracula's name near Bistriţa at the Borgo Pass.

Castle Dracula is located to the north of the city of Curtea-de-Argeş, the old ecclesiastical capital at the source of the river bearing that name, on the peak of a remote mountain rock in the foothills of the Făgăraş range. It had an important role in the defense of the ecclesiastical capital, and tradition holds that the princely church would communicate with the tower of the castle by light signals from the church tower — clearly visible at the castle. It occupies an eerie position and has a commanding view. The castle can be described as remote and inaccessible.

More likely than not, the original castle was built by one of the early Basarab princes in the fourteenth century, as an observation outpost serving the larger Transylvanian castle of Bran on the other side of the mountains, a warning point for discerning attacks from the south. Because of its position near the Hungarian border, the castle was certainly of strategic value to the early Wallachian princes. One factor is more or less certain: when Dracula came to the throne in 1456, only ruins were left of the castle of the Argeş. It had suffered serious damage at the hands of both Turkish and Tatar invaders.

Dracula's decision to rebuild this famous castle provides the opportunity for beginning the discussion of his policies toward the various classes of society at home, the kind of power politics that made him an ideal model for Machiavelli's future *Prince*.

In Dracula's quest for power, one of the central issues he posed was his relationship to the boyar class. Since the birth of the principality, power had always been shared between princes and boyars. Given the brevity of individual reigns (no fewer than twelve had taken place since 1418, which made for an average of just over two years per prince), the absence of primogeniture, and the fact that a boyar establishment had predated the very formation of the principality, effective political sovereignty tilted heavily in favor of the boyars, who were, up to Dracula's time, encroaching upon the authority of the prince. Collective leadership, however, and all that it entails were scarcely compatible with Dracula's overpowering personality, his exalted concept of the role of sovereignty, or his premature idealization of the nation-state. Dracula in this respect may well be viewed as the first modern Renaissance prince of the land, determined to crush the power of the nobility, centralize the administration of the state, and create a military force loyal only to himself, a process well-nigh completed in most of the western states. There were in addition considerations of external policy in Dracula's decision to emasculate the boyar monopoly. With cynical realism, they tended on the whole toward a policy of appeasement toward the Turks, particularly after the fall of Constantinople in 1453. In addition, there were the partisans of Vladislav II, still in hiding on their estates, who had to be eradicated to the last male heir, no matter how young.

The stage was thus set for a massive purge of hostile noble families, carried out by the small loyal force to whom Dracula had owed his throne. In a manner reminiscent of a Louis XIV, Dracula revealed his political philosophy in a quite explicit fashion, in a letter addressed to the mayor of Braşov in 1457: "Pray, think that when a man or prince is powerful and strong at home, then he will be able to do as he wills. But when he is without power, another one more powerful than he will overwhelm him and do as he wishes." These words contain Dracula's whole domestic political program in embryonic form. They are not substantially different from those later to be contained in *The Prince*. This philosophy helps explain why Dracula was so anxious to assuage both the Hungarian king and the sultan during the first two years of his reign. Clearly he wished to deal with unruly boyars first, to strengthen the state, and thus to be able later to face his enemies, both east and west. In some instances, the treachery of individual boyar families was all too obvious and demanded instant action. Such was the case of the boyar Albu the Great, the son of Albu Taxaba, one of the principal followers of Alexandru Aldea, the opponent of Dracula's father, Dracul. With a private army of his own, the younger Albu had organized a revolt just a few months after Dracula had seized power. He was ambushed and then impaled, together with his whole family, whom Dracula considered equally dangerous. Only Albu's younger brother survived; he joined the increasing number of Dracula's opponents who sought refuge at Braşov. Beyond outright revolt, the boyars had deliberately weakened the central government by playing the traditional political game of pitting against each other candidates of the two branches of the ruling family (Dăneşti and Drăculeşti), and even complicating that struggle by added factionalism within each of these two protagonists. It was in the interests of the boyars to choose the weakest possible candidate, the one least likely to intervene in the decisions of the council — hence the instability of the central power and the rapid succession of princes we have noted above. Dracula had the courage to bring this general situation to the fore in a well-known incident narrated to us by the Holy Roman Emperor's meistersinger Michael Beheim and also recalled by an anonymous Turkish historian. The poet refers to the incident in the following words:

He [Dracula] asked the assembled noblemen:
"How many princes have you known?"
The latter answered
Each as much as he knew best.
One believed that there had been thirty,
Another twenty.
Even the youngest thought there had been seven.
After having answered this question
As I have just sung it,
Dracula said: "Tell me,
How do you explain the fact
That you have had so many princes
In your land?
The guilt is entirely due to your shameful intrigues."

With ample proof of the boyars' deceit and treacherous intents, Dracula decided it was timely to inflict upon them an exemplary punishment. He was additionally motivated by learning the details concerning the brutal manner in which his brother Mircea had been suffocated. Revenge for that crime may have provided an additional incentive for the mass impalement of the boyars in the courtyard of his palace, an event that in turn is linked with the reconstruction of his eagle's nest on the river Argeş. The oldest Romanian historical chronicle records the event two centuries later. It had taken place in the spring of 1457, during the Easter celebrations that the boyars were attending at the palace. "He [Dracula] had found out that the boyars of Tîrgovişte had buried one of his brothers alive. In order to know the truth he searched for his brother in the grave and found him lying face downward. So when Easter Day came, while all the citizens were feasting and the young ones were dancing he surrounded them . . . led them together with their wives and children, just as they were dressed up for Easter, to Poenari [a reference to Castle Dracula], where they were put to work until their clothes were torn and they were left naked." In actual fact, this episode, which is also recalled by the Greek historian Chalcondyles and firmly anchored in popular folklore, involved some two hundred boyars and their wives, as well as leading citizens of Tîrgovişte who were equally guilty of plotting Mircea's death. They were seized by Dracula's men as they were finishing their meal in the main banqueting hall of the palace, following the elaborate Easter ritual at the Paraclete Chapel. In Dracula's ingenious mind, one aspect of the punishment had a utilitarian purpose: the reconstruction of the famous castle high up on the Argeş, which would not only provide him with a shelter from his enemies both within and outside the country, but also a safe haven for his princely treasury. On the way out of the chapel the old boyars and their wives were apprehended by Dracula's henchmen and impaled beyond the city walls. The young and able-bodied were manacled and chained to each other and then marched northward under the vigilant eye of Dracula's men. They marched some fifty miles up the Argeş River, until they reached a location called the Source of the River. The journey took them two days. The boyar trek from Tîrgovişte to the site of Castle Dracula was a long and painful one. It undoubtedly claimed many victims long before they caught sight of the ruins of the castle to be reconstructed. The arriving men must have presented a strange sight to the peasants, since the boyars were still dressed in what was left of their fine Easter apparel. Within the villages surrounding the castle site, Dracula had given orders for brick ovens to be built, as well as lime kilns. Under the threat of the whip, the boyars formed a huge human chain extending from the villages to the castle of the Argeş, and passed materials from hand to hand. While some worked up on the mountainside, others were busy making bricks, one vast army of slaves toiling, sweating, building the present castle.

The story does not tell us how long the construction of the castle took — undoubtedly a matter of months, since they simply refortified the earlier abandoned fortress. We do not know the number of victims who fell down the precipice, under the burden of the stones and materials they carried up the mountain, nor the number who died from sheer fatigue and hunger. But the work went on under Dracula's vigilant eye until the castle was completed. In the eyes of the Wallachian peasants, as well as in the lines of the histories, this macabre episode helped establish Dracula's reputation for cruelty, and the mass punishment at Tîrgovişte was in part responsible for creating his nickname, "the Impaler," which henceforth clung to his name. The building of Castle Dracula, carefully planned by Transylvanian specialists in the art of fortress building, was also significant in that it constituted a violation of both Turkish and Hungarian prescriptions that explicitly forbade "a vassal" to protect himself in this manner.

The castle was built on the plan of an irregular polygon, perforce limited by the shape of the narrow plateau, approximately 100 feet wide and 120 feet long, at the summit of the ridge. Its style was that of other Romanian mountain fortresses, which were of Byzantine and Serbian rather than Teutonic design. The surviving semicircular bastions on the southern side and the thick walls built of brick and stone, as well as the strong natural location, made the fortress virtually impregnable and allowed the defenders the possibility of crossfire, in accordance with the latest techniques of war. From what few remains survive, the visitor can still detect the outlines of two of the original five towers, connected by ruined walls, barely visible under a heavy overgrowth of every variety of Carpathian wild flower, greenery, and fungus. The central, or main, tower is in the classical cylindrical form. The thickness of the walls, of stone reinforced on the outside with brick, confirms the popular tradition that Dracula doubled the width of the walls of the earlier fortification so as to be able to withstand the heaviest Turkish cannon fire. These walls, protected by conventional battlements, were originally quite high, and from afar give the impression of forming part of the mountain itself.

Within the fortress there was little room for extensive maneuvering. Each tower could have housed only about twenty to thirty soldiers and an equal number of retainers and servants. Within the main courtyard it would have been difficult to drill more than one hundred men. In the center of that courtyard there was a well, no longer discernible, which was the source of the water supply. According to folklore, there was also a secret passage leading from the well into the bowels of the mountain, emerging in a cave on the banks of the Argeş River. This was probably Dracula's escape route, used in the autumn of 1462 when he fled to Transylvania. The tunnel, say the peasants, was built solidly and reinforced with grooved stones and by boards so as to prevent any mountain cave-ins. The cave along the riverbanks of the Argeş is referred to by the villagers as *pivniţă,* which in Romanian means cellar, by a stretch of the imagination, the cellar deep below the castle at the base of the mountain. A few feet away from the presumed entrance of the secret passage are the remains of a vault. This vault may well constitute the only vestige of a chapel on the site.

When the Turks finally reduced Transylvania to a vassal state in the sixteenth century, Castle Dracula lost all strategic significance and was abandoned as a fortress. What little survived was in great part destroyed by the frequent earthquakes that have their epicenter in the north Carpathian Mountains. These quakes have been recorded about every thirty years in Romania from 1741 onward. This pervasive destruction, however, has served some of the superstitious-minded peasants well in their belief that a "Dracula curse" is associated with this "evil" place. There are those who believe that abandoned fortresses are the domain of the forces of darkness and that one should not pry too deeply into their past — certainly not seek any treasures, even though a golden flame sometimes lights up the sky at night and is taken to mean that the ill-gotten gold accumulated by Dracula still lies in the fortress vaults. Legends such as these are by no means unique to Romania. However, they may help explain why those peasants assigned to various tasks in this lonely place will greet the visitor with the sign of the cross (much as in a Bela Lugosi movie) and are solidly armed with Bibles, intended as a defense against all the evil forces that surround them.

Only two sketches of the castle have been made from the village knoll facing it across the Argeş River. The older painting was done by a Swiss artist, Henri Trenk, in 1860 (the picture is now located at the fine arts museum in Bucharest). Another watercolor, completed in 1885, can be attributed to Ion Butculescu, an amateur historian, a lawyer and relative of one of the authors. At the time of the painting, two of the castle's towers were still clearly discernible.

Of whatever else was within the fortress, there is not a trace today, although the houses of attendants, the princely stables, the pens for domestic animals that provided the castle's needs, the various outhouses that were customarily erected near small fortifications of this nature, and the cell where Dracula's treasure was stored are readily imagined. So is the drawbridge, which evidently existed before the present slender wooden bridge to the peak. The towers must have had some openings, for the peasant ballads speak of candlelight visible from a distance at night.

It is only within the last few years, because of interest generated by the Dracula story, that the country's commission on historic monuments has belatedly decided to shore up the existing towers and battlements. The idea seems to be less to reconstruct the castle than to avoid further deterioration. The walls, however, have been built up to what was probably their original size, so their thickness is apparent, and two of the towers are again quite visible. For Dracula, however, this edifice represented his mountain retreat, his eagle's nest in the Transylvanian Alps, essentially a place of refuge, where the awesome beauty of nature provided a substitute for the perfidy of men.

Many of the old families sought refuge either on their distant mountain estates, in the Transylvanian duchies of Amlaş and Făgăraş, or else they fled to Turkey to await better times. The old boyar class had been virtually decimated, both by impalement and as a result of the sufferings and privations connected with the construction of the castle on the Argeş. All in all, only two out of every three members of the old council in existence at the beginning of the reign survived. Among those names that disappear from the rosters was that of a forebear of one of the co-authors (the man resurfaces only after 1462, in the council of Dracula's brother Radu the Handsome, after Dracula's downfall). The figure given by the German narratives, of 20,000 boyars impaled, is clearly exaggerated. The upper council rarely had more than a dozen spokesmen and six to ten of these held court titles. A somewhat larger figure, however, can be accounted for in terms of boyar families, members of the lesser nobility and the larger number of leading citizens of Tîrgovişte.

To replace these boyars, Dracula created a Napoleon-style nobility of his own. Unlike the custom previously practiced, when a nobleman's confiscated land was given to another member of the same family, Dracula offered confiscated lands and fortunes to new men, some of them of plebeian origin, who thus owed their power entirely to the new prince and had a vested stake in the survival of the regime. A study of the rosters of the boyar council from 1456 to 1462 shows that almost 90 percent of the members were men of lowly class, many of them former free peasants. In addition to these new functionaries, Dracula created a new position, called the *armaş*. The duty of the armaş was to administer the prince's new style of justice, to impose the decisions voted upon by the council, and to execute those guilty of crimes against the state. Some of the armaşi were Romanians, though many were foreigners — Hungarians, Serbs, Turks, even gypsies and Tatars — adventurers for the most part who were well paid and devoid of principles. They were Dracula's "impalers par excellence," the "axes" who fulfilled his awful handiwork. Beheim decries the savage mores prevailing at Dracula's court and denounces the venality, fickleness, and cruelty of the courtiers. His regime of terror certainly could not have endured long without the presence of such mercenaries. There were, however, lack of harmony and bitter conflicts even among the armaşi, who did not have a solid basis of allegiance to the prince, beyond self interest. This tenuous courtier loyalty and the lack of solid support from native boyars, as we will see, help explain the mass defection that occurred at the end of Dracula's reign and ultimately caused his fall.

The same hiring principles applied to other court functionaries, diplomatic envoys, governors of palaces and castles: in fact, all Dracula incumbents. A particularly useful addition to the new regime were the *viteji*, a military nobility recruited from the free peasant landowning class (*moşneni*), who were honored for their bravery on the field of battle. They undoubtedly constituted the officer corps in the large popular army that was raised in times of danger. In addition to a wartime army, Dracula also needed an independent military force that he could use in peace time for repression and policing purposes. For this task he used his personal guard, the sluji. He also had a fairly large force stationed at frontier points such as Rucăr, and forces assigned to his castles under the authority of their governors. They invariably recruited among the free peasants of the respective areas. The establishment of all these military forces was further aimed at reducing the power of the original boyars.

Dracula's sense of the exalted position of his office extended beyond reducing even the new boyars to the status of court servants. In judicial matters, although edicts still bear boyar signatures, we may safely envisage Dracula adjudicating individual cases entirely on his own. In the protocol he insisted upon at court functions, and particularly in receiving the envoys of foreign nations, his autocratic nature is again evident. He had learned these precepts from a past master in the art of ceremony and court etiquette, Sultan Mehmed himself (though the Romanian court titles and traditions were Byzantine). One event illustrating this inordinate concern for "the respect of diplomatic usage" occurred during a reception of a Genoese delegation from Caffa, narrated to us by Michael Beheim:

> I have found that some Italians [i.e., Genoese] came as ambassadors to his court. As they came to him they took off their hats and hoods facing the prince. Under the hat, each of them wore a coif or a little skullcap that he did not take off, as is the habit among Italians. Dracula then asked them for an explanation of why they had only taken their hats off, leaving their skullcaps on their heads. To which they answered: "This is our custom. We are not obliged to take our skullcaps off under any circumstances, even an audience with the sultan or the Holy Roman Emperor." Dracula then said, "In all fairness, I want to strengthen and recognize your customs." They thanked him bowing to him and added, "Sire we shall always serve you with your interests if you show us such goodness, and we shall praise your greatness everywhere." Then in a deliberate manner this tyrant and killer did the following: he took some big iron nails and planted them in a circle in the head of each ambassador. "Believe me," he said while his attendants nailed the skullcaps on the heads of the envoys, "this is the manner in which I will strengthen your customs."

In addition to creating a faithful and servile boyar class, Dracula followed the traditional policy of Wallachian princes brought up in the Romanian Orthodox faith, of dominating the church and using it as an instrument of despotism. Of Dracula's innermost religious convictions and his practices, little is known. We presume that his faith was not deep, that it did not arise from any profound theological convictions, and that it had little bearing on his personal behavior. However, Dracula was often seen in the company of Romanian Orthodox monks. He was known to be particularly fond of the monasteries of Tismana and of Snagov, both of which he often visited. He also liked ritual, a characteristic trait of Orthodox believers. Even when he imposed the death sentence, he insisted upon proper ceremony for his victims and a Christian burial. As a member of the Orthodox faith, Dracula was also sufficiently pre-Lutheran to believe that good works, such as the building of a monastery, could atone more than faith for evil deeds. In his tortured mind cruelty and religiosity were deeply intertwined, and he would occasionally use religious grounds to justify a crime. Dracula was also enough of a medievalist to take his Dragon oath seriously, seeing himself as a Christian crusader against the Infidel.

Patronage — the endowment of land, the granting of immunities and other privileges to monasteries, the building of new religious edifices — was the church's official reward for passive and submissive attitudes. The old Romanian chronicles, as well as oral tradition, credit Dracula with the foundation of several monasteries, the most famous of which was the monastery of Snagov, where his body allegedly lies buried. Dracula himself often resided at Snagov, endowed the monastery with land, and hid his treasure there in 1462 at the time of the Turkish invasion. He had also established in the basement of the edifice a torture chamber where many a boyar enemy perished. With his passion for fortifications, he had transformed the ecclesiastical complex into an island fortress, linked with the mainland by a secret underground tunnel. In times of emergency, as was the case in 1462, the island monastery could give shelter to a numerous population. Other monasteries and churches built by Dracula can be found scattered throughout the country. They were, again, essentially "good works" meant to redeem in the eyes of the Creator. The monastery of Comana, founded in 1461, and the church at Constan-tineşti are Dracula foundations. So is the Church of Saint Nicolae at Tîrgşor, whose inscription, discovered by our late colleague Constantin G. Giurescu, reads: "By the Grace of God I voivode [prince], ruler of Ungro-Wallachia, the son of the great Prince Vlad, have built and completed the church on June 24, 1461." The reason for the erection of this particular Dracula church has nothing to do with the commercial importance of that town, or the fact that Dracula had a princely residence at Tîrgşor. It represented a belated act of atonement, particularly for the assassination of Vladislav II, which had taken place at Tîrgsor. In addition, Dracula gave donations and land to the monasteries of Govora, Tismana, and Cozia, located in northern Oltenia, where he liked to pray. Particularly meaningful were his "donations" to the holy mountain of Athos at the eastern end of the Acte peninsula in Greece, the great holy shrine and cultural center of all the Orthodox churches (Romanian, Bulgarian, Greek, and Serbian), which never submitted to Turkish occupation, even after the conquest of Constantinople. Dracula liked to think of himself as a protector of the whole Orthodox world, not merely the Romanian church. Churches, and monasteries in particular, were obviously important to him not only as defensive fortified bastions, but in terms of general ecclesiastical policy.

As for the gradual expansion of the Roman Catholic faith in his realm, through monasteries established by the Hungarian king on both sides of the Carpathian Mountains (that is, in Transylvania and Wallachia), Dracula looked upon it with suspicion, seeing the monasteries as papal enclaves on his land that eluded his jurisdiction. Their power and influence offended his medieval patriotism. A number of narratives allude to a conflict between Dracula and individual Catholic abbots and monks, many of whom saw their monasteries destroyed and were lucky to escape impalement. Occasionally a monk was able to extricate himself from a difficult position by virtue of his wit, or by simple flattery. On one particular occasion described in a German narrative in the library of Saint Gall, two monks who came to visit the palace at Tîrgovişte climbed to the top of the Chindia Tower and were shown by Dracula the usual scene of horror in the courtyard below, which was strewn with impaled cadavers. Dracula was evidently expecting some form of protest. Instead of reproof, one of the two monks reacted quite meekly, "You are appointed by God to punish the evildoers." The prince hardly expected this enunciation of the doctrine of divine right, and consequently spared and rewarded the monk. His colleague, however, who had the moral strength and courage to disapprove of the crimes, was impaled on the spot.

Whenever he could, even in the case of Catholic monasteries, Dracula would replace foreign incumbents with Romanian appointees of his own. He replaced the powerful French abbot of Cîrţa, in the Făgăraş district, who had been appointed by his father, with a native from Tîrgovişte. The more radical procedure in the case of an unruly foreign abbot was impalement. (As we shall see, the spokesmen of the Catholic church got their belated vengeance by blackening Dracula's name for posterity — thus helping to pave the way for the vampire image.)

Given his opposition to the greater boyars, it would be easy to view Dracula as a proponent of the have-nots, of the peasants, who represented the great majority of Romanians in Dracula's time. Because of his predilections for raising humble men to high rank (the sluji, curteni, viteji, armaşi), some Romanian historians have been tempted to consider Dracula as a kind of Robin Hood, who took away from the rich and gave to the poor. It is a mistake to view Dracula as such a social crusader. He was, after all, a despot (in the modern sense) and a believer in the divine right of the sovereign. Nevertheless, in contrast to the disloyal boyars, the peasantry as a whole looked favorably upon Dracula and rallied to his cause. He in turn took up their cause. He defended the peasants from Turkish demands by refusing to pay the tribute (from 1459 onward) in both money and kind (grain, horses, et cetera), which was computed on the number of existing villages. He also steadfastly opposed all Turkish endeavors to enroll Wallachian children in the janissary corps. Romanian oral tradition emphasized his fairness to peasants in a different way, by stating that in Dracula's time the rich could not buy their way out of punishment as they had done under previous rulers with the traditional baksheesh (bribe) so prevalent in eastern Europe to this day. The peasants, in return for all this, supported Dracula fully during the Turkish campaign of 1462.

There were of course abundant pragmatic reasons for Dracula's pro-peasant stance. He was conscious of the fact that the peasantry constituted over 90 percent of the total inhabitants of the country. He needed their brawn to cut down the century-old Vlasia forest and open up arable land on the Danubian plain, where the black soil was as rich as that of the Ukraine. Turkish documents often referred to the Wallachian plain as the granary of Constantinople. Dracula firmly believed that the strength of the country lay in its agricultural wealth, and the grain had to be sown and cultivated and the crop harvested by manual labor. To encourage these efforts, Dracula granted villages on the plain exemptions from feudal dues. In other instances, he founded new villages. We know their names from local folklore in which Dracula is reverently remembered to this day. Such were the villages of Troianeşti in the Olt district, and Vlădaia and Albutele, closer to the Danube, in the Ilfov district. It was largely with the aim of defending these villages, often located perilously close to the Danube frontier, that Dracula built fortresses, including Bucharest, knowing that the population could find shelter behind the walls in times of danger.

In case of noncompliance with his high standards of work, he was quite prepared to mete out punishment. To see for himself how things were going, Dracula roamed across the countryside in disguise, as a self-styled inquisitor, particularly at night. He discerned how the peasants lived, how well they worked, and what they were thinking about. For those who did not respect his rigid code, he instituted people's courts in individual villages. Sometimes he would take upon himself the role of judge, in the manner of a Saint Louis under his famous oak tree at Vincennes — a clear violation of the jurisdictions of boyar tribunals, which were the bastions of feudal law. In other instances he would stop at individual peasant homes and ask specific questions concerning their lives. Honesty was invariably the best policy, since hypocrisy was a vice Dracula could not tolerate. Hard work, though, was particularly emphasized and laziness abhorred. Whenever he encountered a libertine or rake, Dracula lost his temper and imposed punishment, as witnessed in the following paraphrased Romanian peasant ballad:

> One day Dracula met a peasant who was wearing too short a shirt. One could also notice his homespun peasant trousers, which were glued to his legs, and one could make out the sides of his thighs. When he saw him [dressed] in this manner, Dracula immediately ordered him to be brought to court. "Are you married?" he inquired. "Yes, I am, Your Highness." "Your wife is assuredly of the kind who remains idle. How is it possible that your shirt does not cover the calf of your leg? She is not worthy of living in my realm. May she perish!" "Beg forgiveness, my lord, but I am satisfied with her. She never leaves home and she is honest." "You will be more satisfied with another since you are a decent and hardworking man." Two of Dracula's men had in the meantime brought the wretched woman to him, and she was immediately impaled. Then bringing another woman, he gave her away to be married to the peasant widower. Dracula, however, was careful to show the new wife what had happened to her predecessor and explain to her the reasons why she had incurred the princely wrath. Consequently, the new wife worked so hard she had no time to eat. She placed the bread on one shoulder, the salt on another, and worked in this fashion. She tried hard to give greater satisfaction to her new husband than the first wife and not to incur the curse of Dracula.

The image of Dracula as a friend of the poor has had to overcome examples of even sterner retributions in the oral traditions of the Romanian people. Perhaps the most tragic incident involving mass punishment of the have-nots, one that is referred to in all the narratives —

German, Russian and Romanian — was Dracula's ridding the country of the beggars, the sick, and the poor. The Romanian version of that particular incident is as follows:

> Having asked the old, the ill, the lame, the poor, the blind, and the vagabonds to a large dining hall in Tîrgovişte, Dracula ordered that a feast be prepared for them. On the appointed day, Tîrgovişte groaned under the weight of the large number of beggars who had come. The prince's servants passed out a batch of clothes to each one, then they led the beggars to a large mansion where tables had been set. The beggars marveled at the prince's generosity, and they spoke among themselves: "Truly it is a prince's kind of grace." Then they started eating. And what do you think they saw before them: a meal such as one would find on the prince's own table, wines and all the best things to eat which weigh you down. The beggars had a feast that became legendary. They ate and drank greedily. Most of them became dead drunk. As they became unable to communicate with one another, and became incoherent, they were suddenly faced with fire and smoke on all sides. The prince had ordered his servants to set the house on fire. They rushed to the doors to get out, but the doors were locked. The fire progressed. The blaze rose high like inflamed dragons. Shouts, shrieks, and moans arose from the lips of all the poor enclosed there. But why should a fire be moved by the entreaties of men? They fell upon each other. They embraced each other. They sought help, but there was no human ear left to listen to them. They began to twist in the torments of the fire that was destroying them. The fire stifled some, the embers reduced others to ashes, the flames grilled most of them. When the fire finally abated, there was no trace of any living soul.

The main justification for this crime was that it was an attempt to rid the country of useless vagabonds. Dracula's own words have survived in the collective memory of the Romanian people: "These men live off the sweat of others, so they are useless to humanity. It is a form of thievery. In fact, the masked robber in the forest demands your purse, but if you are quicker with your hand and more vigorous than he you can escape from him. However, these vagabonds take your belongings gradually by begging — but they still take it. They are worse than robbers. May such men be eradicated from my land!"

In Dracula's defense one might allege that these vagabonds, infirm and destitute people who roamed the countryside, occasionally invading cities and preying upon the rich instead of working, constituted a social plague. These people were a threat to the prosperity of the land and gave his country a poor reputation. One specialist in the history of Romanian medicine has suggested also that Dracula, through this action, was attempting to rid the country of the plague, a constant scourge on the lower Danube. In addition he may have been trying to liquidate the problem of the gypsies, the vagabond people, notorious for their thievery and wrongdoing. When on one occasion a condemned gypsy leader protested to the prince that death by impalement or fire was contrary to their law, Dracula ordered him to be boiled alive in a huge cauldron — and then, as an added refinement, compelled the members of his tribe to eat the flesh of the culprit, an act of forced cannibalism. In most instances, however, gypsies, if caught in a crime or misdemeanor, were given the option of enrolling in Dracula's army, where they were distinguished by the motley-colored cattle hides that they wore, a fact noted by one of Romania's first great eighteenth-century epic poets, Ion Budai-Deleanu. His poem, *Ţiganiada,* the first written in the Romanian language, focused on Dracula's role as the leader of a gypsy army against the Turks.

Though primarily interested in promoting the farming efforts of the peasant class, who in return remember their prince reverently, Dracula did not neglect the interests of the merchants and artisans; on their behalf he took on the German Saxon merchants of Transylvania. Indeed, Wallachia's geographical position placed it on the important crossroad linking western Europe to Hungary and Transylvania to Constantinople and the Near East. Traffic had been temporarily disrupted by the Turkish conquest, but was bound to continue with Turkish encouragement after 1453. One classic anecdote involves an important merchant from Florence, who spent some time in Tîrgovişte on his way to Constantinople with a carriage laden with both money and goods. As he reached the capital, the merchant immediately went to the princely palace and asked Dracula for servants who might watch over him, his merchandise, and his money. Dracula ordered him to leave the merchandise and the money in the public square and to come to sleep in the palace. The merchant, having no alternative, submitted to the princely command. However, during the night, someone passing by his carriage stole 160 gold ducats. On the next day, early in the morning, the merchant went to his carriage, found his merchandise intact, but 160 gold ducats missing. He immediately went to Dracula and told him about the missing money. Dracula told him not to worry and promised that both the thief and the gold would be found. He ordered his servants to replace the gold ducats from his own treasury, but to add an extra ducat. He commanded the citizens of

Tîrgovişte immediately to seek out the thief, saying that if the thief were not found, he would destroy the capital. In the meantime, the merchant went back to his carriage, counted the money once, counted it a second time and yet again a third, and was amazed to find all his money there with an extra ducat. He then returned to Dracula and told him: "Lord, I have found all my money, only with an extra ducat." The thief was brought to the palace at that very moment. Dracula told the merchant: "Go in peace. Had you not admitted to the extra ducat, I would have ordered you to be impaled together with this thief."

It is relevant to note that Dracula in this instance made all the citizens of Tîrgovişte collectively responsible for finding the culprit, under threat of destroying their city, an extremely harsh stance. Another narrative confirms the fact that because of such severe measures thievery became virtually unknown in Wallachia by the end of Dracula's reign. The most poignant story is that of a golden cup purposely left by Dracula near a certain fountain located near the source of a river. Travelers from many lands came to drink at this fountain, because the water was cool and sweet. Dracula had intentionally put this fountain in a deserted place to test dishonest wayfarers. So great was the fear of impalement, however, that so long as he lived no one dared to steal the cup, and it was left at its place.

Dracula's objectives in using terror at home thus included ending feudal anarchy through the subjugation of the boyar class; preventing disorders wrought by thieves, gypsies, and vagabonds; and ensuring the security of merchants and their goods at a time when roads were hazardous, to say the least. "There must be security for all and sundry in my land" was a popular watchword attributed by the peasants to Dracula. Almost to the end of his career, the peasants accepted the fact that intrinsic values such as these could be enforced through the harshest means if necessary. Indeed, Dracula is remembered most reverently by the Romanian people, as we shall see.

In addition, there was a strong puritanical strain in him, which accounts for both his good works and some of his worst acts of terror. Most narratives seem to agree that he wished to introduce a new system of ethics in his country, laying emphasis on personal morality. "Dracula so hated evil in his land," states the Russian narrative, "that if someone lied or committed some injustice, he was not likely to stay alive, whether he was a nobleman or a priest or a monk or a common man." One example taken from Romanian folklore will serve to demonstrate this puritanical strain:

If any wife had an affair outside of marriage, Dracula ordered her sexual organs cut. She was then skinned alive and exposed in her skinless flesh in a public square, her skin hanging separately from a pole or placed on a table in the middle of the marketplace. The same punishment was applied to maidens who did not keep their virginity, and also to unchaste widows. For lesser offenses, Dracula was known to have the nipple of a woman's breast cut off. He also once had a red-hot iron stake shoved into a woman's vagina, making the instrument penetrate her entrails and emerge from her mouth. He then had the woman tied to a pole naked and left her exposed there until the flesh fell from the body, and the bones detached themselves from their sockets.

Regardless of motivation, savage acts of this nature, the hallmarks of Dracula's reign, serve to emphasize a cruel and perhaps irrational streak in his personality. At such moments, he emerges as a murky character from *The Thousand Nights and One Night,* an Oriental tyrant, a monster who may well vie with Ivan the Terrible for the title of the most gruesome psychopath of history. Apart from the methods of imposing death, what shocks one is the number of victims Dracula amassed within the short span of a six-year rule. Estimates range from a minimum of 40,000 victims to a maximum of 100,000, a calculation made by the papal nuncio, the bishop of Erlau, near the end of Dracula's career in 1475, clearly an exaggerated number even if one includes his Turkish war victims as well. These victims included people of all nationalities (Romanians — from Moldavia, Wallachia, and Transylvania — plus Bulgarians, Germans, Hungarians, and Gypsies), all classes (boyars as well as peasants), all religions (Catholic, Muslim, Orthodox, Jewish) and men, women, and children. By our insensitive twentieth-century standards these numbers may appear insignificant. However, the figures far exceed those of the so-called massacres of the fifteenth, sixteenth, and even eighteenth centuries. The wholesale massacre of Protestants during the night of Saint Bartholomew in Paris (August 24, 1572), which made even Ivan the Terrible indignant, accounted for only 5,000 to 10,000 victims, while during Robespierre's reign of terror (1793–1794), no more than 20,000 to 25,000 victims perished on the guillotine. The number of Dracula victims, even if exaggerated, is all the more telling, when it is recalled that France's total population in 1715 was 18,000,000 inhabitants, whereas the total population of Wallachia in Dracula's time did not exceed half a million.

It was, however, and as noted, not only the matter of killing on a massive scale that shocked contemporaries, but the manner and refinements used in imposing death. Dracula's favorite method of execution, which has immortalized him among artists of crime, was impalement. According to the various narratives — German, Russian, Hungarian, Turkish, Romanian — stakes stood permanently prepared in the courtyard of the palace of Tîrgovişte, in various strategic places, in public squares, and in the vicinity of the capital. Dracula was often present at the time of punishment. Usually, it is said, the stakes were carefully rounded at the end and bathed in oil so that the entrails of the victims should not be pierced by a wound too quickly fatal when the victim's legs were stretched wide apart and two horses (one attached to each leg) were sent cantering in different directions, while attendants held the stake and body firmly in place. Not all of Dracula's impalement victims were, however, pierced from the buttocks up. Judging from several prints, men, women, and children were also impaled through the heart, the navel, the stomach, and the chest.

Nor was impalement the only form of punishment. Dracula decapitated, cut off noses, ears, sexual organs, and limbs. He blinded, strangled, hanged, burned, boiled, skinned, roasted, hacked ("like cabbage," specifies a German narrative), nailed, buried alive, and had his victims stabbed. He also exposed them to the elements and to wild animals, and built secret trapdoors to drop the wretches on cunningly located stakes below. If he did not practice cannibalism, the German storyteller mentions that he compelled others to eat human flesh, as was the case with the gypsies. He also made use of the wheel, hot irons, and other forms of medieval torture. Turkish sources state that on one occasion he smeared salt and honey on the soles of the captives' feet and allowed animals to lick them for indefinite periods of suffering. The papal legate Modrussa recapitulated some of the stories related to him by King Matthias about the refinements of Dracula's cruelties. Modrussa reported to Pope Pius II, for example, how, in his years of reign before 1462, Dracula had killed 40,000 of his political foes:

> He killed some of them by breaking them under the wheels of carts; others, stripped of their clothes, were skinned alive up to their entrails; others placed on stakes, or roasted on red-hot coals placed under them; others punctured with stakes piercing their head, their navel, breast, and, what is even unworthy of relating, their buttocks and the middle of their entrails, and, emerging from their mouths; in order that no form of cruelty be missing, he stuck stakes in both breasts of mothers and thrust their babies onto them; he killed others in other ferocious ways, torturing them with varied instruments such as the atrocious cruelties of the most frightful tyrants could devise.

Tursun Bey, a Turkish chronicler who wrote at the end of the fifteenth century, depicts the following macabre scene:

In front of the wooden fortress where he had his residence, he set up at a distance of six leagues two rows of fence with impaled Hungarians, Moldavians and Wallachians. In addition, since the neighboring area was forested, innumerable people were hanging from each tree branch, and he ordered that if anyone should take one of the hanging victims down, he would hang in his place.

From descriptions such as these the term "the forest of the impaled" was coined.

In addition to physical torture, Dracula had a predilection for various forms of moral torture: he liked to obtain confessions prior to punishment, to put a man in the wrong before he was executed. Dracula placed inordinate importance upon the use of words, and greatly prized dialectical talents: a clever answer to a twisted question could occasionally save a man's life. Those who failed to pass the ordeal, however, faced certain death.

Such physical and moral suffering must of course be viewed in the light of the standards and morality of his time. Mass killings, and the execution and torture of political opponents together with their families, were hardly Dracula's inventions. Dracula's mentality was not very different from that of Louis XI, the Spider King, who had a predilection for hanging young boys on the branches of trees and placed his enemies in cages. Dracula's cruelty was no worse than that of Ferrante (Ferdinand) of Naples, who, having killed most of his political opponents, had his victims mummified and placed in the royal museum, where they were shown to his guests. The massacres carried out by the Italian "signori," whether the blood feuds between the Odi and the Baglioni at Perugia or the Orsini and Colonna in Rome, or those of Ludovico Sforza, the Moor, at Milan, Pope Alexander VI and his illegitimate son Cesare Borgia, or the notoriously evil Sigismondo Malatesta of Rimini, reflect equally the low ethical standards of the period.

Even the favorite torture, impalement, though never before practiced on so wide a scale, was not a Dracula innovation. It was known to Asiatic people, and practiced by the Turks, as well as by other Balkan rulers, including Dracula's cousin Stephen of Moldavia. (In 1473, Stephen had 2,300 of his Wallachian prisoners impaled through the navel.) The German Saxons of Transylvania had written legal codes in which impalement was specifically described as a suitable form of punishment for a variety of serious crimes.

But no matter how carefully we account for Dracula's crimes by placing them in the context of his times and even seeing motivation for some, it is a matter of record that in the end he was abandoned by all his people. Many of his contemporaries, even his henchmen, felt that no one was really safe from impalement at the hands of this villain. One cannot adopt the adage *"tout comprendre, c'est tout pardonner,"* especially as some of Dracula's atrocities seem to have been motivated only by a streak of irrationality. Dracula, in other words, was on occasion guilty of senseless butchery.

Although we are unwilling to indulge in a Freudian analysis of Dracula's personality, the nature of some of his crimes, particularly vis-à-vis women, suggests sexual abnormalities that have never been explained by historians. The ritual and manner of impalement, watching his victims eat flesh, the cutting of sexual organs—all point to morbid sexual deviation. In this connection, one anecdote mentioned in the Russian narrative seems to confirm Dracula's anger toward women. On one occasion, relates the Slavonic narrative, one of Dracula's mistresses pretended that he had made her pregnant. Dracula was angered by what he evidently expected to be a lie. He first had his mistress examined; then, realizing that he had been made an object of ridicule, had her womb cut open from her sexual organs to her breasts. As the unfortunate woman lay dying, writhing in excruciating pain, Dracula cynically remarked: "Let the world see where I have been."

What can explain the savagery of such crimes? The answer that suggests itself even to a nonspecialist is that Dracula may have been partially impotent. The ritual of impalement may have provided a satisfaction that substituted for his own inadequacy.

As we review Dracula's domestic policies, several factors besides the atrocities he committed stand out. Dracula's mentality and his politics can in part be labeled as representative of an age that witnessed the final disappearance of feudalism, the emergence of the centralized nation-state, and the rise of a middle class. In the case of Dracula's state, the arguments for "modernization," for subjugating the boyars, were all the more cogent, since he faced imminent danger from outside, threatening the very existence of his principality. Bearing this in mind, even his use of impalement can sometimes be explained on utilitarian grounds. The use of these terror tactics against the German cities of Transylvania will provide a good case in point, to which we shall now turn.

CHAPTER 5

Transylvanian Terror

EVERY twentieth-century movie buff associates the fictitious "Count Dracula" with Transylvania. In many ways this association fits the real Vlad Dracula. In a historic sense, these upland regions of the western portion of modern Romania — a vast plateau of mountains and foothills bordered by the eastern and western Carpathian mountains — was in fact "Dracula country." Vlad Dracula was born in Sighişoara, Transylvania, he was educated there early in life, and his first wife hailed from that province. It was from Transylvania that he came to assume his throne, and it was in that province that he hoped to find moral as well as material support against his enemies both at home and abroad. It should also be added that the commercial relations between Transylvania and Wallachia had always been close. Most of Dracula's correspondence is to be found in the archives of Sibiu and Braşov; when things did not work out in Wallachia, Dracula sought asylum in Transylvanian cities such as Sighişoara, Braşov, or Hunedoara. This relationship was intermittently darkened by a variety of incidents that grew to tragic proportions and need an explanation.

His relationship with the German Saxon community was particularly uneven. When the Hungarian kings completed the conquest of Transylvania, they needed colonists to settle on their new lands. They appealed essentially to German colonists, who responded enthusiastically with massive migrations, first during the twelfth century and later at the close of the thirteenth, following the extensive destruction of townships and the massacres that accompanied the Mongol invasions of Genghis Khan and his successors. These Germans were collectively known as Saxons, because of their use of Saxony as a staging area on their trek eastward. In fact, they came from every part of Germany: the Rhineland, the Moselle area, Brunswick, Westphalia, and Luxemburg. Most of them settled in the southern and northern portions of Transylvania, building powerful, fortified townships — in effect, privileged, self-governing communities with a powerful voice in the Transylvanian parliament. The Germans in Transylvania were officially recognized as a "nation," though under the ultimate authority of the princes of Transylvania. Identical privileges had been granted to the less populous Szeklers (whose Asiatic ancestry we have already noted), who, like the Germans, were Catholics, Catholicism being the only established religion in Transylvania. The citizens of these fortified towns were governed by a mayor and a city council, which had a great deal of independence and maintained a loyalty to their German homelands, to which they were tied by sentimental, religious, and cultural bonds. They also, consequently, tended to favor the interests of the Habsburg family, the rulers of Austria. In fact, each city conducted a foreign policy of its own, not always coincident with that of the Hungarian king or his local representative, the prince of Transylvania. So long as Ladislas V Posthumus, a member of the Habsburg family, was king of Hungary, there were no problems of allegiance. When he died in 1458, however, most of the German townships of Transylvania threw their loyalty to the Habsburg Holy Roman Emperor Frederick III, one of their kin, rather than siding with the Hunyadis, whom they considered aliens.

We have already mentioned by their Romanian names a number of these Transylvanian German towns, which in those days were known by German equivalents. The most important were Braşov, the largest center; Sibiu; Sighişoara, Dracula's birthplace; Sebeş; and Bistriţa, the setting Bram Stoker uses. The populations of these townships, ranging from 4,000 to 10,000 inhabitants, espoused traditional German values: hard work, frugality, and efficiency. They developed a great variety of goods destined for more than local consumption and organized according to traditional principles of the medieval guilds. There were butchers, shoemakers, tailors, clockmakers, goldsmiths, jewelers, textile and silk manufacturers, and metalworkers, all of whom took pride in the good quality of their workmanship, the high standards of which became known throughout southeastern Europe. They catered particularly to the refined tastes of the wealthy upper classes. As noted, one specialty that had aroused the interest of military leaders, including the sultan, was the manufacture of firearms made of heavy steel or bronze. The cannon foundries and bombard factories of Braşov and gunpowder workshops of Sibiu became quite famous — indeed the German arms manufacturers of Transylvania were the Krupps of the fifteenth century, fully conversant with the latest techniques of war. Also substantially adding to the wealth of the Germans were the monopolies granted to them by the Hungarian kings over the rich gold, silver, and copper ores that had been mined since antiquity in the Transylvanian Alps.

Given this development of local industry and connections with their former homeland, the German townships naturally began to engage in a very lucrative east-west trade. It followed essentially two different routes. The northern route, centered on the city of Bistriţa, carried Saxon goods to some twenty-five German ports like Hamburg and Danzig along the Baltic seacoast, which had formed an association of their own, often referred to as the Hanseatic League. Braşov and Sibiu, on the other hand, conducted a much larger volume of trade, which followed the two southern passes leading from Transylvania to Wallachia, Turnu Roşu, and Bran. Their merchants traveled to the principal cities of Wallachia, Cîmpulung, Tîrgovişte, and Tîrgsor, and the ports of Brăila and Chilia on the Danube delta, and finally, by sea, to Constantinople and even beyond. From Wallachia the Saxons imported grain, flax, hemp, horses, and various other farm animals. Spices and other refined goods from Asia would also cross Wallachian territories in the opposite direction, though the German balance of trade was always favorable and the difference was made up in hard cash — the currency of Venice or Florence being generally preferred.

German-Wallachian trade, then, centered on market towns such as Tîrgovişte and Tîrgsor, where important fairs were held and the Saxons could display their goods. The Germans also made use of such towns as warehousing centers for goods in transit farther east. Insofar as fiscal policy was concerned, German goods were, if sold in Wallachia, subject to certain import duties, in accordance with past usage; if they were shipped outside Wallachia, the merchants were charged an export tax. The point of restricting commerce to certain towns was that the prince could thereby exercise control over the influx of foreign goods and protect native merchants from foreign exploitation. The collection of export and import duties obviously benefited the Wallachian treasury and helped to pay the mercenary soldiers needed for the army. Levying tariffs also tended to enhance the prosperity of the selected towns.

To round off our image of these German people who had settled on the borderlands of European civilization, we should add that the Teutonic Order of Knights, which had played a crucial role in civilizing and Christianizing the Slavs during an earlier period and had built a string of fortresses from the Baltic to the Carpathians, played a far smaller role in Transylvania during the fifteenth century. The powerful fortresses that they had built, such as Bran, which guarded the city of Brașov during the thirteenth century, had been placed under the control of the cities that they were meant to defend. In Dracula's time, the order, which had lost both power and prestige following its defeat by the Poles at the battle of Tannenberg, was considered untrustworthy by the Hungarian kings and confined its activities to the defense of a region known as the Banat, the region of southwest Transylvania around the Danube shoe, which extends into present-day Yugoslavia, where they controlled a number of important forts.

Most of Dracula's activities involved two Transylvanian districts with a strong concentration of German settlers. One was the area in the vicinity of Brașov, referred to in the old documents as Burzenland (now Țara Bîrsei), which included a dozen smaller townships and many villages of mixed ethnic origin. The other district, far more German in character, lay in the vicinity of the city of Sibiu, and as described by Emperor Sigismund's biographer, Eberhard Windecke, as Sieben Burgen (seven fortresses), a name still used by the Germans to describe all of Transylvania. Both Țara Bîrsei and the "Seven Fortresses" were located within the duchies of Făgăraș and Amlaș, traditional possessions of the Wallachian princes in Transylvania proper. Since these regions contained populations of mixed ethnic origins, they were a constant source of contention with the Hungarian kings, who preferred to forget that there were dozens of purely Romanian townships and villages within the boundaries of these duchies.

In order to understand fully the "terror" activities that Dracula aimed at the "privileged" German communities of Transylvania, it should be recognized that, even in this prenational age, Romanians who shared their native tongue and Orthodox religion with him formed a majority of the population of Transylvania (roughly 500,000 total inhabitants in the fifteenth century) and enjoyed no rights. Considered as a "people without a history," most of them were serfs attached to the lands of either Hungarian, Szekler, or Saxon landowners. The Romanian upper class in Transylvania had been virtually destroyed. The only ones who survived were those families that, out of self-interest — the case of Hunyadi was typical — decided to become Hungarians and adopt the Catholic faith.

Nonetheless, the vast majority of Romanians clung to their language, which was taught in the family, given the absence of schools, and to their Orthodox church, which continued to function even though it was not a "recognized" religion and there were no Orthodox Romanian bishoprics in Transylvania at this time. Priests in the various peasant parishes continued to be ordained by the metropolitan of Moldavia or Wallachia, who thus helped keep religion alive among the Romanians of Transylvania. Sometimes the oppressed Romanian population would revolt or even join with Hungarian serfs against the nobility, as was the case with the Bobîlna uprising in 1437. Repressed politically by the Hungarian kings and religiously by no fewer than three inquisitions, somehow Romanian national and spiritual life survived at a very modest level. This is reflected in the quaint village churches built entirely of wood (the people were not allowed to build in stone) that are still standing today.

Because of its extraordinarily beautiful, varied, and at times forbidding countryside, the diversity of language, races, religions, and traditions, the impact of both western and eastern cultural patterns, and the commercial prosperity and industry of its towns, Transylvania indeed presented a most unusual, perhaps unique, microcosm of the full range of east-west civilization. These facts provide the chief explanation for its having attracted the attention of so many travelers from Dracula's time onward. Its wealth was both a blessing and a curse for the country; it became a magnet in the interplay of hostile and conflicting political interests.

When Dracula became prince in 1456 he had every interest in maintaining good relations with all the German Saxon cities — indeed, the latter had been instructed, by the Hungarian king, Ladislas V, to support Dracula's quest for the Wallachian throne. It was, in fact, because of the support he had received from the Braşovians, among whom he had many friends, that Dracula wrote a most cordial letter (September 6, 1456) to the mayor and the city councilmen, whom he described "as honest men, brothers, friends, and sincere neighbors" (*honesti viri, fratres, amici et vicini nostri sinceri*). Shortly thereafter he signed a commercial treaty with the Braşovians and the district of Ţara Bîrsei, which contained the following provisions: (1) Dracula would help defend the Transylvanian Saxons against the Turks; (2) in case of need, he would be granted political asylum in the city; (3) the merchants of Braşov and of the region were given the right to barter unimpeded in certain towns such as Rucăr, Tîrgovişte, and Tîrgsor, as had been the practice theretofore. They could sell their wares directly to the customers and buy their raw materials from the producer — the only obligation being that of paying the usual Wallachian customs duties, upon entry. Both sides undertook not to give protection to their political enemies, and not to confiscate the goods of their respective merchants, no matter what the provocation. In the same document Dracula swore renewed fidelity to the young king of Hungary. In essence, the economic treaty somewhat liberalized and confirmed existing privileges. A similar treaty was signed with the city of Sibiu, since each township maintained a policy of its own. It would be fair to presume that Bistriţa and the other more important German cities throughout Transylvania obtained identical commercial advantages.

Such auspicious beginnings were not destined to endure. Before long, the Wallachian prince committed some of his worst atrocities at the expense of the Germans in Transylvania. These have been described in great detail by those Germans who survived.

Among the causes for Dracula's increasing hostility toward the German Saxons were international factors. A new conflict had arisen between László Hunyadi, who had inherited all his father's titles and was ostensibly still commander-in-chief, and the Hungarian Habsburg king, Ladislas V, who was supported by the powerful Count Ulrich Cilli (related by marriage to the late Emperor Sigismund) and ultimately by the Holy Roman Emperor Frederick III. As governor of Belgrade, Hunaydi had invited the young king to make an official visit to the city, which had heroically resisted Mehmed's formidable onslaught. Shortly after the king had entered the fortress with his retinue (which included Count Cilli), the drawbridge leading to the fortress was suddenly closed, cutting off both the king and Count Cilli from their bodyguard, which was deliberately kept outside the fortress walls. On the first day of the royal visit, in admittedly confusing circumstances, Count Cilli was assassinated by one of László Hunyadi's hired henchmen — an act of revenge for the numerous indignities that his father had suffered at the hands of a man who had consistently opposed him. Young King Ladislas V Habsburg, now totally at the mercy of Hunyadi, expected a similar fate, since it was known that Hunyadi had his sights set on the Hungarian crown. The king, however, stayed calm and was allowed to leave the fortress unharmed. But he meditated on his vengeance. There is no question that the real reason for the arrest, trial, and death sentence for László Hunyadi the following year (1457), the imprisonment of his young brother Matthias, and the formal confiscation of the vast Hunyadi estates by the king, though linked to the crime at Belgrade, were a result of the broader struggle for power that had always existed between Cillis and Hunyadis.

In general, the events at Belgrade marked the beginning of a struggle for power between the Hunyadis and the Habsburgs, both of whom wanted the Hungarian crown. Following László's death, the leaders of the Hunyadi faction were Erzsébet Szilágy, John Hunyadi's widow, and Mihály Szilágy, her brother. They were not only determined to avenge the death of their kin, but now they openly worked for the downfall of László Habsburg. The new Hunyadi candidate to the throne was to be László's youngest brother, Matthias, who was still in jail.

What was Dracula's attitude toward this complex power play in neighboring Hungary? Although he had sworn allegiance to the Habsburg boy king, Dracula's loyalties lay more strongly with the family that had helped secure for him the Wallachian throne. Michael Szilágy turned to the Wallachian prince for help, and it is clear from the existing correspondence that the two leaders considered themselves brothers in arms. As the struggle between the Habsburgs and the Hunyadis broke into the open, King Ladislas V was supported by his former guardian, the Holy Roman Emperor Frederick III, and the German cities of Transylvania. Dracula supported Szilágy, and thus he became the enemy of the German towns.

The initial phase of his undeclared war against the Saxons took place in northeastern Transylvania, when the German population of Bistriţa revolted against Mihály Szilágy during the summer of 1457, allegedly because of fiscal abuses of the Szilágy administration. Szilágy immediately appealed to Dracula to help him quell the disturbance. Even though Bistriţa was fortified, the Dracula-Szilágy forces were able to penetrate into the town, and their soldiers looted and burned the homes of the suspected leaders of the insurrection. Those rebels who survived fled southwest toward Braşov and Sibiu. Dracula was rewarded by Szilágy with the gift of a castle located at the Borgo Pass, close to the medieval city of Rodna, only the ruins of which have survived. (The fact that this is precisely the location Bram Stoker used in the opening chapters of his famous novel lends additional support to the view that the Anglo-Irish author expended some effort in research attempting to base his novel on authentic history.)

Evidently persecution of Germans at Bistriţa had aroused the ire of all the German cities of Transylvania, primarily Sibiu and Braşov, as well as that of the Szeklers under the command of their powerful Count Oswald Rozgony, now captain general of all the royal forces in Transylvania. They were all the more indignant toward Dracula since it was rumored that, notwithstanding all his declarations of friendship, he had, shortly after his accession to power, sent an embassy to Constantinople to renew his vassal relationship with the sultan. Dracula, in turn, was furious with the Braşovians, whom he had considered allies by virtue of the generous trade concessions that he had made. The terrain was obviously propitious for further acts of hostility on both sides.

The mayor of Braşov resorted to the traditional weapon of encouraging subversion in Wallachia by espousing the cause of the Dăneşti rival, in this instance, Dan III, the brother of Vladislav II, whom Dracula had slain at Tîrgsor in 1456, and a friend of the Habsburgs. Dan, who now established his headquarters at Braşov, had himself crowned by dissident boyars and styled himself "Dan III, by the Grace of God Prince of Ungro-Wallachia, Duke of Făgăraş and Amlaş," much in the manner of Prince Mircea, Dracul, or, for that matter, Dracula himself.

At Braşov Dan was surrounded by a regular court and took up residence in a small palace in the Romanian district outside the city walls, on the edge of a hill called Tîmpa. Nearby stood the small wooden Orthodox church of Saint Nicolae, where his court worshipped and where he was presumably crowned. The names of Dan's boyar supporters are known to us; some of them were large landowners in the Făgăraş district. Others had left Wallachia to save their lives following the mass impalements described in the last chapter. Among them was a former chief treasurer called Albu, the only surviving member of a famous family that had been rooted out by Dracula because they were partisans of Vladislav II. It should also be noted that one boyar from the Făgăraş district who supported Dan III, Bogdan Doboca, owned the village of Şercaia.

The city council of Sibiu and its mayor viewed the imposing of Dracula's authority on Bistriţa with equal alarm and, like the Braşov authorities, decided to champion the claims of yet another rival candidate to the Wallachian throne. The blow was all the more galling since it involved none other than Dracula's half-brother, also known as Vlad the Monk. (He was, as noted, the fruit of Dracul's relationship with Călţuna, a Transylvanian woman of lowly estate.) Vlad the Monk was equally successful in drawing to his support a number of dissident boyars, including Vintilă Florescu, who was later rewarded with high office for his support. Vlad the Monk established his headquarters in the town of Amlaş. Among his most prominent supporters were two wealthy German merchants. One was Peter Gereb de Weresmarth, Count of Roşia, who had been elected mayor of Sibiu several times in Dracula's lifetime, along with his numerous sons. Peterman de Longo Campo, the other, was a former Wallachian of German origin who played a considerable political role in German imperial circles. For instance, he is known to have accompanied King Sigismund of Luxemburg at his coronation in Rome. Peterman also owned land within the duchy of Amlaş: the villages of Noul Săsesc, Cacova, and Vale. His son Jacob possessed Satul Nou. That all these villages along the Hîrtibaciu River were owned by Dracula's political foes provides the explanation for the terror experienced in that valley during the summer of 1457. In order to ingratiate himself with his German patrons, Vlad the Monk promised to enhance the generous commercial concessions granted by Dracula in 1456 by extending free trading rights to the ports at Brăila and along the whole line of the Danube — a most profitable concession that the Saxons had never previously enjoyed.

Yet a third candidate, who like Vlad the Monk ultimately became prince of the land (1481 and 1482–1495), was another member of the Dăneşti clan, Basarab Laiotă, a son of Dan II. He was the most cultured of the candidates, holding a degree from a Braşov institution of higher learning. Like the others, he made the usual promises to Romanian boyars and German merchants who cared to support his cause — though his appeal was not as strong as that of his relative Dan III or that of Vlad the Monk. He also eventually became prince of Wallachia following Dracula's assassination in 1476.

Dracula decided to take up the challenge posed by these rival pro-German candidates by canceling the commercial concessions he had initially granted to the Saxon merchants in 1456 and engaging in a trade war on his own terms. At first he simply extended the "most favored nation clause," formerly enjoyed exclusively by the Saxons, to the merchants of Wallachia and those of other nations such as the Genoese of Caffa and the Florentines, who frequently traveled through his country. The following year, Dracula obligated the German Saxons to unpack their wares in transit at various frontier points such as Rucăr or at certain specific towns such as Tîrgovişte, Tîrgsor, and Cîmpulung. In these centers Dracula gave Wallachian merchants priority in purchasing German goods, even below fair market value. The Wallachian merchants thus acquired the right to resell the Saxon goods within the country and throughout the Balkan peninsula, thus reducing the role of the Germans to wholesaling. This inevitably affected them financially. For a time the Germans ignored these measures and attempted to carry on the trade much as they had done before, while trying to elude Dracula's customs officers located at the border. Their attempts to avoid customs simply became another factor accounting for the fury and enormity of Dracula's terror raids on the German territories from 1458 to 1460.

In fairness to Dracula it should be stated that he initially attempted to resolve both the commercial and political challenge through diplomatic means. Dracula sent two diplomats, the boyar Mihail and the head of his chancellery, a boyar called Priboi, to Sibiu in an attempt to persuade the mayor of Sibiu, Oswald, to give up his support of "a Wallachian priest [Vlad the Monk] who had established himself in *his* [that is, Dracula's] Duchy of Amlaş with the connivance of the authorities." A similar request was made to Braşov in regard to Dan III. Since neither city chose to respond, Dracula decided to teach the Germans an opening lesson in international good manners, which would serve as a fair warning. Without the formality of a declaration of war, a small mobile cavalry force, led by Dracula in person, struck with lightning speed across the mountains in the spring of 1458. He took the shortest route from his castle on the Argeş, crossed the Lovişte country, and thence followed the valley of the Olt River by way of the Cozia monastery (where the tomb of his grandfather, Prince Mircea, can be admired to this day). He then moved his force through the guarded pass at Turnu Roşu, the Red Tower ("red," according to local legends, because it was permanently stained with the blood of the Turks who had repeatedly tried to take it). From there his men scaled the mountains following the valley of the Hîrtibaciu River, where the properties of Vlad the Monk's German patrons were located.

The German manuscripts from the monasteries of Saint Gall and Lambach describe the fury of Dracula's attacks in "the land of the forests." He destroyed the villages of Hosman, Caşolṭs, and Satul Nou, all possessions of the wealthy merchants or Romanian boyars who supported Vlad the Monk. From Amlaş Dracula's troops attacked Ţara Bîrsei, the region controlled by the supporters of Dan III, near Braşov. He made the village of Bod a wasteland by killing all of the inhabitants except some prisoners, whom he took and later impaled at Tîrgovişte. Dracula's one notable failure was his inability to capture the village of Codlea near Braşov, according to the Lambach manuscript. Hearing of Dracula's atrocities, the villagers resisted valiantly. Dracula's captain had to report to the prince: "I cannot carry out your instructions, for the inhabitants are brave and well fortified, and they fight with great courage." Dracula's response was to have this captain immediately arrested and impaled "in a horrible way." At the town of Talmeş, Dracula had the city burned and the people "hacked to pieces like cabbage." Dracula's ally Mihály Szilágy was unable to take the highly fortified city of Sibiu on October 9, 1458. Instead, Szilágy set up his headquarters in Sighişoara, perhaps in the very building where Dracula had been born.

After recalling his own Wallachian merchants home from Transylvania, Dracula had all the Saxon merchants who did not comply with the new rules for unloading their wares apprehended and impaled on the spot. Michael Beheim informs us that there were 600 such merchants from Ţara Bîrsei on their way to Brăila with their goods. Dracula ordered most of their wares confiscated and had the merchants impaled. Others he assembled "in a huge cauldron which was adapted with holes so that their heads could peer out. He then ordered boiling water to be poured over the cauldron and boiled them alive."

A group of forty-one Saxon youths who had come to Wallachia on the pretext of learning the Romanian language were impaled, because Dracula thought that they had actually been sent as spies. "I do not wish them," wrote Dracula defensively, "to gain knowledge so that they might spy in my land." Indeed the German argument that "they were sent to Wallachia in order to learn Romanian" is quite unconvincing. Could they not have learned Romanian equally well in Transylvania, where the majority of the population spoke that language in their homes as fluently as did the Wallachians? It is more than likely that these youths were spies, instructed to foment discontent and subversion, to pave the way eventually for Dracula's replacement by one of his numerous exiled rivals. In the meantime, altered political circumstances that had taken place in Hungary facilitated some sort of a compromise. The sudden death of the young King Ladislas V Posthumus on December 9, 1457, at Prague, in rather mysterious circumstances (poison was suspected) caught everyone unaware and changed the political chess game. Mihály Szilágy had for some time backed his young nephew, Matthias, for the Hungarian throne. Matthias was elected Hungarian king by the diet on January 24, 1458, though he was not crowned. Szilágy hoped to continue to act as governor of Hungary and tutor, in view of Matthias's youth and inexperience. Szilágy, who had closely collaborated with Dracula since the Saxon revolt in Bistriţa, was now prepared to act as mediator in this dispute, hoping that Dracula's "destructive raids" and "warnings" had sufficiently chastened the German Saxons. This calculation was to prove correct. Like Szilágy, the king also wished to maintain friendly relations on his border, since he needed the support of the German cities, which continued to remain suspicious of Dracula in spite of the recent agreement. To further ease tensions, the king sent one of his cleverest diplomats, a great nobleman of Polish origin, to negotiate with Dracula. His name was Benedict de Boithor. When the diplomat arrived at Tîrgovişte, the prince ordered him to sit with Dracula at his table in the castle, which was, not unexpectedly, surrounded by dead and dying victims impaled on stakes. In front of the main table Dracula had put a large stake gilded in gold. Dracula asked the ambassador, "Tell me, why did I place this stake here?" The ambassador was frightened, but he summoned up his courage and replied, "Lord, it would appear that some great man committed some crime at your expense and that you wish to reserve for him a more honorable death than that meted out to humbler men." Dracula answered, "You spoke well. For you are the representative of the great king Matthias, and I have reserved this stake for you!" The ambassador contended, "Lord, if I have committed some crime which deserves the death penalty, do what you think is just, for you are an impartial judge, and it would not be you responsible for my death but I alone." Dracula burst out laughing and said, "Had you not answered me properly, you would be on that stake now!" Instead, Dracula honored the man and gave him presents. The prince closed the audience with the words "You are fully worthy of being an ambassador of a great ruler, since you have mastered the art of speaking to another great sovereign. But do not send any ambassadors to me who have not been properly educated in the art of diplomacy." Parallel negotiations with representatives of Braşov continued for some time in the fall of 1458, though in the end Dracula placed under house arrest the 500 German representatives sent to Tîrgovişte. On November 23, 1458, an accord was reached with Braşov at Sighişoara, where Szilágy resided. The Braşovians agreed to surrender Dan III, and his boyar supporters were also to be extradited. The city would pay Szilágy 10,000 florins for war damages. In exchange Dracula would restore the commercial privileges of both towns. Dracula seemed to accept these terms, for on December 1, 1458, he wrote to the mayor of Braşov: "Know that I shall keep the word ordered by my brother and Lord Mihály Szilágy. Your men can travel in our land freely to buy and sell without worry and without prejudice as if they were in their own country."

Mutual suspicions and bad faith on both sides contributed to make the agreement signed at Sighişoara almost a dead letter from the start. On the one hand, the Germans had never seriously intended to surrender to Dracula their refugee candidates to the Wallachian throne, who included Dan III; on the other, new tensions arose between nephew Matthias and his uncle Mihály Szilágy, as the ambitious boy king, who had lingered in jail for so many years, was impatient to be his own master and soon planned to get rid of his cumbersome guardian. Such tensions were bound to have their effect on Dracula, who sided with Szilágy, the man with whom he had so often collaborated. Matthias, on the other hand, preferred to stake his future on the support of the German Saxon townships and brought no pressure upon them to comply with the terms of the earlier agreement.

In the winter of 1459 Dracula organized one of his most devastating raids on Transylvanian soil, with the clear intention of trying to seize Dan III and his supporters. Advancing along the valley of the Prahova River, he delivered his first blows in the vicinity of Braşov, where he burned villages, forts, and towns, burned the crops to deprive the population of food, and killed men, women, and children as he progressed. He focused his attention on the exposed Braşovian suburbs, especially the Spenghi and Prund areas, which were located outside the walls of the fortress. This was the Romanian section of town, where Dan III and his dissident boyars resided. Under cover of darkness Dracula's men burst across the lightly fortified wooden palisade surrounding the section. He then proceeded to burn the whole suburb, including the old chapel of Saint Jacob, built in 1342, located at the foot of Tîmpa Hill; it was never restored. He took as many captives as he could find and impaled them "lengthwise and crosswise," according to Beheim's narrative. Their bodies were strung on Tîmpa Hill above the chapel. Dracula meanwhile was seated at a table having his meal; he seemed to enjoy the gruesome scenario of his butchers cutting off the limbs of many of his victims. Beheim tells us the additional detail that the prince "dipped his bread in the blood of the victims," since "watching human blood flow gave him courage." The stage was thus set for Dracula's later reputation as a blood drinker or vampire, and his subsequent fictional reincarnation as Count Dracula. As we will see, this episode at Tîmpa Hill did more to damage Dracula's reputation than any other act in his whole career. On this occasion Dracula also displayed the perverted black humor that is attributed to him in Russian narratives. A boyar attending the Braşov festivity, apparently unable to endure any longer the smell of coagulating blood, had the misfortune to hold up his nose and express a gesture of revulsion. Dracula immediately ordered an unusually long stake prepared for the would-be victim and presented it to him with the cynical remark: "You live up there yonder, where the stench cannot reach you." The boyar was immediately impaled.

Dracula and his men then attacked the church of Saint Bartholomew, also located outside of the Braşov walls. It still exists, the oldest Romanesque church in all Transylvania, dating from the thirteenth century. He "burned the church, together with its treasures, chalices, and priestly vestments." Finally, he even dared to make a quick foray inside Braşov, where he attempted to burn the famous Black Church. However, from his point of view, the entire expedition was a hollow failure: Dan III and his court, who had been forewarned, had gone into hiding on a boyar estate before the attack. They were not among those captured and impaled.

Dracula's horrors and his wanton destruction of property provided the young Prince Dan III with a formidable weapon against Vlad. He appealed to the "honest and good citizens of the city of Braşov and of Ţara Bîrsei . . . to all their brethren, their friends, their relatives and sons who had lost a dear one because of the actions of this lawless, cruel, and faithless tyrant responsible for torturing and killing people aimlessly and devastating whole areas" to support him. For good measure he added that "Dracula had sold himself to the Turks." Although the first accusations were probably quite justified, Dracula had not at the time surrendered to the Turks. Indeed, 1459 was a particularly bad period in Wallachian-Turkish relations, for it was the first year that Dracula refused to pay the promised tribute. Regardless, this propaganda by Dan provided good material to be exploited at will by Dracula's future political enemies.

In March 1460, Dan III, with the support of Braşovians, took the offensive against Dracula. He seized Făgăraş and Amlaş, traditional fiefs of the Wallachian princes, and arrested and killed Dracula's supporters along the way. Then Dan organized a full-scale invasion of Wallachia, though he failed to arouse the local Romanian population. The main encounter with Dracula took place at the Wallachia-Transylvania border, near Rucăr. Dan lost the skirmish, and only seven of his boyars managed to escape.

A macabre fate awaited Dan himself. Upon his capture by the Wallachians, Dracula "ordered his priest clothed in the formal liturgical funeral vestments to read the mass for the dead," a kind of extreme unction for Dan, who was very much alive. Then Dracula forced the unfortunate prince to dig his own grave, following which Dracula himself cut off Dan's head. Beheim again makes reference to Vlad's perverted sense of humor in stating that "he reserved for Dan a death worthy of 'The Prince' he styled himself." He killed all the captured boyar followers of Dan by impalement.

Once Dan and his main supporters were out of the way, the Braşovians sent their leading citizen, Johann Gereb, to negotiate a truce with Dracula. But Dracula was not ready to sign the peace with any Transylvanian township, so long as other rivals there, such as Vlad the Monk, still constituted a threat to his throne. His ally Mihály Szilágy had repeatedly demanded that Sibiu abandon its support of Vlad the Monk, but without results. Dracula therefore determined to bring this formidable opponent to his knees as well.

Thus, during the summer of 1460 Dracula organized his final raid on Transylvania. This time he attacked townships and villages in the district of Amlaş known as the "Land of the Forest" or Unterwald, where Vlad the Monk was hiding. The meistersinger Beheim gives the exact date of the attack as falling on the feast day of Saint Bartholomew in the year 1460: August 24. Dracula struck in the early morning after "passing through the great forest", with his cavalry force. He burned the town of Amlaş and impaled all the citizens, a priest having led the procession to the burial scene. (It is interesting to note that 114 years later, in 1574, Catherine de' Medici and her son, Henry, the duke of Anjou, made Saint Bartholomew's Day equally infamous through one of the most brutal mass exterminations in history, the Saint Bartholomew Massacre, when all the Protestant leaders in Paris were killed.)

Dracula's raid on Amlaş was aimed at eliminating any remaining dissident resistance and at killing rival contenders to his throne, especially Vlad the Monk. Dracula knew, for instance, that one of the principal advisers of the dead Dan III, the boyar Bogdan Doboca, was hiding in the village of Şercaia, in the Făgăraş district. So he had the entire village razed to the ground; it had to be completely repopulated in the following century. Similar was the fate of the village of Mica. The narrator Beheim tells us that Dracula burned or destroyed half the communities in the Amlaş district, including the capital city by that name. He "assembled all the citizens and all those he could find" from other villages and hanged them on hooks and pitchforks, after having had his men hack them to pieces with knives, swords, and sabers. Amlaş was reduced to a ghost town, as it still is today, and other villages such as Sălişte, Apodul de Sus, and Tilişca were similarly destroyed. Beheim claims that altogether some 30,000 Germans were killed during this Dracula raid on the district of Amlaş.

No help for the Germans was forthcoming from the Hungarian king, Matthias, or the Transylvanian governor, Mihály Szilágy, whose forces were instructed to observe neutrality. Matthias, who had not as yet consolidated his authority, had shown little interest in this brushfire that was burning within the confines of his realm, despite the human toll. Dracula, on his part, had studiously avoided attacking the king's garrisons posted at various fortresses within the areas that he had terrorized.

Still, both parties had an interest in working out a settlement. On October 1, 1460, a peace treaty was signed at Braşov between Dracula's representatives and the city council. There were four main provisions: (1) Braşov was to surrender all the Romanian boyars who had taken shelter on its soil, while Dracula was prepared to do the same with the enemies of the city who had sought asylum in Wallachia; (2) all commercial privileges obtained by the German cities from Dracula in 1456 were to be restored, canceling the various restrictions Dracula had placed on German trade; (3) the cities of Braşov and Sibiu, the various townships of Ţara Bîrsei, and the region of the "seven fortresses" would pay Dracula maintenance money for an army of 4,000 mercenaries to fight against any impending attack by the Turks; and finally, (4) Dracula agreed to pay the German merchants of Sibiu and Braşov war compensation for the destruction of property that he had caused. That last provision must have angered Dracula a great deal. But there was little that he could do, since King Matthias himself guaranteed the peace treaty. Similar treaties were arranged with Sighişoara, Bistriţa, and other German towns.

Despite the fact that this treaty signified that Dracula had to abandon his protectionist economic policies, it was a kind of victory for him. For the two years from 1460 to 1462 he knew that his western front was secure, and he could afford to turn against a far more dangerous rival, Sultan Mehmed II.

But these raids and accompanying atrocities against the Germans of Transylvania during the years 1457 and 1460 were to have a long-range impact that reached far beyond the borders of Romanian countries. Those German Catholic monks who were fortunate enough to escape from their monasteries, which had been reduced to ashes, brought with them to the west what in essence became the first Dracula "horror stories." Thus, Dracula in his own lifetime became a subject of horror literature. At the monastery of Saint Gall in Switzerland, at Lambach near Salzburg, and at the Melk Abbey on the Danube River in Lower Austria — all Benedictine houses — these refugees related their harrowing escapes to the other monks. These stories were copied down, mostly by scribes, and in turn used at the opportune moment as propaganda against the prince by the Hungarian chancellery. Among the refugees who had fled Dracula's terror was a Bernardine lay brother who is simply referred to as "Brother

Jacob.'' He was to become the chief informant to the Swabian minnesinger Michael Beheim. Among the later German texts that included
Beheim's account, one printed at Strassburg in 1500 was prefaced by a
woodcut showing Dracula seated at a table surrounded by rows of
impaled cadavers. This image suggests clearly that the bloodthirsty Count
Dracula of fiction and movies was born from the loins of the bloody
practitioner of terror in Transylvania.

CHAPTER 6

The Struggle Against
Mehmed the Conqueror

THE war between Dracula "the Impaler" and Mehmed II "the Conqueror" was bound to happen; the only question was the timing. Having grown up with Mehmed, Dracula was aware of the sultan's insatiable desire for conquests and his great ambition to be ruler of all Europe as well as Asia. Mehmed had declared, after all: "I am young and rich and favored by fortune, so I intend to surpass Caesar, Alexander, and Hannibal by far." He planned to strike at the pillars of European civilization and bring it tumbling down into his control. Though Dracula ruled a comparatively small country, he was quite as determined and proud as the sultan himself. And he was not about to give in without a struggle to the sultan's designs on his country.

Dracula realized that he had to avoid a two-front war at all costs. It would be difficult enough fighting the Turkish army, which would outnumber his own three to one, without having to worry about an attack from the west by the Germans of Transylvania or their allies. This was one of the major reasons behind Dracula's decision to seek a permanent peace with Transylvania. Indeed, he hoped to secure Hungarian and Saxon help in his crusade against the infidel Turks. Perhaps little did he realize that the European Christians had no deep sense of a need to unify against the Turkish onslaught, while the Turks were inflamed by the idea of the Holy War of Islam. After all, if you were a Christian who fell in battle, you no longer had the assurance that you would go to heaven as in the heyday of crusading, but if you were a Muslim, there was absolute certainty that if you died in a war for the spread of Islam, your soul would be propelled to an earthlike paradise, where lovely young maidens would serve you tasty drinks.

The Dracula campaign of 1462 must be evaluated in its European context. After the failure of the sultan's army to take Belgrade in 1456, the sultan's immediate aim was to consolidate and stabilize the front by securing the banks of the Danube River at the very least. This meant not only a renewed attempt to capture Belgrade but also control of the mouth of the Danube, the western coast of the Black Sea, and such strategic fortresses as Chilia and Akkerman, technically in Moldavian territory. One of the sultan's janissary commanders, who has left us a remarkable account of the Turco-Wallachian struggle, simply identifies himself as "the Janissary of Ostrovitza" (a site in present-day Yugoslavia). He stated the problem in a soldier's unsophisticated language: "You, my happy master, must know that so long as Chilia and Akkerman are in the hands of the Romanians and the Hungarians possess the fortress of Belgrade, the capital of Serbia, we shall not be able to conquer the Balkans." The sultan accepted this advice, and in this respect he was thinking in remarkably modern strategic terms: control of the Danube and the Black Sea were in fact interrelated. Seizure of the Danube was the primary objective, since the river, which has its source in the Black Forest of Germany, represented the traditional highway for eastern invasion of the west. It was like a dart aimed at the soft underbelly of his western enemies, a means of penetration into Europe. In addition, control over Bulgaria, Serbia, and most of Greece having been seized, it was logical that the sultan should also wish to transform Wallachia into a province of his empire. Besides, Mehmed had been irked by the ambivalent policies pursued by both Dracul and Dracula, on whose help he could not really count despite their status of vassals.

Enea Silvio de' Piccolomini, Pope Pius II, who had succeeded the ineffectual Calixtus III in 1458, was, like Dracula, one of the few statesmen in Europe who understood the nature of the Ottoman threat. As mentioned previously, an aristocrat from Siena, educated in the traditions of Renaissance humanism, having dissipated his early youth in mundane pursuits, illicit adventures that included the fathering of several illegitimate children and the writing of profane literature, he experienced a change of heart after he entered religious life. Once ordained a priest, he devoted his skills at the Council of Basel to saving the papacy from the danger of "democratic" government implied in substituting for papal rule a college of cardinals. He also helped pave the way for the union between Orthodoxy and Catholicism at the Council of Florence in 1439.

His unusual negotiating abilities had caught the eye of the Holy Roman Emperor Frederick III, who invited him to serve as a chief councillor in his chancery, being virtually in charge of imperial diplomacy. He had also acted as an educator to the young king of Hungary, Ladislas Posthumus, as we know, and wrote for the exclusive use of the emperor's ward a pedagogical treatise that is still worth reading today. When elected pope, he was remarkably tolerant of dissent, to the point that the great English historian Lord Acton describes him as "the founder of freedom of speech." In spite of, or perhaps because of, his humanistic background, Pius II understood the Ottoman threat to Europe after the fall of Constantinople and the need to organize a great crusade, which would involve not only the west but the surviving free states of eastern Europe. Well informed through a network of diplomats and spies, the pope had made a study of the sultan's psychology and modi operandi. Among the eastern European leaders, he was to become most intrigued with Dracula. He made frequent mention of his name in his *Commentaries* and in other treatises, at times in favorable terms.

Pius II launched the idea of this new crusade by summoning a great council of the church in the cathedral of Mantua on September 26, 1459, with invitations sent to all the leading powers of Europe. His two-hour inaugural address drained his already feeble health but left an indelible impression on those few delegates who had cared to attend. He exhorted his spellbound audience to "take up the cross" in stirring and inspiring words. Nothing of the kind had been heard since the great crusading Council of Clermont in the eleventh century. The pope saw virtually no limit to Mehmed's ambition; he warned his audiences, "Every victory for him will be a stepping-stone to another, until after subjecting all the Christians of the west, he will have destroyed the Gospel of Christ and imposed that of his false prophet over the entire world!" To substantiate his claim and to fire up his audience, the pope brought forth witnesses, refugees from various parts of the Balkans, to describe their sufferings and privations at the hands of the Turks. But those few delegates in attendance from Burgundy, Milan, and Hungary were largely unresponsive; appeasement was the order of the day.

The emperor Frederick III, on whose behalf the pope had worked diligently in past years, promised an infantry force of 32,000 and 10,000 cavalrymen, a promise, as it turned out, worth no more than the paper it was written on. This egoistic psychopath was more interested in consulting astrologers who told him that he still had a good chance of subverting the power of his main rival for the crown of Hungary, Matthias Corvinus.

England was in no position to join any crusade, since the Wars of the Roses were still exhausting the country. The imperial German representative, Gregor von Heimburg, was totally uncooperative, giving social strife and boundary disputes among the German states as his excuse. The ever-timid French king Charles VII and his successor, Louis XI, the Spider King, were more absorbed with succession to the kingdom of Naples than crusading against Mehmed. In Italy, King Alfonso V, who had paid lip service to crusading, had died on July 27, 1458, and his bastard son, Ferrante, soon recognized by the pope as rightful ruler, was more concerned in resisting French ambitions.

The overall attitude of indifference was best revealed in the words of the famous Sigismondo Malatesta, Lord of Rimini, member of one of the most powerful families of Italy, who combined the cleverness of a fox with the courage of a lion. Replying to a critic who had faulted him for favoring the Turks, he said, "I serve him who pays me more," and actually made war with the pope. This cynical reply also reflected thinking in Florence, Milan, Genoa, and Venice, all deeply interlocked in political or commercial competition with one another. Venice, the greatest maritime power in the Aegean and eastern Mediterranean, whose possessions were most immediately threatened by the Turkish advances, made financial demands of the pope which they knew were impossible to fulfill: payment for 8,000 men to man their ships, 50,000 cavalry, and 20,000 infantry — all to be covered by the empty papal treasury.

Among the central and eastern European states, George Poděbrady, king of Bohemia since 1458, was not really interested in fighting the Turks, who did not yet threaten his own borders. It took all his efforts to restore the badly shattered authority of the crown of Saint Wenceslas after the religious and civil disobedience by Catholics and the successors of the Hussites. The Polish king, Casimir IV, also duke of Lithuania, had evidently learned the lesson of his predecessor, Ladislas III, who had died at the debacle at Varna in 1444. Poland was too distant and involved in its own struggles against the German Teutonic Order to do much else than protest by diplomatic notes. The Russian ruler, Ivan III, grand duke of Moscow, was even more geographically remote from the scene and was clearly preoccupied with internal feudal and religious strife. Russia was still not free from the Tatar yoke. Stephen of Moldavia, Dracula's cousin and ally, evinced little interest in crusading at that time, and instead vented his wrath against the Hungarian king, who had given shelter to the man responsible for the assassination of his father. He chose to place himself as a vassal to the Polish king and waited upon events to determine his future course of action. Even the Albanians, who had resisted for so long under their great hero Skanderbeg and upon whom the pope counted for aid, took this inopportune moment to sign a three-year truce with the Turks.

Ironically, both at Mantua and later at Rome, representatives of eastern Asiatic powers, mostly Muslims, showed more enthusiasm for the war against the Turks than did western European Christians. Among them, the sultan's own brother-in-law, Uzun Hazan, "Lord of the White Sheep," who controlled part of Iran, was ready to fight and promised to raise 5,000 troops. The lord of "Little Armenia" came to Rome with an offer of 150,000 troops. Sensing support in numbers and dreaming of the possibility of an eastern coalition that could help launch a two-front war against the Ottoman Empire, Pope Pius II sent a monk in papal service, Fra Ludovico da Bologna, on a mission to various eastern capitals to gather support for such a project. As a result, some strange and obscure characters came to the Roman curia: among them was a certain George VIII of Imeretia, self-styled "King of the Persians"; a prince of Georgiana or Great Iberia, the sustenance of whose corpulent body reportedly required two hundred pounds of meat a day. Other exotic types were Dadian Liparit, ruler of Mingrelia, on the eastern shore of the Black Sea, who declared that he would raise 60,000 troops, and Rabia, lord of Abkhazia; Ismail Bey of Sinop also promised to help the war effort. The lord of Karaman in Asia Minor, a perennial enemy of the sultan, promised to raise 40,000 "Goths and Alans" to fight under the banner of the surviving Greek emperor of Trebizond against Mehmed II.

The Congress of Mantua formally came to a close on January 14, 1460, when the pope issued a bull proclaiming the three year crusade, implying the usual pardon of sins to all who undertook it. A new religious association, the Order of Saint Mary of Bethlehem, was created to commemorate the occasion. One hundred thousand gold ducats was to be raised by the Roman curia to pay for a force of 50,000 men. But even the pope admitted one month later that the odds for success were not in his favor.

Virtually the only European ruler who immediately planned a positive response to the papal appeal was Dracula, and that is perhaps why the pope initially had such high regard for the Romanian warlord. Having signed a treaty with the Transylvanian Saxons in 1460 and renewed his oath of loyalty to the Hungarian king, Dracula had his western flank covered and was poised to resume the vows he had inherited from his father as a member of the Dragon Order. King Matthias Corvinus's enthusiasm was measured by his inability to be formally invested with the crown of St. Stephen; Emperor Frederick III filled his response with pious and encouraging words, but mentioned no specific dates for joining the crusade.

Sultan Mehmed II, who was well aware of the unenthusiastic response of the European powers to the pope's appeal at Mantua, felt that this was the opportune time to strike and seize control of the remaining free Balkan states. His immediate objective was the city of Smederevo (Semendria), the final symbol of Serbian independence. The city fell easily to the Muslim onslaught in 1460; in turn the Turks threatened Bosnia, a Slavic principality religiously subverted to Islam. Pressures once again increased against Belgrade, the strategic fortress under Hungarian rule, which protected the course of the Danube, leading to Buda and Vienna itself. These moves were followed by Vizier Mahmud's diplomatic mission to the despot of Morea, a Byzantine stronghold that had survived the fall of Constantinople. He persuaded the incumbent, a member of the famed imperial Paleologus dynasty, to give up his throne, assuring him safe passage to Italy. The latter fled there on March 7, 1461. Clad in the white garb of a penitent, he strode into Saint Peter's Basilica in Rome, into the presence of Pope Pius II, and presented the Holy Father with a famous relic, the head of the Apostle Andrew, which had once been preserved on the island city of Patras but had been removed because of the Turkish onslaught. Both Mistra, one of the queen cities of the Aegean, and Corinth similarly surrendered virtually without a struggle.

Dracula was understandably upset by these events of the end of 1461. He saw resistance to the Turks gradually petering out in the Balkans as the few surviving free territories were either conquered or made their peace with the sultan. Among the warriors who opted for resistance was his close ally Mihály Szilágy, belatedly reconciled to his nephew King Matthias. By a stroke of ill fortune Mihály Szilágy was captured by one of the sultan's officers, the bey Mihaloğlu Ali, while on a reconnaissance mission in Bulgaria, shortly after the fall of Smederevo. His companions were immediately killed and mutilated. Szilágy himself was brought to Constantinople and tortured in the sultan's presence. Mehmed was interested in obtaining detailed information on Hungary's military preparedness at Belgrade and Chilia and the extent of Dracula's commitments to the Hungarian king. We presume that Szilágy did not reveal any military secrets and that it was for his courageous silence that he was most cruelly executed by being sawed in half — a familiar Turkish method of imposing death. One can readily imagine the impact of Szilágy's death —

that of a man he had always considered as a brother — on Dracula, with his strong eye-for-eye and tooth-for-tooth ethic.

The initial indication that relations between Dracula and Mehmed II had cooled considerably is evident from a letter addressed by the Wallachian prince to the city elders of Braşov, dated September 10, 1460: "An embassy from Turkey had now come to us. Bear in mind that I have previously spoken to you about brotherhood and peace . . . the time and the hour have now come, where the Turks wish to place upon our shoulders . . . unbearable difficulties and . . . compel us not to live peacefully with you. . . . They are seeking ways to loot your country passing through ours. In addition, they force us . . . to work against your Catholic faith. Our wish is to commit no evil against you, not to abandon you, as I have sworn. I trust that I shall remain your brother and faithful friend. This is why I have retained the Turkish envoys here, so that I have time to send you the news." These detained Turkish envoys may have been the victims of the famous nailing of the turbans to the heads of the Turks, which is described in the German, Russian, and Romanian narratives. (As mentioned, Dracula had also nailed their caps to the heads of Italian envoys from Caffa.) Dracula's action in this second matter amounted to deliberate provocation of Mehmed II, who, given his character, was bound to react in kind.

A tense Turco-Wallachian situation resulted from the above-mentioned circumstances. The reason for the final breakdown of relations and for the opening of hostilities between Dracula and Mehmed must be sought in Turkish attempts to tighten the loose terms of existing treaty obligations, as a preliminary step toward incorporating Wallachia into the empire. For instance, the tribute of 10,000 ducats a year had been paid by Dracula only until 1459. Wallachia was thus three years in arrears, owing the sultan 30,000 ducats, a very heavy burden, which ultimately fell on the peasants in the 222 villages of the country. (Each village, on average, could raise only 45 ducats.) In theory the tribute and the many other "gifts" to a variety of Turkish officials from the grand vizier downward had to be brought to the sultan in person by the prince. Preoccupied by his campaigns against the Germans of Transylvania, Dracula had never paid such homage to his Turkish masters as convention prescribed, yet another cause for offense. The Turks had also requested no fewer than 500 boys destined for the janissary corps, a demand that was not generally required of vassal states, as opposed to actual Turkish territories. Violating that provision, Turkish recruiting officers had been seen crossing the Danube frequently in certain regions of Wallachia such as Oltenia, where the quality of "manhood" was thought to be good. Such incursions had been resisted by Dracula by force of arms, and the Turkish Danubian commanders, when caught, were apt to find themselves on the extremities of stakes. In fact, such violations of territory practiced by both sides were considered added provocations, and they embittered Turko-Wallachian relations. Raiding, pillaging, and looting were endemic from Giurgiu to the Black Sea coast, and the Danube itself often froze during winter, allowing easy crossing. The Turks had also succeeded in securing control of various fortresses and townships on the Romanian side of the river, including the formidable fortress of Giurgiu, built by Dracula's father, Dracul; these provided advanced operational offensive points for them. In spite of these provocations, the sultan, the bulk of whose army was involved in a struggle with his Asiatic enemy Uzun Hazan Pasha, was playing for time, and ostensibly took the lead in attempting to resolve his differences with Dracula. He invited the Wallachian prince to discuss their differences either at Constantinople or at some mutually convenient city within the confines of his Empire.

Dracula, a wily negotiator who had learned his lessons from experience, immediately suspected a trap such as had been sprung on his father at Gallipoli in 1442. His main objective was also to gain time, and, if possible, allay the sultan's suspicions until his own forces were militarily prepared to deliver an initial strike. In a missive dispatched to Mehmed at the end of November 1461, Dracula alleged that his country had been bled white and his treasury exhausted by the three years of struggle with his German political foes in Transylvania and by domestic upheaval among the boyars. He therefore could not pay the arrears in taxes he owed to the sultan, nor could he leave his capital, "for if I should leave my country my political opponents would invite the Hungarian king to rule over my domains." Only in the event that the sultan immediately sent one of his pashas to "watch over [the] country" would Dracula volunteer to make the trip to Constantinople. As additional proof of his good faith and his desire to remain the sultan's ally, he was ready, even contrary to treaty obligations, to "provide many children and horses, so that the sultan may not reproach me for not having served him well, and I will count the amount of the tribute and add gifts of my own." Dracula also indicated that he was willing to discuss a mutually acceptable frontier on the Danube River.

The sultan, detecting a possible deal in the works and worried about the continuing conflict in Asia Minor, accepted Dracula's proposal and sent a diplomatic mission to Tîrgovişte, led by a half-Greek, half-Serbian official, Hamza Pasha, bey of Nicopolis, a chief falconer of the realm. This was to be the last official mission from the sultan to Dracula negotiating in apparent good faith.

In the meantime, Mehmed intercepted letters written by Dracula to the Hungarian king that proved that Dracula had negotiated a military alliance with the king. Now convinced of Dracula's insincerity, Mehmed hatched what he thought to be a clever plot to apprehend the Wallachian prince and forcibly bring him to Constantinople. A new meeting place for negotiations was designated by Hamza Pasha outside the island fortress of Giurgiu; there Dracula was to be ambushed and kidnapped. Yet another Turkish envoy, a renegade Greek in Turkish service, Thomas Catavolinos, was to proceed to Tîrgovişte to accompany Dracula to this place. He was to keep the Turkish commander at the citadel informed at various stages on the road of the progress of the party, giving the precise time when the Wallachian leader was likely to leave his capital and reach the fortress. Forewarned of the plot, Dracula artfully played the cat-and-mouse game to the hilt; he went, but took the precaution of ordering a superior cavalry force to follow his small number of attendants at a distance. A letter from Dracula to King Matthias from the fortress of Giurgiu on February 2, 1462, makes it quite evident that the Wallachian prince suspected a trap: "By the grace of God, as I was journeying to the frontier, I found out about their trickery and slyness, and I was the one who captured Hamza Bey in the Turkish district and land, close to the fortress called Giurgiu." Dracula had both Hamza Pasha and the Greek Catavolinos captured; they were destined to face a theatrical death.

Dracula then attacked and captured the fortress of Giurgiu, which his father had built at great sacrifice but which had fallen into Turkish hands in 1447. Disguising himself as a Turk and giving orders in fluent Turkish, he persuaded the garrison commander to open the gates of the fortress. And then, in Dracula's own words, "our men, mixing with theirs, entered and destroyed the fortress, which I immediately burned." After looting the place for good measure, according to the Italian traveler Donado de Lezze, Dracula "personally cut the noses and ears off two slaves." The successful attack on Giurgiu, coupled with a well-executed ambush of two high-ranking Turkish officials, was, to say the least, tantamount to a declaration of war.

Dracula was to strike next all along the Danube, taking the offensive at a most propitious moment, since the sultan was still involved in a campaign on the northern shores of Asia Minor. So the Turks were unable to respond quickly to the Dracula challenge.

During the winter of 1461–1462 Dracula waged the first and remarkably successful phase in the Turco-Wallachian war. In responding positively to Pope Pius II's call for a crusade against the Turks, Dracula was attempting to duplicate the successes of Hunyadi during the forties. The fact that the winter was unusually cold that year actually facilitated his war operations, since the frozen Danube River could be crossed with impunity along both banks. Much of the actual fighting took place on Bulgarian soil that was controlled by the Turks.

The key to Dracula's wartime strategy was speed, boldness, and ruthlessness. He forced his troops to cover the distance of some 800 kilometers in two weeks, from the Danube heel facing present-day Yugoslavia to the delta and the Black Sea. With his army divided into smaller forces under individual commanders, Dracula's principal aim was to capture those ports along the Danube, such as Giurgiu and Turnu, which lay on the Romanian bank, the points from which the Turks had launched sallies deep inside his territory. An equally important objective was the systematic destruction of towns on the Bulgarian side of the river that the Turks might use as fording places. He also aimed at depopulating the area, destroying food and other supplies the Turks might need for their future offensive, thus making a Turkish invasion more difficult. Ultimately Dracula's campaign, like Hunyadi's, had a liberating aspect, to free the Christian population of Bulgaria from Turkish control, though he would need the help of the Hungarian king to carry that objective out to its logical end. Since Hungarian help was not forthcoming, many Bulgarians in the Danube area fled with Dracula's troops after the Turkish onslaught and sought asylum in Wallachia.

In his letter to the Hungarian king, Matthias Corvinus, dated February 11, 1462, Dracula boasted of his achievements, especially the numbers of enemy killed, a fact confirmed by the German chronicle from the monastery of Melk. Dracula wrote:

> I have killed men and women, old and young, who lived at Oblucitza and Novoselo, where the Danube flows into the sea, up to Rahova, which is located near Chilia, from the lower Danube up to such places as Samovit and Ghighen. We killed 23,884 Turks and Bulgars without counting those whom we burned in homes or whose heads were not cut by our soldiers. . . . Thus Your Highness must know that I have broken the peace with him [the sultan].

Dracula also included some gruesome statistics concerning the exact number of men killed (both Turks and Bulgarians) in the various townships on both banks of the Danube, which enables us to follow the precise course of his attack. At Giurgiu itself there were 6,414 victims; at Eni Sala, 1,350; at Durostor, 6,840; at Orsova, 343; at Hîrsova, 840; at Marotin, 210; at Turtucaia, 630; at Turnu, Batin, and Novograd, 384; at Sistov, 410; at Nicopolis and Ghighen, 1,138; at Rahova, 1,460. It is worth noting that Dracula did not destroy the port of Vidin because, he stated, "from that point onward the Turks can do no great damage." To impress King Matthias further with his accuracy, Dracula counted the heads, noses, and ears cut off, then placed them in two bags and sent them to Buda through his envoy Radu Farma. These figures did not include the thousand or so Turkish troops and their two commanders, Hamza Pasha and Thomas Catavolinos, who were manacled, marched to the vicinity of Tîrgoviște, and impaled. Taller stakes were reserved for the two Turkish commanders.

Dracula was pleased with what he had accomplished, for "had the Turks wished to bring their ships from Constantinople to the Danube they no longer have fording points, because I have burned, destroyed, and laid waste their towns." Dracula had reasserted his control over the whole length of the Danube River down to the delta and Black Sea region. In essence he also reestablished Wallachian supremacy in the province of Dobruja, which had been won by his grandfather Mircea (Durostor and Eni Sala were both located in that province).

Sultan Mehmed was still busy besieging the city of Corinth in May, but he made an initial attempt to punish Dracula for his daring by sending his grand vizier, Mahmud, a part-Serbian, part-Greek renegade and an able diplomat used by the sultan in various successful Balkan missions, to lead an army to destroy Brăila, the largest Wallachian port on the Danube. Overreaching his official instruction, Mahmud, having captured the port, organized a full-scale military offensive involving some 18,000 Turkish troops and launched deep sallies into Wallachian territories, pillaging and burning villages along the way and taking the population away in bondage. When Dracula heard from his scouts of these atrocities, he force-marched his army and caught the vizier's rear guard near Brăila, as the Turks were trying to make their way back to the right bank of the Danube. According to the Italian chronicler de Lezze, Dracula's forces destroyed a good part of Vizier Mahmud's army; only 8,000 Turks survived.

This humiliation proved to be the last straw. Mehmed gave up the siege of Corinth and decided to launch a full-scale invasion of Wallachia. Dracula's control of the Danube, however, meant that the sultan would be compelled to invade the country by land from Bulgaria, rather than using the usual water route (the Black Sea and the Danube). The fleet would be used only as an ancillary weapon after a landing had been effected. From a strategic point of view, given the hopeless disparity of forces, Dracula had two options: he could either disperse his troops at diverse locations along the river to prepare for a number of Turkish landing points, or alternatively, had the main Turkish offensive taken place by way of the Danube, he could have made use of amphibious operations, as his father had done in 1446, following the fleet on land by using his fast-moving cavalry to confront the sultan's army at any disembarkation point. As things stood, the element of surprise in the Turkish attack was greater, since Dracula could not anticipate the precise landing spot, once the Turkish army could proceed to the Danube from their assembly point in Bulgaria.

Meanwhile, the prince's extraordinary exploits on the Danube were greeted in western Europe by mixed awe, admiration, and praise. It seemed as if the days of the great Hunyadi had returned. A new hope of liberation spread throughout the enslaved lands of Bulgaria, Serbia, and Greece. The Transylvanian towns of Braşov, Sibiu, and Bistriţa were among the first to hear the good news, which then spread on to Buda, Prague, Vienna, and even to western capitals. Venetian diplomats such as Pietro Tommasi at Buda, Domenico Balbi at Constantinople, the Cardinal de Saint Angelo, the papal nuncio, and Florio de Reverella, representing the duke of Ferrara (both stationed at Buda), and the representatives of Milan, Ferrara, Bologna, and other Italian states became absorbed in their dispatches with Dracula's Danubian offensive. Ultimately their missives reached the careful eyes of Pope Pius II, who henceforth became an admirer of Dracula's military talent. The Venetian representative at Buda, Pietro Tommasi, in particular turned into a self-styled advocate who pleaded Dracula's cause, with the knowledge that the contents of his reports would go straight to Rome. He expressed the hope to the Venetian senate that once the promised subsidies were sent from Rome and Venice on March 4, 1462, "the Hungarian king will do all he can to help Dracula. . . . He promised that he would descend at the head of his army and cross into Transylvania." This was of course wishful thinking. An English pilgrim to the Holy Land, William of Wey, who had happened to sojourn on the island of Rhodes on his way home, wrote that "the military men of Rhodes, upon hearing of Dracula's campaign, had Te Deums sung to the praise and honor of God who had granted such victories. . . . The lord mayor of Rhodes convened his brother soldiers and the whole citizenry feasted on fruit and wine.'' The Genoese from Caffa in the Crimea sent envoys to Dracula informing him that his campaign on the Danube had saved them from an attack by some 300 ships that the sultan had planned to send against them.

From a psychological point of view, knowing of the impressionable Turkish mentality, Dracula's deliberate use of terror on the Danube to frighten the Turks had in essence been successful. At Constantinople itself there was an atmosphere of consternation, gloom, and fear. Some of the Turkish leaders, haunted by the awesome reputation of the Lord Impaler (''Kazîglu Bey''), as they began to call him, were apparently contemplating flight across the Bosporus into Asia Minor.

However, as a realist Dracula now anticipated the full furor of the sultan's revenge. His immediate aim was to revive the idea of a crusade, which the pope had proclaimed at Mantua, since he knew that at best he alone could only delay a Turkish invasion. He made the usual appeal to the Christian powers in both the east and west, as well as to the Muslim enemies of the sultan. ''Your Majesty must know that I have broken the peace with them not for *our sake,* but for the sake of the honor of Your Highness. . . . The Holy Cross, and for guarding all of Christianity and strengthening the Catholic law.'' Messages such as these were ultimately intended to reach the pope, whom he knew to have a vested interest. The Greek historian Laonicus Chalcondyles, later citing Dracula's words, in his history *Historiarum demonstrationes . . .* accentuated the urgency of Dracula's appeal:

> You know that our land is a neighbor to your land. . . . You also may have heard that the sultan has set up a huge army against us. If this land of ours is subjugated, please realize that they will not stay content with our land but will immediately make war on you, and the inhabitants of your land will suffer great misfortunes at their hands. So now is the time: by helping us, you really help yourself by stopping their army far from your own land and by not allowing them to destroy our land and harm and oppress us.

In order to secure a hard-and-fast military alliance with the Hungarians, Dracula expressed his readiness to conclude a marriage with a member of Corvinus's royal family. This meant that he would have to abandon his Orthodox Christianity and become a Roman Catholic. But, since the church council of Florence had formally reunited the two churches in 1439 this did not represent any serious problems of a theological or religious nature. In those days, changes of religion for marital purposes were quite common, especially among the ruling families. Dracula also informed the king that if Matthias and his own troops were unable to fight, then at least he should "send aid from the Szeklers and Saxons," his old political enemies. The Wallachian prince warned that the aid must be forthcoming by April 23, 1462, the feast of Saint George, an ominous date in Romanian folklore, since Saint George is also the slayer of dragons, a possible reference to his commitment to the ideals of the Dragon Order. Other diplomatic envoys went scurrying about in search of help to such remote locations as the capital of Armenia and Georgia, which was at war with the sultan. More realistically, he appealed on May 17 to the khan of the Tatars in the Crimea and to the Genoese of Caffa, who were equally threatened by Mehmed.

In essence, Dracula was reverting to the traditional Romanian view of his small country as an advanced bastion of Christianity defending the frontiers of Europe against the barbarism of the Orient. In an uncanny and prophetic way he foresaw the inevitable Turkish expansion should the king not respond to his urgent plea. "If, God forbid, we should fail, the consequences of such a Turkish victory would be severe for all Christianity," he wrote. Sixty-four years later, in 1526, following the disastrous battle of Mohácz, Matthias's successor, Louis II, and the flower of the Hungarian nobility perished at the hands of another ambitious sultan, Süleyman the Magnificent, as most of Hungary was subsequently transformed into a Turkish province.

The expected help from the Hungarian king failed to materialize, since Matthias preferred to keep his army in reserve, pending the solution of the conflict with Emperor Frederick III, who continued to hold the crown of St. Stephen, which alone could give legal sanction to Matthias's rule at Wiener Neustadt. In a sense the Hungarian king looked upon Dracula's vassal army as the first line of defense of Hungarian territory. The small Hungarian garrison stationed at the fortress of Chilia was given instructions to collaborate with the Wallachian leader, should it be attacked by the Turks. For the time being, though, this was the extent of Hungary's commitment to the crusade. (It provided some justification for use of papal and crusading funds.)

In the meantime, Sultan Mehmed concluded his successful campaign in Asia. The empire of Trebizond, a last Christian enclave in Anatolia, had fallen, the sultan signed a truce with the Moslem prince of Karaman and had also conquered Sinop. He was thus free to use the full brunt of his forces to punish Vlad's temerity. On May 17, 1462, Mehmed the

Conqueror finally set out with the bulk of his army from Constantinople in person, thus emphasizing the importance he attributed to this campaign. The sultan's aim was not merely to punish his unfaithful vassal for his amazing effrontery, but to transform Wallachia into a Turkish province. The Greek historian Chalcondyles speaks of "the largest Turkish force that had been assembled since the conquest of Constantinople" (a force certainly larger than that which attacked Belgrade in 1456). He estimated the total strength of the Turkish army at 250,000 men. Tursun Bey, the Turkish historian, mentions 300,000. The Venetian envoy at Buda, Tommasi, was probably more accurate than either. He gauged a total regular force of 60,000, excluding some 20,000 to 30,000 irregulars from various subjugated provinces.

The official Turkish court historian, Enveri, has left us a vivid picture of this vast array of soldiers who had assembled in what is now Plovdiv late in May, to receive words of encouragement from the sultan himself. The sultan inspired enthusiasm in his elite contingents by appealing to the spirit of the holy war and sharpening their desire for revenge for the inhuman acts committed against fellow Ottomans by the infidel "Kazîglu Bey." In the fore were of course the fearsome janissaries, pedestrian soldiers, the chosen praetorian guard, always close to their master, the sultan's bodyguards, with their long, black mustaches, exotic headgear of feathers and white beaks that fluttered in the wind, wearing chain mail under long mantles lined with calfskin and fastened with costly belts. Behind them came the *sipâhis,* the feudal cavalry force and perhaps the most colorful arm, wearing elaborate high white turbans and riding on swift Arabian stallions with rich harnesses; these men had been recruited from among the landed Ottoman gentry throughout the Balkans. The advance guard was composed of slave soldiers — the *saiales* or the sacrificial troops — who could buy their freedom should they perchance survive. Protecting the flanks were the *silahdârs,* custodians of the sultan's weapons. The *azabs,* wearing long robes of green and reddish hue, struck terror in their enemies because of the use of their long spears, particularly deadly in pursuit. The *acings* were the archers, who also wielded pikes; the *beshlis* handled firearms. At the center of the sultan's assembled army stood the famed Turkish artillery, 120 cannons in all, manned by the cannoneers, not all of whom were Turks. The latter had turned the scales of battle against the Byzantines at the siege of Constantinople. Because of the virtually unpassable roads, the marshy conditions of the countryside, and the thickly forested belt, they were to prove far less effective in Wallachia, and in fact delayed the progress of the army, because they had to be pulled by slow-moving oxen, bison, or black buffaloes. More important to the smooth functioning of the sultan's armed forces were the *ceausi,* or ushers, considered "the eyes and ears of the sultan." They watched over the regular progress of each unit, ready to use the whip or even behead anyone guilty of hesitation or cowardice. On the left and right flanks marched the allied contingents from Europe and Asia, each force under its individual governor, or *beylerbeyi.* In addition there were the engineers, who built roads and pontoon bridges; those responsible for setting up the camps at night; and the artisans and workers, such as wheelmakers, ironmongers, tailors, cobblers, musicians, cooks, and other camp followers without any specific function. One should add the women reserved for the night pleasures of the men. A particularly important role was played by the priests (*ulema*) of Islam and the muezzin, who, in the absence of minarets, called the troops to prayer with a clarion call at sundown. There were court astrologers, for Mehmed consulted his horoscope in making important military decisions. For transportation purposes, oxen, buffalo, bison, and horses were used, but particularly dromedaries (one-humped camels) from Africa, because of their resistance to heat and ability to go long distances without water. Since Dracula had destroyed all the ports on both sides of the Danube River, the sultan's navy, consisting of 150 ships, never succeeded in playing a major part in the war and mainly confined its activity to attacking Brăila and Chilia and, in the end, evacuating the troops. The army was under the personal command of the sultan, who had assembled the most tried military leaders of the Empire: Grand Vizier Mahmud, the beys Turahanoğlu Omer, Mihaloğlu Ali, Evrenos Beioğlu Ali, Delioğlu Umur of Janina, Mihaloğlu "Iskender," Nesuh of Albania, plus Radu the Handsome, whose role in the sultan's headquarters became increasingly significant as the campaign progressed. Another unlikely ally whose betrayal will be explained was Steven the Great, who directed the attack on Chilia. The official historians, whose accounts are invaluable in following the progress of the Turkish forces, also formed part of the immediate entourage. Among them were Enveri, Hodja Husein, Asîk Pasha Zade, and Constantin Mihailovič, known to us simply as the "Janissary of Ostrovitza" evidently of Serbian origin, who has left us an eyewitness account of the more important operations.

Dracula's army paled in comparison with the mighty Ottoman forces. As always happened in times when the survival of the country was in jeopardy, Wallachia experienced virtually a mass levy of all able-bodied citizens, which entailed the mobilization not only of men of military age, but also of women and of children from the age of twelve up, and included gypsy slave contingents. There are various estimates of the strength of Dracula's army: the Russian narrative gives us a total of 30,900 men; Domenico Balbi, the Venetian ambassador, mentions 30,000; Pietro Tommasi 24,000, a figure also accepted by Modrussa, the papal legate. We tend to accept the figure of the Russian ambassador of roughly 30,000, divided between 22,000 foot soldiers and the balance a fast-moving cavalry force. Dracula's newly elected boyars and their retinue, fighting under their individual standards, formed a very small proportion of the army. The majority of the older families of the land stood aloof and kept hidden in their mountain hideouts or had fled to Transylvania. The bulk of Dracula's army was composed of peasants and officers raised to their rank by virtue of their military abilities alone. They wore their long white tunics or shirts, tied at the waist by broad, heavy belts, often along with vests lined with sheep's wool or of thick animal skins to ward off the blows from the Turkish soldiers. They carried axes, scythes, hammers, or scimitars, as well as swords, bows, and arrows. The boyars on horseback wore armor under their long Byzantine robes and were equipped with lance, sword, and dagger, much in the manner of the feudal cavalry in the west. The townsmen had no distinctive uniform beyond the colors of their respective guilds, which paid for their inadequate firearms and helped finance the bombards, a small, unsafe bronze artillery piece that had to be loaded from the front, and the few small cannon they could afford. In addition Dracula had a personal guard of his own, composed of mercenaries from many lands; it included a small retinue of gypsies, who were pardoned of crimes for as long as they served him. His system of scouts was very efficient and kept him regularly informed of the progress of the Turkish forces and camp locations. The scouts were invariably local people intimately familiar with every topographical detail of the terrain to which they were assigned. They acted very much as a partisan force would, collaborating with the local population. Very effective was Dracula's cavalry, which was responsible for swift hit-and-run attacks either into the Turkish camps or against stragglers who were cut off from the main body of the Turkish army.

Morale among the Wallachians was extremely high, particularly at the beginning of the campaign, since the peasants were fighting in defense of their homelands. Like Napoleon, Dracula had a talent for inspiring enthusiasm in his men; he exhorted them to glorious and sometimes sacrificial action. "It would be better," he told his men at the beginning of the campaign, "that those who think of death should not follow me."

Chalcondyles records that during one of the battles, the sultan captured one of Dracula's soldiers, who was brought before the sultan for questioning. Mehmed II promised the man all sorts of rewards, including the granting of a noble title, if he would reveal Dracula's battle plans or his secret hiding place. But the soldier remained silent and refused to answer any questions. So the sultan used threats. He told the soldier that he would break him on the wheel, skin him, or bury him alive, but all to no avail. The peasant stood his ground, and finally, sensing his end was near, he told the sultan, "I realize that my life is in your hands and that you will order me to be killed, but you will find out nothing from me about my master Dracula. I want to die for my country and not betray him." The sultan was angry at first but, upon reflection, he told the man, "If your master had many soldiers like yourself, in a short time he could conquer the world!" Conversely, Dracula was severe against those who did not live up to these high standards. The Russian narrative relates that after a battle Dracula would examine the wounds of his men. Those who were wounded in the front parts of their bodies were rewarded, but those who were wounded in the back were impaled, with the reproach "You are not a man but a woman," because they had been cowards and had fled the scene of battle.

Keenly aware of the disparity of numbers, Dracula kept close watch on the Danube as his scouts reported the advance of the main Turkish force from Plovdiv to Vidin (one of the few ports that had not been destroyed the previous winter), where an initial attempt at disembarkation was made. Volleys of well-aimed arrows drove the Turks back to their ships. Finally, during the first week of June 1462, an advance contingent of the Turkish army attempted its first major landing on the Romanian bank at Turnu, a port that had been badly damaged by Dracula but was still usable. The sultan's intention was to sail up the Olt river and strike at Dracula's capital city of Tîrgoviște. In fact, when the elite corps of janissaries crossed the Danube under cover of darkness, on Friday, June 4, using seventy barges commandeered from local fishermen, some miles away from Dracula's main camp, the Wallachian prince was caught by surprise.

An eyewitness, the Serbian-born janissary Constantin of Ostrovitza, has left us a graphic description of the Turkish disembarkation:

> When night began to fall, we climbed into our boats and floated down the Danube and crossed over to the other side several miles below the place where Dracula's army was stationed. There we dug ourselves trenches, so that cavalry could not harm us. After that we crossed back

over to the other side and transported other janissaries over the Danube, and when the entire infantry had crossed over, then we prepared and set out gradually against Dracula's army, together with the artillery and other equipment that we had brought with us. Having halted, we set up the cannon, but not in time to stop three hundred janissaries from being killed. The sultan was very upset by this set of circumstances, as he witnessed the great battle from the other side of the Danube and was unable to come over himself. He was afraid that all the janissaries might be killed. . . . Seeing that our side was greatly weakening, we defended ourselves with the 120 guns which we had brought over and fired so often that we repelled the prince's army and greatly strengthened our position. . . . And Dracula, seeing that he could not prevent the crossing, withdrew. After that the emperor crossed the Danube with his entire army and gave us 30,000 coins to be distributed among us.''

The janissaries landed first, followed by the azabs, the Asiatic troops from Anatolia, and the bulk of the sipâhis from Rumelia. The sultan, together with Dracula's brother Radu, who was in charge of 4,000 horsemen of his own, figured prominently at the vanguard of the Turkish force.

From this point onward, Dracula resorted to what is known as "strategic retreat," the device invariably used by an outnumbered army. The idea was to draw the superior enemy force deep into his own territory. The Romanians depended on the physical varieties of their terrain for defense: the marshy soil near the Danube, the dense Vlasia forest extending deep into the plain, and the impenetrable mountains. According to Romanian tradition, the forest and the mountains were the cradle that ensured the survival of the Romanian people through the ages. Another tactic used by Dracula in wearing down his enemies was "scorched earth," creating a vast desert in the path of the invading army. As Dracula's army withdrew northward, abandoning territory to the Turks, they depopulated the area, burned their own villages, and set fire to the cities, which were reduced to ghost towns. Boyars, peasants, and townspeople alike, together with their families, accompanied the retreating armies, unless they could find shelter in isolated mountain hideouts or inaccessible island monasteries such as Snagov, where many of the wealthy had sought refuge. In addition, Dracula ordered the crops systematically burned, poisoned all the wells, and destroyed the cattle and all other domestic animals that could not be herded away. Dracula even ordered dams to be built to divert the waters of small rivers to create marshes that might impede the progress of the Turkish cannon by miring them down. His people also dug huge pits and covered them with timber and leaves with the purpose of trapping men, camels, and horses. Contemporary sources confirm this scenario of desolation that greeted the Turkish armies. The Greek historian Michael Ducas stated, "Dracula removed his entire population to the mountains and forest regions, and he left the fields deserted. He had all beasts of burden herded up the mountains. Thus, after having crossed the Danube and advanced for seven days, Mohammed II found no man, nor any significant animal, and nothing to eat or drink." His compatriot, Chalcondyles added, "Dracula had hidden the women and children in a very marshy area, protected by natural defenses, covered with dense oak forest. And he ordered his men to hide themselves in this forest, which was difficult for any newcomer to penetrate." On the Turkish side, the comments are very much the same. Hodja Husein, a veteran of the campaign, complained that "the best azabs of the Turks could find no springs . . . no . . . drinkable water." Mahmud Pasha (the vizier who had earlier attacked Brăila), who was sent ahead of the main army with a small contingent of men, thought that he had finally found a place to rest. "But even here," Hodja Husein wrote, "for a distance of six leagues there was not a drop of water to be found. The intensity of the heat caused by the scorching sun was so great that the armor of the janissaries melted like a lighted candle. In this parched plain, the lips of the fighters for Islam dried up. Even the Africans and Asians, used to desert conditions, used their shields to roast meat." Certainly a contributing factor to the sufferings and death endured by the Turkish army was the fact that the summer of 1462 by all accounts was one of the hottest on record.

Along with "scorched earth," Dracula used guerrilla tactics, in which the elements of surprise and intimate knowledge of the terrain were the keys to success. The Italian traveler Michael Bocignoli reported, "Dracula, preparing his cavalry at night and sometimes even during the day, would often emerge from roundabout, relatively unknown paths and attack the stragglers foraging for food, who had departed from the main Turkish force. At times Dracula would even attack the main force when it least expected it, and, before they could rally, he would again take refuge in the forest without giving his enemy an opportunity to give battle on equal terms." Stragglers who remained behind the main body of the Turkish force were invariably cut off, killed, and most likely impaled. One most insidious technique, almost unheard-of at that period, was what could truly be termed a fifteenth-century form of "germ" warfare. Dracula would encourage all those affected by lethal diseases, such as leprosy, tuberculosis, syphilis, and particularly the bubonic plague (which ultimately made its presence felt in the ranks of the Turkish army) to dress in Turkish fashion and intermingle with the soldiers. Should they perchance survive their illness, and be successful in contaminating any Turk who might die as a result of his catching the disease in question, it was sufficient to bring the dead man's turban back to Dracula's camp, and the infected Wallachian would be richly rewarded. In that same vein, Dracula set free hardened criminals, who were encouraged to kill Turkish stragglers.

Such tactics of attrition worked, as Dracula knew they would from his intimate knowledge of the Turks that he had gained as a child living among them. Not only were the resources (both in men and materiel) of the Turkish army greatly diminished, but the morale of the rank and file, the officers, and even that of the sultan declined under the strain. This general breakdown of will was to play an important part in Mehmed's eventual decision to withdraw.

The Turks advanced towards Tîrgovişte along a path dictated by the necessity of providing fodder and water for horses and camels in addition to food for the men. The itinerary was probably as follows: from Turnu the Turks marched northward to the monastery of Glavacioc. Then they turned westward toward Bucharest, and northward again to the island monastery of Snagov — neither of which was captured. Finally they marched to the capital, Tîrgovişte. Just before the sultan could reach Tîrgovişte, Dracula staged a last-ditch night attack on the Turkish camp in an endeavor to kill the sultan himself. Given the low morale of the Turkish force, killing the sultan could prove to be the last straw; it could cause a total collapse in morale, which might compel the army to withdraw. It was a desperate gamble.

The so-called "night of attack" took place on June 17, 1462, and, according to the Turkish chronicler Enveri, it lasted from three hours after sunset until four the next morning, in a mountainous region south of Tîrgovişte, thus at the foothills of the Carpathian Mountains. The following is the pro-Romanian account of the event, attributed to a veteran in Dracula's army, but possibly dictated by Dracula himself. It was recorded later by the papal legate Niccolò Modrussa in conversation with Dracula in Buda, and was transmitted in a diplomatic dispatch to the Roman curia:

> The sultan besieged him and discovered him in a certain mountain
> where the Wallachian was supported by the natural strength of the

place. There Dracula had hidden himself along with 24,000 of his men who had willingly followed him. When Dracula realized that he would either perish from hunger or fall into the hands of the very cruel enemy, and considering both eventualities unworthy of brave men, he dared commit an act worthy of being remembered: calling his men together and explaining the situation to them, he easily persuaded them to enter the enemy camp. He divided the men so that either they should die bravely in battle with glory and honor or else, should destiny prove favorable to them, they should avenge themselves against the enemy in an exceptional manner. So, making use of some Turkish prisoners, who had been caught at twilight when they were wandering about imprudently, at nightfall Dracula penetrated into the Turkish camp with part of his troops, all the way up the fortifications. And during the entire night he sped like lightning in every direction and caused great slaughter, so much so that, had the other commander to whom he had entrusted his remaining forces been equally brave, or had the Turks not fully obeyed the repeated orders from the sultan not to abandon their garrisons, the Wallachian undoubtedly would have gained the greatest and most brilliant victory. But the other commander (a boyar named Galeş) did not dare attack the camp from the other side as had been agreed upon. . . . Dracula carried out an incredible massacre without losing many men in such a major encounter, though many were wounded. He abandoned the enemy camp before daybreak and returned to the same mountain from which he had come. No one dared pursue him, since he had caused such terror and turmoil. I learned by questioning those who had participated in this battle that the sultan lost all confidence in the situation. During that night the sultan abandoned the camp and fled in a shameful manner. And he would have continued to this way, had he not been reprimanded by his friends and brought back, almost against his will.

Modrussa reported that had Dracula's commander Galeş's courage been equal to Dracula's, or had the Turks wavered in their response to the sultan to stay at their command posts, the Wallachian "would have undoubtedly won a great victory."

Chalcondyles gives a slightly different version of these events, adding a few details of his own. According to the Greek chronicler, Dracula rushed into the Turkish camp with some seven to ten thousand troops and was able to drive the Asian troops backward. Aided by torches and flares, the Romanians tried to reach the sultan's red tent. But they mistakenly went for the tent of two viziers, Mahmud and Isaac. This error and the noise created gave the Ottoman cavalry time to mount their horses and the janissary guards surrounded the sultan's tent for protection. The sultan was alerted, and the janissaries warded off Dracula's attack. The sultan then ordered his janissaries to rally under Mihaloğlu Ali Bey and pursue Dracula and his troops. As a result, 2,000 Wallachian soldiers were taken prisoner, and Dracula himself may have been wounded. Even the Janissary of Ostrovitza, who was an eyewitness to the event, was not altogether successful in playing down the psychological impact of the event as he wrote: "Although the Romanian prince had a small army, we always advanced with great caution and fear and spent nights sleeping in ditches. But even in this manner we were not safe; for during one night the Romanians struck at us. They massacred horses, camels, and several thousand Turks. When the Turks had retreated in the face of the enemy, we [the janissaries] repelled the enemy and killed them. But the sultan had incurred great losses." Given such testimony, the losses incurred by the Turks were undoubtedly heavy. According to Domenico Balbi, Dracula lost 5,000 men and the Turks 15,000, although these figures appear rather high and may have included minor skirmishes that followed the actual night attack. In any event, the night attack was an act of extraordinary temerity, which is celebrated in Romanian literature and popular folklore. It also represented Dracula's last attempt to save his capital.

A few days later the sultan was ready to attack Dracula's capital city of Tîrgovişte, his main objective. The gates of the city were closed and defenders were ready to man the walls and towers recently refortified by Dracula for precisely such a contingency. With the cannons in place, the city was prepared for a prolonged siege. According to Chalcondyles, as the advance guard of the Turkish army reached a site 27 leagues north of the city (a distance of roughly 60 miles), they reported a most gruesome sight, perhaps the most infamous of all Dracula's "horror scenes," the so-called forest of the impaled. Strung along a mile or so in picket-fence fashion in a huge semicircle, thousands of stakes of various heights held the remaining carcasses of some 20,000 Turkish captives; their bodies were in a state of complete decomposition, due to the heat of the summer and the ravages of ravens and other Carpathian birds of prey, many of which had made their nests within the skulls and skeletal remains of the victims. Barely recognizable because of the higher stakes used in deference to their position were the remains of the Greek Catavolinos and Hamza Pasha, who had been impaled months before. The tattered remains of their gaudy vestments fluttered against the evening sky. The entire area reeked with the stench of death — the smell of rotting flesh.

Dracula had deliberately stage-managed this sinister spectacle as part of his terror tactics to destroy whatever spirit was still left in Mehmed after the unsuccessful assassination attempt a few days before. Indeed, "the forest of the impaled" was horrible enough to discourage even the most stout-hearted officers who witnessed the scene. Mehmed himself all but admitted defeat, in a statement reproduced by Chalcondyles, which included mixed sentiments of awe and admiration: "What a desolate spectacle this was for the Turks and even for the emperor himself! So overwhelmed by disbelief in what he saw, the emperor said that he could not take the land away from a man who does such marvelous things and can exploit his rule and his subjects in this way and that surely a man who had accomplished this is worthy of greater things." Confusing sultans at several centuries' distance, and giving the sultan credit for an aggressive response never made in reality, Victor Hugo, writing his *Légende des Siècles* (*The Legend of the Centuries*), recalls this particular incident in these famous lines:

> *Vlad, boyar of Tarxis, nicknamed "the Devil,"*
> *Refuses to pay the sultan tribute,*
> *Seizes the Turkish ambassadors and has all of them killed*
> *On thirty stakes, planted at the side of the road.*
> *Murad rushes forth, burning crops, barns, and lofts,*
> *Defeats the boyar, captures twenty thousand men.*
> *Then around the huge black battlefield*
> *Constructs a huge wall built of solid rock*
> *And causes horrible wailing cries heard in the battlements*
> *Where he immured and bricked in the twenty thousand captives,*
> *Leaving holes so that one might see their eyes in the shade,*
> *And departed, having written on their somber walls,*
> *"Murad, carver of stones, to Vlad, planter of stakes."*

In actuality, that night the sultan ordered that an especially deep trench be dug around the Turkish encampment to keep out the Impaler. The next day Mehmed gave orders for the retreat. In his eyes, Dracula's country was not worth the price of victory.

As the Turkish army retreated eastward toward Brăila, where the Turkish fleet weighed anchor, plague began to make its appearance in the Turkish ranks. To the sultan, who regularly consulted astrologers, it seemed as if he and his men were under Dracula's curse.

Despite this retreat, in late June (June 22) the war took a curious twist, as Dracula's cousin Stephen took this opportunity to betray the man who had helped him gain his throne. With Turkish help, he attacked the fortress of Chilia, which was in the hands of a joint Wallachian and Hungarian garrison. Let us recall that the two families were related by marriage; the two cousins had spent several years at Suceava as students; they had fought side-by-side against Poland at the battle of Crasna in 1450; they had fled to Transylvania in each other's company after Stephen's father's assassination in 1451. On June 28, the Venetian envoy Balbi informed his senate that the fortress of Chilia was attacked by Stephen's army, which had been waiting to effect a juncture with the Turkish feet. "They besieged the town," he wrote, "during 8 days but could do nothing. Many Turks died in the process. Then they returned in shame, defeated by the Hungarian garrison and Dracula's 7,000 men." In the course of the attack Stephen was hit by a piece of shrapnel, which wounded his left calf so profoundly, or else was so badly doctored, that he never recovered from that wound to the end of his life. The superstitious peasants stated that that was to be his punishment for the betrayal of Dracula, if not the result of the Wallachian prince's curse.

The conflict between Dracula and Stephen, which has elicited much controversy among Romanian historians, has a simple explanation. Stephen had his own priorities — he was less interested in treaty obligations than in assuring the survival of Moldavia, should the fortress of Chilia fall to the Turks. Besides, there was a Hungarian contingent at Chilia, along with the Wallachian troops, and Stephen was at odds with the Hungarian king. Matthias Corvinus had, as previously mentioned, given political asylum to Stephen's father's assassin, Petru Aaron. (The Chilia episode also was important for Matthias. Since Hungarian forces were involved in fighting the Turks, he had a pretext, albeit a weak one, to justify acceptance of the papal subsidies, which were intended to foster the crusade.)

On June 29, during the month of Ramadan, the sultan's army reached Brăila and had that port burned as a final act of defiance. By July 11, the sultan and his bedraggled troops arrived in Adrianople. The troops marched into the city late at night (most of the horses and camels had perished) for fear of arousing the suspicions of the local population, who would have suspected that the campaign had ended in failure. Next morning, festivities were held to commemorate the "great victory over Dracula"! The army finally returned to Constantinople, where the thin and haggard faces of the returning veterans could hardly mask the severity of the defeat that they had suffered. Court historians persisted, however, in representing Mehmed as having won a great victory against the faithless Impaler!

There can be no question that Sultan Mehmed had suffered the most humiliating defeat of his career at the hands of Dracula, and that his plans to reduce Wallachia to a Turkish province had failed dismally — as had projects of further expansionism in central Europe. This did not necessarily signify that Dracula had won the war. A deft move made by Mehmed was to leave his protégé Radu the Handsome with a small contingent of Turkish soldiers in the Bărăgan region of Wallachia to attempt to win over the boyars, the townspeople, and the peasants at large; he was to try to convince them to recognize him as prince of the land in Dracula's place. The Turks in turn would respect the ancient autonomy of the country as they had done before, on the condition that Radu would recognize Mehmed as his sovereign lord. Nothing, in fact, was to be changed in the Wallachian-Turkish relationship except the person of the prince, since Dracula was clearly unacceptable to the Turks.

What Sultan Mehmed had failed to do by military force, Radu and the boyars eventually succeeded in achieving by diplomacy — though the freedom of Wallachia had in essence been ensured by Dracula's stubborn resistance. It is conceivable that Radu had strengthened his links with the boyar hierarchy by marrying, according to the late George Florescu, one of Romania's leading genealogists, Maria Despina, the sister of Vintilă Florescu, a prominent enemy of Dracula, who had quit or been expelled from the boyar council when Dracula became prince in 1456.

Prince Radu (the future Radu the Handsome) has far too often been dismissed by historians as just an attractive bisexual youth with a finely chiseled face, regular features, and particularly beautiful green-blue eyes that had helped to win the heart of two successive sultans, but a man totally lacking in intelligence and statesmanship. Clearly the sultan's minion, he was showered with gifts by Mehmed and maintained a small court of his own at Constantinople throughout the campaign, composed in part of Wallachian boyars. Though there was initially no thought on the sultan's part of establishing Radu on the throne, Dracula's brother had exploited his presence at the sultan's side in Wallachia since the beginning of the campaign, by contacting dissident boyars; he made it his business to keep informed of what they were thinking through a network of spies and other sycophants. It was probably at his suggestion that dissident boyar delegations began to appear in the sultan's camp as of the first week of June, urging Mehmed to rid the country of the heinous Impaler and replace him with his attractive and peace-loving brother.

Moreover, they alleged, Dracula was the candidate of the Hungarian king, Matthias (a fact of which the Turks had of course been aware since the peace treaty of 1460), whereas Radu would be loyal to his natural liege lord, the sultan, with whom he was tied by bonds deeper than friendship. Arguments such as these may well have given Mehmed his cue when his campaign against Dracula began to fail.

Radu's appeal to the Wallachian people from his headquarters in the Bărăgan, paraphrased by the historian Chalcondyles, provides further proof of his astute political and propagandistic instincts and also demonstrates his attitude of "sweet reasonableness."

> I am aware of the mighty forces that the sultan controls, which sooner or later he will use to lay waste what remains of your country. If we continue to oppose him, we shall be despoiled of all that is left to us. Why do you not reach an agreement with Sultan Mehmed? Only then will you have peace in the land and in your homes. Are you aware that there are no cattle, no horses, no farm animals, no food left in this country? Surely you have borne such sufferings long enough because of my brother, because you were loyal to this man who was responsible for more suffering than any other prince.

Dracula's demented reign of terror through impalement had simply lasted too long. No one really felt secure from his terrible and inquisitorial vindictiveness. Besides, now that the Turks had withdrawn the bulk of their forces there was no further need of terror. Radu would restore all the ancient rights of the land, acknowledge the sultan as his lord, and pay the tribute. However, he would allow no Turk to settle on Romanian soil, nor would he force Wallachian youths to be inducted into the janissary corps. Here was Radu promising the nation a blander, more humane rule without stakes.

Radu's appeal to the nation proved irresistible. In the first instance the old nobility was won over. The boyar class, the real rulers of the land, had firmly believed, since the fall of Constantinople, that the realities of power dictated a policy of friendly cooperation with the Turks; they felt that continued collaboration with Hungary or with the papal crusade would in the long run lead to the extinction of the autonomy they had achieved. The peasants and merchants, on the other hand, had had enough of war and privation and were anxious to return to work, now that the independence of the country was no longer in danger. Though the Turkish army had been badly emasculated, losing about a third of its force, Dracula's losses were equally heavy, and he could less afford them. Despite a final victory at Buzău on June 26 against Evrenos Pasha, the last military encounter between the two armies, the number of defectors from Dracula's army to Radu's force was on the increase. In fact, Dracula's army was gradually melting away, leaving the prince without a throne and only a small number of personal bodyguards and mercenary soldiers. With his back to the wall, Dracula's instinct dictated retreat toward the Carpathian Mountains, toward his famous, virtually impregnable eagle's nest, where resistance was still possible. He would rely on guerrilla tactics in the mountainous terrain that he knew best. Final salvation, however, could come only from King Matthias of Hungary, whose army, he hoped, was finally moving toward Transylvania in response to his persistent appeals for help.

CHAPTER 7

Imprisonment and Death

W I T H the defection to Radu of the majority of boyars and many of the Romanian people, Dracula's army simply melted away. It was but natural in these circumstances for the escapee to attempt to reach the Transylvanian border and seek help from the Hungarian king, his so-called ally whose assistance he had so far sought in vain. It was equally logical that Dracula and his few partisans should avoid the plain and the major cities, by the middle of September completely under Turkish or Radu's control. Dracula headed toward his famous castle hideout on the southern slopes of the Transylvanian mountains, at the Hungarian-Wallachian frontier, a logical point of departure for Braşov, where the Hungarian king, should he come to Dracula's aid, would establish his headquarters. The castle had, after all, originally been built by Wallachian slave labor specifically for such an emergency. The precise road Dracula traveled from eastern Wallachia can be largely retraced with the help of local folklore. It is likely that he stayed within the protective shadow of the Sub-Carpathian mountains, crossing the Teleajen, Prahova, and Dîmboviţa rivers, climbing quite high up near their sources. On that path Dracula likely passed through the villages of Cheia, Sinaia, and Cetăţeni. Tradition states that Dracula sought refuge in the castle rock at Cetăţeni overlooking the Dîmboviţa. Finally, he crossed the Argeş River, a few miles to the west, and reached his impressive mountain retreat.

There is one valid argument for the authenticity of the stories collected from the village surrounding Castle Dracula: all the narratives end precisely at the moment when Dracula crossed the border into Transylvania, demonstrating that no matter how imaginative the peasants could be, they related only events that they personally could have witnessed.

We shall paraphrase a classic folkloric narrative of Dracula's last moments of resistance on Romanian soil. Knowing of Dracula's hideout, Prince Radu ordered the Turkish forces to pursue his brother along the valley of the Argeş River. Reaching the village of Poenari, they encamped upon a bluff that commanded an admirable view of Dracula's castle on the opposite bank of the Argeş. From this vantage point, Radu and his Turkish allies set up their cherrywood cannons and small bronze artillery bombards. At Poenari to this day there is a field known as Tunuri ("the field of cannon"). The bulk of the Turkish janissaries descended to the river, forded it, and encamped at the foot of the Castle Mountain. The Turkish bombardment of the castle began without much success, because of the light caliber of the Turkish guns and the thickness of the castle walls. The orders for the final assault were to have been given the following day.

During that night, one of Dracula's relatives who had been enslaved by the Turks years before, mindful of his family allegiance, decided to forewarn the Wallachian prince of the great danger he was incurring by remaining in the fortress. Undetected, during the pitch-dark, moonless night, the former Romanian, who was a member of the janissary corps, climbed to the top of Poenari Hill, a short distance from Dracula's castle, and then, armed with a bow and arrow, took careful aim at one of the dimly lit openings in the main castle tower, which he knew contained Dracula's quarters. At the end of the arrow he had pinned a message advising Dracula to escape while there was still time. The Romanian-born Muslim witnessed the accuracy of his aim: the candle was suddenly extinguished by the arrow. Within a minute it was relit by Dracula's Transylvanian concubine; she could be seen reading the message by the flickering light. What followed could have been recalled only by Dracula's intimate advisers within the castle, who presumably witnessed the scene. Peasant imagination, however, reconstructed the story in the following manner. Dracula's mistress apprised her husband of the ominous content of the message. She told him that she would "rather have her body rot and be eaten by the fish of the Argeş than be led into captivity by the Turks." She then hurled herself from the upper battlements, her body falling down the precipice below into the river, which became her tomb. A fact that tends to corroborate this story is that to this day the river at that point is known as Rîul Doamnei, or the

"Princess's River." Apart from a brief notice in the Russian narrative, this tragic folkloric footnote is practically the only reference anywhere to Dracula's so-called wife, who is permanently enshrined only in local memories.

Surrounded by an overwhelming Turkish force, Dracula decided to attempt to escape across the mountains by subterfuge. According to tradition he left through a secret passage leading to the banks of the river; his party's horses were allegedly shod backward to confuse potential pursuers. A local peasant clan, simply identified as the seven Dobrin brothers, helped him get away. He needed their assistance because the ascent and the descent of the three-thousand-foot Făgăraş slopes were no easy task for the forty-one-year-old prince, and there were no passes at that point. The upper slopes are rocky, treacherous, and often covered with snow or ice even in summer. The precise escape route was mapped out by the Dobrins. Popular folklore names the sources of rivers, clearings, forested areas, even rocks, that provided landmarks along the way he took. Peasants in the area say that Dracula rewarded the Dobrins by taking them up on a mountain peak and donating all the land "as far as the eye could see" in return for their loyalty. Tradition states that Dracula officially confirmed this donation by inscribing it on rabbit-skin scrolls, and that these scrolls are preserved by the free landowning peasants in the village of Arefu, even in present-day socialist Romania. It is interesting to note that collectivization of land has never been applied in this mountain region. As he descended the Transylvanian slopes, the former prince, still at the head of a small mercenary force, decided to establish his headquarters at the Hungarian fortress of Königstein ("the King's Rock"), the ruins of which have survived. A small fortress had been originally established by John Hunyadi at the mountain summit of the Făgăraş to protect Braşov from Turkish attack. There Dracula would await news from his scouts of the precise date of King Matthias's expected arrival at Braşov, only a few miles away to the north, to decide on his future course of action.

During the fifteenth century, even allowing for the slowness of travel of a large royal retinue accustomed to comfortable quarters, the snail's pace with which King Matthias and his army progressed from Buda to Braşov hardly reflected great eagerness on Matthias's part to meet his so-called ally, with whose plight he was all too familiar. Matthias had left Buda on July 15; by August 10 he had barely reached the Hungarian city of Szeged. Ten days later he crossed the Transylvanian border and reached Turda only on September 17. By the thirtieth of the month he was at Sibiu, where the king and his court decided to spend the whole month of October discussing the various options created by the explosive situation of Dracula's defeat and Radu's inauguration as prince, and the consequences it would entail for Hungary and crusading policy. Matthias finally reached the Ţara Bîrsei and Braşov area only in November, taking up residence in a castle still known as the little fortress (Cetăţuia), now completely restored, on the peak of a hill. He was in time to attend the celebrations of the feast day of Saint Martin, one of the patron saints of the German Saxons, when tradition entitled the king to collect a poll tax from every German household, badly needed for his depleted treasury. Although the slowness of the king's progress in Transylvania did not augur well for those who still believed in his commitment to the papal crusade, he kept up the pretense that he had crossed the border to come to the help of Dracula. At least the minnesinger Michael Beheim professed to believe in the sincerity of the king's intentions: "We are told that the king of Hungary declared himself ready to come to the aid of Dracula with a large army, set in motion from the city of Buda. He took the shortest route toward Transylvania and Kronstadt [Braşov] with his army, which had numerous counts, barons, lords, knights, and servants in it, and it seems there was a great deal of excitement in the city [Braşov]." The king also sent reassuring messages to Pope Pius II to the effect that he would soon attack the Turks on the Danube. Bonfini, King Matthias's official historian, reaffirmed this view. "The king," he wrote, "was proceeding to Wallachia in order to liberate Dracula from the Turks . . . and he would give a relative of his to the Wallachian prince as a wife" — a reference implying that Matthias, at least at that time, was looking favorably on Dracula's request for a matrimonial union with the Hunyadi family, aware that his previous lady companions were illicit. Others at Buda, allegedly well informed, also professed to believe in the sincerity of the king's intention. Indeed, Sultan Mehmed's defeat in Wallachia, followed by his humiliating return to Constantinople, created admirable conditions for a successful anti-Ottoman crusade.

When he finally learned that King Matthias had reached Braşov, Dracula joined him from his mountain retreat and took up residence in the Scheii district, the Romanian section of town which lay outside the city gates. Dan III had at one time resided there. Like any realistic condottiere, Dracula was keenly aware of the fact that he was no longer in control of the situation. The two men met in what is now the town hall, still standing in the old German section, and they maintained a pretense of negotiations, according to Beheim, "during a five-week period." It was the first time that the two leaders had met as adults, and Dracula was in a position to take measure of Matthias's enigmatic personality, disguised by his diminutive bullish figure and rather plain exterior, high forehead, and deepset but shifty eyes. Hard political realities soon exploded the euphoria of the initial embrace. Far from being the awesome impaler prince, Dracula was little more than a political refugee with a few henchmen on foreign soil, who had lost the support of his war-worn country. His hated brother, Radu the Handsome, a minion of the sultan, was now on the throne but had maintained the traditional autonomy of the country. In essence, Dracula was a supplicant whose only assets were past promises, which meant little in an age where power was the only language that rulers understood.

There were good reasons for Matthias's lack of openness in negotiating with Dracula. In early August 1462 Radu had sent a boyar delegation to Braşov, offering not only to renew the commercial concessions that Dracula himself had previously conceded in 1460 but adding a sum of 15,000 ducats for additional compensation. On the fifteenth of that month, Albert de Istenmezö, vice-count of the Szeklers, no great friend of Dracula, recommended to the authorities of Braşov and Bran to give official recognition to Radu and observe the peace with the Turks. Similar negotiations were later carried out by Radu's boyars at Sibiu. Matthias was inevitably informed of Radu's recognition by the two powerful German cities, and even before he arrived at Braşov in November, Matthias had been won over to their view. He not only gave official recognition to Prince Radu the Handsome, but also signed a five-year armistice with the sultan. This pact freed Mehmed II to plan yet another strike against his enemy, the ruler of Karaman in Anatolia. There is a good deal of speculation on the determining role played by Matthias's official court astrologer, an Italian by the name of Antonio della Camera, who had accompanied the king at Braşov, in the latter's decision to abandon his erstwhile ally Dracula and to recognize Radu as prince in November. It was rumored at Braşov that the astrologer was in the pay of powerful German banking interests, in Nuremberg and Augsburg, that had also worked for Dracula's demise. Matthias finally signed an armistice with Mehmed, evidently abandoning the projected crusade, for which important sums of money had been duplicitously gathered.

The principal reason, however, for Matthias's decision to recognize Radu (and to abandon Dracula and the anti-Ottoman crusade) had little to do with German or Turkish politics. Rather it was due to events in Vienna, where Emperor Frederick III, trying to impose additional taxes

(6,000 florins), found himself in the embarrassing position of being besieged by the citizens of his own capital, in the royal palace (the Hofburg) on October 15. When a delegation of rebels traveled from the imperial capital to Braşov in November to offer the Hungarian king nothing less than the Habsburg estates (an offer that in turn opened up the possibility of succeeding to the imperial crown), this proved to be the clinching factor in turning Matthias's attention to events in the west. All these events help account for King Matthias's decision to proceed with the arrest of his one-time ally Dracula.

The plot was carefully hatched by the king's men in a manner reminiscent of the ambushes that had been sprung in the past by Dracula himself. When, after weeks of fruitless talks, Dracula finally suggested to Matthias that they embark on the campaign to liberate Wallachia from his brother's and Turkish control, the king gave him a body of soldiers under the leadership of Jan Jiškra of Brandýs, a former Slovak Hussite leader, who in return for money had made his peace with the Habsburgs, and more recently had sold his services to the Hungarian king. Jiškra had little love for Dracula and resented the latter's support of the Hunyadis during the internal strife in Hungary when he had espoused the imperial cause. The small contingent, composed of a few remaining Dracula mercenaries, Hungarians, and Slovaks, were ostensibly to provide the vanguard for a larger Hungarian force that was to have followed under the command of King Matthias and transformed the operation into a full-fledged crusade. The troupe traveled along the traditional commercial road through Christian, Tohanu-Vechi, Zărneşti, and Bran to the customs point at Rucăr that would lead to the ancient Wallachian capital of Cîmpulung across the Transylvanian mountains. At the basin of the Dîmboviţa River, the party reached the fortress of Königstein (Piatra Craiului), where Dracula had established his headquarters a few weeks before while awaiting Matthias's arrival at Braşov. He was at last on what was technically Wallachian territory and in his heart of hearts rejoiced, because, according to Beheim, "he thought he was in his own land."

Once arrived at Königstein Castle on December 5, a majestic location at the summit of the Făgăraş Mountains, Dracula's contingent and their war wagons were slowly lowered down from the high fortress to the Valley of the Saxons (Valea Sasului) below. To the north loomed the majestic, lofty snow-covered Carpathian Mountains; from the castle walls there was a sheer thousand-foot precipice straight down a wall of stone, wholly inaccessible from the valley below. It was only on December 6, when almost all of Dracula's soldiers had been lowered by ropes and pulleys to the lush, green valley of the dam built below, that the famous Slovak mercenary seized Dracula as his prisoner, under secret orders from the Hungarian king. Dracula was unable to resist. Far below in the valley, in the village of Dîmboviţa, Dracula's men cried out loudly but in vain for their captured master. At that point there was nothing much they could do to save him.

The fortress of Königstein had been carefully chosen by Matthias precisely because it lay in the king's personal domain, not under the control of the municipality of Braşov, which wished to claim jurisdiction over this important prisoner in order to condemn him to death for his inhuman crimes against the Saxons of Transylvania. Jiškra brought Dracula back to Braşov, but once he was within the city walls, the Slovak was replaced by the more trustworthy Hungarian bodyguard. The royal retinue and its important prisoner then left for Alba Iulia, where Beheim, by far the best informed, tells us that Dracula was imprisoned at the fortress of Iersiu. It was only there that some form of judicial inquiry into Dracula's conduct was set in motion by the Hungarian king to justify his arrest. However, the party left Iersiu before the inquiry was completed. Then they proceeded by way of Mediaş, Turda, Cluj, and Oradea, and crossed the actual frontier of Hungary near Debrecen. They finally reached Buda by Christmas of 1462.

Despite all the precautions that had been taken by King Matthias, the arrest of Dracula, only months after he had been universally greeted as a hero in the successful war against Mehmed, created a good deal of consternation among the European powers, particularly in Venice and Rome, where important sums had already been spent in the name of crusading. The problem was not a merely local matter. It became a cause of concern for all those powers that had a stake in the anti-Ottoman struggle. King Matthias was badly in need of a legitimate explanation for his drastic action.

Some extraordinary documents seemed to provide the king with the most damning justification for Dracula's arrest. These were three letters bearing Dracula's signature, written from a place called "Rothel" and dated November 7, 1462, only copies of which have survived, allegedly intercepted by spies of the king. One of these letters was addressed to Mehmed himself, another to the renegade Vizier Mahmud, and the third to Prince Stephen the Great of Moldavia. All three seem to reveal an unaccountable change of attitude and policy on Dracula's part. First, according to the document, Dracula addressed Sultan Mehmed in abject and servile terms such as "emperor of emperors" and "lord and master.'' Dracula ''humbly begged forgiveness for his crimes,'' ''offered his services to the 'Turks' to campaign alongside the sultan, to conquer Transylvania and Hungary, and ''offered even to help in seizing the person of the Hungarian king.'' Because of the style of writing, the rhetoric of meek submission (hardly compatible with what we know of Dracula's character), clumsy wording, and poor Latin, most historians consider these letters to be forgeries. It was hardly conceivable that Dracula would have been foolish enough to write letters of treason while he was on Hungarian territory, far removed from the Ottoman forces to whom he appealed. The clinching argument is that, in spite of various attempts at localizing ''Rothel'' (Turnu Roşu, Cisnădie, and Rucăr have all been mentioned as possible substitutes), no satisfactory identification has thus far been made.

We believe that the ''Rothel'' letters were clever forgeries (like the more famous ''casket letters'' manufactured a century later by Queen Elizabeth's partisans to indict her rival Mary Stuart in the eyes of Europe) aimed at blackening Dracula's reputation and making him appear a traitor to the Christian cause. The probable author of the forgery was one Johann Reudell, the Catholic chaplain of the famous Black Church at Braşov, which had earlier been looted by Dracula during his terror raids. The church is now labeled ''Black'' since it had at one time been half burned down by the Turks. Because of its pure Gothic lines and its rich collection of priceless carpets, given by Turkish merchants to buy the goodwill of the city authorities, it is still one of the main cultural sites in the city. Knowing that the chancelleries of Venice, Milan, Rome, and Vienna, whom the letters were intended to influence, were totally ignorant of Transylvanian place names, Reudell, perhaps not very imaginatively, simply used an adaptation of his surname as a place name, ''ex Rothel.'' This mystery eluded all the Dracula sleuths until the Romanian historian Radu Constantinescu recently proved this startling subterfuge on the basis of material available at the Braşov archives. In this respect, Reudell truly espoused the hostile sentiments of the German Saxons, who never forgave Dracula's atrocities during the period from 1457 to 1460. Apart from indicting Dracula as a traitor, Saxon documents also portrayed him as a demented killer and psychopath, as one of the worst tyrants of mankind, ''who had killed many German men, women and children in Transylvania aimlessly and deserved execution for his crimes against humanity,'' according to Chalcondyles. Materials such as these were too good to be ignored by the scribes and propagandists of the Hungarian chancellery, whose duties were to elevate their master in the eyes of

Europe. It was in this manner that the first anti-Dracula tracts found their way into the foreign-affairs concerns at Venice, Milan, Vienna, and Rome. The "Rothel letters" and other damaging evidence against Dracula were later included in the *Commentaries* of Pope Pius II. It was one of the first eloquent demonstrations of the effectiveness of propaganda even in the fifteenth century.

On the whole, European reactions to the official explanation stemming from Buda were cautious. Among the first powers to be informed of the reasons for Dracula's arrest were the doge of Venice, Cristoforo Moro, and the senate of the Venetian republic, through Moro's able spokesman at Buda, Pietro Tommasi, who blithely reported on the explanations of the Hungarian court in succeeding dispatches without even minimal comments. The senate, however, reading in between the lines of the ambassador's report, was not entirely satisfied by the official explanation and requested of Tommasi additional facts concerning the "precise circumstances of Dracula's arrest." Unable to provide them, the ambassador, who was a skillful diplomat and had undoubtedly become aware of the Hungarian chancellery's sophisticated manipulation of the circumstances of Dracula's arrest, refused to convey deceitful information to his home government any longer and tendered his resignation — a request that was refused by the senate. But the Hungarian court, through its spies, who intercepted even diplomatic correspondence, decided that the Venetian diplomat simply knew too much and expelled him from Buda as persona non grata. This angered the Venetian republic, which instructed its new ambassador, Giovanni Aymo, "to find out the truth on the character of the negotiations between Dracula and Matthias" and whether Matthias had signed a secret truce with the Turks. In the light of these instructions, it is clear that Venice, at least, did not believe in the official explanations given by the Hungarian king.

If there was skepticism on the side of Venice, there was even more open cynicism displayed in Rome at the papal court, though initially Pope Pius II thought it prudent to accept the explanations of the Hungarians at face value. However, the Roman curia, familiar with Dracula's heroic exploits on the Danube, also found it difficult to accept that this foremost crusader should suddenly decide to betray his Dragon oath and seek the support of the sultan. It was with the purpose of learning the truth that Pius II sent a new papal legate at Buda, Niccolò Modrussa, to learn what really occasioned Dracula's arrest by King Matthias. Modrussa was instructed to approach the king in person and if possible get to know Dracula. (It was largely as a result of these instructions that Modrussa, who obtained an audience with the detainee, was able to leave us a most detailed description of the Wallachian prince's physical traits, which corresponds closely to the brushstrokes of the unknown Renaissance artist who painted the prince at the Hungarian court.) Other contemporaries also expressed concern about Dracula's arrest, among them the Pole Jan Dlugosz, who dared accuse King Matthias of having acted in concert with the Turks — an obvious allusion to the truce which had been signed with Mehmed. Even the Hungarian court chronicler, Bonfini, vaguely alluded to the fact that concerning Dracula's arrest, "the king had acted in opposition to general opinion." It was evident that Dracula's imprisonment had created an embarrassing "diplomatic problem" that it was in the king's interest to resolve. His explanations and rationalizations for his failure to embark on a crusade were simply rejected by the majority of European statesmen and diplomats.

The problem of Dracula's imprisonment in Hungary for "some twelve years," as the Russian ambassador, Kuritsyn, would have it, poses serious historical problems. New evidence seems to suggest that once safely out of the reach of the Germans of Transylvania, Dracula was placed under house arrest as a distinguished prisoner. He was initially confined at Buda in the fortress of Vác and later incarcerated in the beautiful summer palace at Visegrád, located on a hill above the scenic Danube bend, where King Matthias entertained his important guests. Dracula's unofficial prisoner status is confirmed by the fact that his name does not figure on the roster of political detainees listed in the high-security jail called Solomon's Tower, on the banks of the Danube, which has been beautifully restored. Within the large complex at Visegrád, which is today the site of careful archaeological investigation and partial reconstruction, was centered the flowering culture of the Hungarian Renaissance. Like the Medici of Florence, King Matthias evidently liked to think of himself as a true patron of learning and the arts. He used Visegrád to impress foreign visitors with the material splendors of his age, reflected in the countless artistic treasures in the main palace, recently rediscovered.

At Visegrád Dracula was occasionally invited into the king's presence and became a subject of interest among courtiers and diplomats in view of his ambiguous reputation. Many of the anecdotes about Dracula that later circulated throughout Europe were written at the time of his so-called imprisonment. Well-known portraitists were encouraged to come to Buda to capture his physical traits on canvas. It is likely that the original less-than-life-size portrait, a copy of which has survived in the so-called monster gallery at Castle Ambras in the Tyrol, was originally commissioned by King Matthias himself.

When Matthias signed the armistice he had earlier concluded with the Turks, and a delegation from Sultan Mehmed finally made its appearance at the Hungarian summer court, the king received the Turkish diplomats in the presence of Dracula. He knew of the psychological impact that this confrontation would entail — the awesome "Impaler Prince," even as a captive, had the power of sending shivers down the spines of the Turkish delegates. It was a way of signaling to the king's foes that Matthias would keep Dracula in reserve, just in case the sultan violated the provisions of that treaty. In essence, Dracula had become a living legend at the court of the Hungarian king.

Two separate accounts of Dracula's activities in jail mention bizarre behavior. The narrative of the Russian ambassador, Fedor Kuritsyn, tells us, "It is said of him that even while in jail he could not cure himself of the evil habit of catching mice and having birds bought at the marketplace, so that he could punish them by impalement. He cut off the heads of some of the birds; others he had stripped of their feathers and then let loose." This strange behavior is confirmed by a few suggestive details in a letter from Gabriele Rangoni, Bishop of Erlau, to Pope Sixtus IV in 1476. The bishop wrote, "Unable to forget his wickedness, he caught mice and, cutting them up into pieces, stuck them on small pieces of wood, just as he had stuck men on stakes." It is unlikely that either of these accounts could have been copied from the other, so the historian must deem them at least possible, however strange the behavior may seem, suggesting that there may have been more than a streak of irrationality in Dracula's "impalement fetishism."

The shift in the fortunes of Frederick III after the Vienna uprising were probably in part responsible for King Matthias's softening of his attitude toward his fearsome political prisoner. By December 1462 the Viennese uprising against the Holy Roman Emperor had been brutally repressed through the intervention of King George Poděbrady of Bohemia, Matthias's father-in-law and leader of the Bohemian Hussites. He had thus extricated Frederick III from a humiliating situation. Though Matthias now renounced all ambitions over the ancestral Habsburg estates of his rival, he was all the more intent upon securing the holy crown of St. Stephen of Hungary, which had been promised to him by the emperor in an earlier agreement at Graz. Frederick, however, had never made good his promise and continued to keep the crown, which alone conferred legitimacy, safely hidden in his imperial palace at Wiener Neustadt, just in case he might take the fancy of becoming king of Hungary. However, prodded by the papacy and by the promise of 80,000 gold crowns from King Matthias, Frederick III, in his characteristically unpredictable manner, finally agreed to implement the earlier accord and surrender the crown to King Matthias. This occurred in June of 1463, when Matthias sent a delegation of 3,000 formally attired knights from the best families of Hungary to bring back the precious jeweled crown in exchange for the promised sum. The formal investiture of King Matthias took place the following year in the ancient cathedral of Esztergom with the customary pomp and ceremony. It was the first formal coronation since the days of Ladislas V, and there followed weeks of feasting and merriment in the Hungarian capital. At last, the son of the great Hunyadi could be considered the legitimate king. One fact that had not escaped the attention of the gathered nobles of the Hungarian establishment was the presence of a little man with almond eyes, a feathered cap, and a severe countenance. Dracula had been invited to the ceremonies of inauguration; he sat in a choice seat reserved for the best families of the land. These were certainly auspicious omens.

Matthias's triumphant coronation was offset by the tragic death of Pope Pius II in 1464, an event that saddened Dracula and those who still believed in the ideal of crusading. Knowing his end was near, the pope freely vented his disillusionment with the Christian states. He was particularly disappointed with the Hungarian king, who had pocketed over 40,000 ducats from the papal curia and from Venice, in part, it was suspected, to defray the costs of reclaiming the crown of St. Stephen. In a somber spirit, the pope addressed the college of cardinals, ready to sacrifice his own person and lead the new crusade that he had proclaimed five years before: "We know it is a serious matter for a man of our age and that we shall go to certain death in one way or another. . . . We must die one day and we do not mind where, provided we die well." These were the prophetic words of a man who knew his days were numbered. Having assembled a ragtag army of some 2,000 ill-clad and poorly armed volunteers from every part of Europe (somewhat reminiscent of Capistrano's dedicated crusaders who had saved Belgrade in 1456), the pope managed to reach the marshes of Ancona, where he waited for the Venetian transport ships that were to carry his force across the Adriatic. He finally caught sight of the sails of the galleys in the distant horizon on the morning of August 14; then, racked by pain and exhausted by fevers induced by the insalubrious August sun, Pope Pius II expired on August 15, while his army was celebrating the Feast of the Assumption.

Following his death, the crusaders simply melted away, almost as precipitously as they had gathered.

Pius II's successor, the Venetian Pietro Barbo — Pope Paul II — openly reproved the Hungarian king for having used crusading subsidies for political ends (that is, the purchase of the Hungarian crown). Now that he was the legitimate successor of St. Stephen, Hungary's first Catholic king, who owed his crown to the papacy, it was increasingly embarrassing for Matthias to justify his continued lack of action against the Turks.

Developments in both Wallachia and Moldavia were to provide the Hungarian king with a solid pretext for reconsidering his inaction. Having duly recognized Radu the Handsome as legitimate prince in November 1462, Matthias was willing to continue this relationship so long as Radu respected a policy of balance between his allegiance to Mehmed and his vassalage toward Hungary. Ironically enough, the first blow to disturb that balance occurred when Stephen the Great of Moldavia, Dracula's cousin, successfully attacked the fortress of Chilia on the Danube, held by the Wallachians in January of 1465. It had taken Stephen two years to avenge the humiliation he had suffered in 1462.

Stephen's capture of Chilia, always considered a particularly important strategic outpost by the Hungarians, was indirectly responsible for the worsening of relations with King Matthias, who eventually attacked the Moldavian prince in the fall of 1467. The Hungarian king, however, was decisively beaten by the Moldavians at the battle of Baia-Mare in December of that year, being severely wounded in the course of battle. Radu the Handsome, still technically an ally of the Hungarians as well as the Turks, could hardly afford to accept the loss of that important fortress without a further challenge, and thus in 1470 began a campaign of attrition between himself and his cousin. Given the increasing dependency of Radu on the Turks, Stephen's intention was clearly to oust Radu from the Wallachian throne and replace him with a more energetic Dăneşti protégé of his own, Basarab III Laiotă. Stephen's campaign against Radu began in earnest in the fall of 1473. The crucial encounter took place about thirty miles from Bucharest on the Vodnău River. Though he was supported by a Turkish contingent, Radu, never known for his courage in battle, abandoned his troops and took refuge in the fortress of Bucharest. The Moldavians captured the city of Bucharest on November 24, 1473, and proclaimed Basarab Laiotă prince. Part of the considerable booty of war captured by Stephen included "all Radu's treasures, all his vestments, his standards, and flags." Most humiliating was the capture of his wife, Maria Despina, and his beautiful daughter, Maria Voichiţa, whom Stephen later took as his second wife. Throughout the year 1474 the struggle for the Wallachian throne raged on. Radu, who had withdrawn to Giurgiu, had the support of the Turks, but the Hungarians were fast losing interest in his fate. Radu's forces were again beaten by Stephen's troops, and Basarab Laiotă, who had made his peace with the Turks, retained the Wallachian throne. Dracula's brother Radu died in January, 1475, as the result of a long bout with syphilis. He was buried at the monastery of Tînganu near Bucharest, while his wife and daughter remained in Stephen's hands. Only Vintilă Florescu, one of Radu's boyars, attempted to keep the princesses' spirits up by assuring Maria Despina that efforts were being made to obtain her release.

The death of Radu the Handsome and the defection of Basarab Laiotă to the Turks provided Matthias with a valid argument to set plans in motion for Dracula's rehabilitation and to launch his long-delayed crusade against the Turks. The Russian diplomat Kuritsyn records that following the death of Prince Radu, the king sent an emissary to Dracula with the question: Would he wish to become prince of Wallachia as he had been before? Would he be willing to convert to Catholicism? The stipulation was that if not, then he would be obliged to die in prison. In short, the king made a proposal that Dracula could ill afford to refuse. The prospects of complete freedom and reassuming a position of power were certainly worth a Catholic mass. So Dracula abandoned Orthodoxy and became a Roman Catholic. With this conversion, the Hungarian king could finally accept an offer that Dracula had made as early as 1462: namely, to marry within the extended family of the Hungarian king. The most likely choice was Ilona Szilágy, daughter of Mihály Szilágy, Matthias's uncle (hence a cousin of Matthias). It should also be recalled that Dracula had been closely allied to Mihály Szilágy in his early struggles in Transylvania and even later when the powerful voivode of Transylvania lost favor with the king himself. The marriage took place, and Dracula was able to add a new heraldic insignia to his coat of arms: the blackbird, symbol of the Corvinus family. (John Hunyadi's wife was a Szilágy.)

This new set of circumstances freed Dracula to move into an imposing house in Pest, across from Buda, where he lived in a princely manner and where at least one of his two sons was born, one brought up at the Hungarian court and the other raised by the bishop of Oradea. Dracula's eldest surviving son, named Mihnea, the product of an illegitimate liaison, was also living at the Hungarian court.

Anecdotes, however, continued to circulate concerning Dracula's unusual traits — in this case his fanatical concern for protocol — even in his new palatial surroundings. According to the account of Kuritsyn, a criminal had sought refuge in Dracula's courtyard. Officials of the king, chasing him, came into Dracula's courtyard in search of the escapee. But Dracula reacted to this intrusion into his private domain with sword in hand. He cut off the head of the chief officer who was holding the criminal and let the criminal go free. His men fled in terror and complained to a judge, informing him about what had happened. This judge and his men went to the Hungarian king to lodge a complaint against Dracula. The king then sent a messenger to Dracula, who was told to ask the Wallachian, "Why have you committed such a crime?" And Dracula replied, "I did not commit any crime. It is the police official who committed suicide. Anyone will perish in this way, should he, like a thief, invade the house of a great ruler such as myself. If this man had come to me first and had explained the situation to me, and if the criminal had then been found in my own home, I myself would have delivered the criminal over to him and would have pardoned him." When the king was told about this, he began to laugh and marvel at the candor of his new relative.

Florio de Reverella, the representative of the duke of Ferrara, an Italian republic always threatened by Venice, reported that he was very satisfied to learn that "the so-called Dracula, in whom so much hope had been vested, [was] finally a free agent" by July 18, 1475. Similar positive reactions came from the representatives of Milan, Venice, and the papal legate, the bishop of Erlau. There was a generally jubilant reaction to the good news, for none of the diplomats assigned to Buda who were really familiar with the events of 1462 had ever placed much faith in the Hungarian king's attempts to revile the reputation of the Wallachian prince. Matthias, through his action, had finally rehabilitated Dracula's reputation completely. He implicitly admitted that the earlier charges leveled by the Germans were false and that he now shared others' belief in Dracula's innocence.

Though Dracula did not assume the Wallachian throne at once, the stage was definitely set for that move. The king's nod toward Dracula was aided by news of aggressive actions by Sultan Mehmed against Bosnia, a state torn by pacifism and pro-Turkish sentiments displayed by Bogomil heretics. Matthias Corvinus saw this as a direct threat to Hungary. The Ottomans had also attacked the remaining valuable Genoese-dominated colonies in the Crimea, at Caffa, and bordering the Azov Sea. In addition, the sultan had extended his direct authority over the Crimean Tatars — a threat to Poland and even to the distant Moscovite state.

Given these fresh dangers, the newly elected pope, Sixtus IV, called for a renewal of the European Christian coalition of states against Ottoman expansionism. Special emphasis was placed on the roles of Hungary, Poland, Transylvania, Wallachia, Moldavia, and Bohemia. Since the Venetian settlements in the Balkan area were also being directly menaced, the senate in Venice was ready this time to respond with ships and troops, not merely words and money.

Stephen of Moldavia, former foe of the Hungarian king and vassal of Poland's Casimir IV, responded warmly to the call with the words "We are ready to resume the struggle for the defense of Christendom with all the power and heart which Almighty God had chosen to invest in us." Since Stephen's protégé on the Wallachian throne, Basarab Laiotă, had veered too much toward the Turks, the Moldavian ruler was ready to make overtures to Dracula. Thus, during the summer of 1475, Stephen was ready to make amends for his betrayal and end the feud with his cousin Dracula, which had done so much harm and divided the two Romanian principalities. Stephen sent his personal envoy, Ion Ţamblac, to King Matthias with the formal request that Dracula be once again established on the throne. "I asked," wrote Stephen on June 5, 1475, "that Basarab Laiotă be replaced by another prince, Dracula, with whom we can reach an agreement. I made this request of the Hungarian king, that he might give his support to that prince with whom we have good intelligence."

The Hungarian king, a master of procrastination, followed his usual cautious ways. At first he summoned a meeting of the Hungarian nobles in order to secure their support. Then he appealed for money and arms to the German townships of Braşov, Sibiu, and Bistriţa to fight the Turks. Finally he levied a special crusading tax of a gold florin per household from each family in the Hungarian kingdom. Only after these moves did he appoint Dracula in January of 1476 as his "captain" to be able to lead the campaign he was planning in Bosnia, which was now in the hands of the Turks. However, he was not yet prepared to consider Dracula as the official candidate for the Wallachian throne.

Dracula, who had previously been treated so often as persona non grata in Transylvania, was able to set up his headquarters at Arghiş and to ask for 200 florins from the mayor of Sibiu, Thomas Altenberger, for the upkeep of his court. At this point in time his nickname "Dracula" was evidently not only accepted by most foreign rulers and diplomats but also used by the Wallachian ruler himself in official correspondence. For example, in a letter to Braşov, dated August 4, 1475, written from

Arghiş, Dracula, in sending one of his boyars, one Cîrstian, to the Hungarian king with a request that a castle be readied for him at Braşov, signs the letter "Wladislaus Dragwlya." The request was never acted upon — presumably because Matthias Corvinus was well aware that anti-Dracula sentiment still ran high in that city. Instead, Dracula proceeded southward in October 1475 to Merghindel, to help plan the campaign with Matthias to recover Bosnia during the winter of 1475–1476. Thus, at the head of an army of about 5,000 soldiers, Matthias led the crusade to liberate Bosnia, with Dracula and the exiled Serbian despot Gregorević under his command.

The bishop of Erlau, Gabriele Rangoni, duly reported to Pope Sixtus IV this first military exploit of Dracula since his confinement; the pope was understandably interested in the progress of the new crusade. These forces met with initial success, liberating the Bosnian city of Šabac on February 8, 1476. Flushed with victory, the Hungarian king returned in triumph to Buda, leaving the army under the command of Dracula and Gregorević. Their next military objective was the Bosnian city of Srebreniča, a well-known silver-mining center. Givern the absence of the king, Dracula reverted to the kinds of tactics that had earned him his fearful reputation during previous encounters with the Turks. He reconnoitered the area by sending out 150 Hungarian cavalrymen, disguised as Turks. They succeeded in entering Srebreniča the evening before the monthly market day. Their task for the next morning was to create confusion among the vendors and the populace at large, so that the defenses would be paralyzed when the main attack took place. The tactics were successful. After seizing control of the town, Dracula had the surviving Turkish garrison members impaled and the place burned to the ground. He and his officers pillaged the homes of the wealthy merchants, seizing silver, gold, carpets, and other precious objects as booty of war.

After the victory at Srebreniča, Dracula's army proceeded to loot and kill the garrisons of the neighboring towns of Kuslat and Zwornik. The enormity of Dracula's crimes came to the attention of the papal legate, Gabriele Rangoni, who reported on these cruelties with obvious relish and bias. "He tore the limbs off the Turkish prisoners and placed their parts on stakes . . . and displayed the private parts of his victims so that when the Turks see these, they will run away in fear!" The bishop of Erlau had apparently been informed of Dracula's earlier crimes against the Turks, particularly the infamous forest of the impaled that had so impressed Mehmed II. In this context, the pope's representative added the amazing statistic that "while he was Prince of Wallachia, he killed about 100,000 human beings by means of the stake or by other frightful punishments'' (a figure evidently exaggerated).

When Dracula returned to Transylvania in March 1476, his chief task was to try to persuade the Hungarian king to give official sanction to his candidature to the Wallachian throne, and to help him overthrow his rival, Basarab Laiotă, who had sold himself to the Turks. His impressive victories in Bosnia helped his cause, as did the diplomatic support of his cousin, Stephen of Moldavia. As early as January 1476, the Hungarian parliament had thrown its weight behind him, as had the governor of Transylvania, Johann Pongrác, and the German cities of Transylvania. Basarab Laiotă evidently got the message and no longer considered himself, in terms of the citizens of Sibiu and Braşov, their friend.

Matthias finally gave Dracula his support. He was ready to give him a Hungarian army to help reconquer the throne. The planning for this last campaign took place during the summer of 1476 at Turda in Transylvania, where Dracula had set camp. The Hungarian king had entrusted supreme command of this expedition to Stephen Báthory, a member of the Ecsed branch of that powerful Hungarian family. Dracula's army of 8,000 infantry and 13,000 cavalry had come from Hungary and Transylvania. Even though Báthory's military expertise was somewhat shaky — in fact, he could not even read a war map — the Hungarian king saw fit later to reward him by making Stephen governor of Transylvania from 1479 until his death, a position then held by many of his successors. (This Stephen Báthory was the great-uncle of the notorious ''Blood Countess,'' Elizabeth Báthory [1560–1614], a genuine living vampire, who reputedly butchered some 650 girls, in order to bathe and shower in their blood, because she thought such cosmetics kept her skin looking young and healthy. Later writers would draw upon this connection and attribute to Dracula vampire practices that came from the legends surrounding this ''Countess Dracula.'')

Though Stephen Báthory was technically commander-in-chief of the army aimed at restoring Dracula to the Wallachian throne, actual leadership was shared by Dracula and the Serbian despot Vuk Branković, the heir to that particular family's claim to the throne of Serbia. The entire operation was planned as a joint effort involving Hungarian, Transylvanian, Moldavian, and Wallachian troops, as well as a small Serbian contingent. Dracula and Vuk Branković warned Prince Stephen of Moldavia not to begin his struggle against the Turks until additional forces had arrived from Transylvania. The idea was to effect a juncture with the Moldavian forces before engaging the enemy. Unfortunately,

One of the more famous portraits of Sultan Mehmed II by the Venetian Renaissance artist Gentile Bellini (1429–1507).

Pope Pius II (Enea Silvio de' Piccolomini) (1458–1464), opening the Congress in the Cathedral of Mantua on September 26, 1459, to launch the crusade against the Turks. From a fifteenth-century fresco at the Cathedral of Siena.

King Matthias Corvinus, son of John Hunyadi, king of Hungary, 1458–1490. Print from *Mausoleum Regi Apostolici*, Nuremberg, 1660, p. 316.

An artist's impression of King Matthias's summer palace at Visegrád on the Danube bend, where Dracula was under house arrest from 1462 to 1474. The castle walls extend to the Danube, where Solomon's Tower is located. The palace of the king lies on the summit of the hill. Even if Dracula was detained at the tower he would often have been present at the palace when important delegations (particularly Turkish diplomats) visited.

Solomon's Tower at the palace of Visegrád, where high security prisoners were held by King Matthias of Hungary.

Dracula was probably detained at the main palace of the Hungarian king, which is now largely in ruins.

Photograph by George Florescu

Chapel of Snagov, where
according to tradition
Dracula lies buried, as it
looked in 1931 shortly
after the Rosetti-Florescu
excavations, before
repairs and restoration.

With permission of Mr. Dinu Rosetti, Archeological Excavations at Snagov, Bucharest, 1935

The 1931 excavations at
the tomb at the Snagov
altar footsteps, where
Dracula was said to be
buried. No casket was
found, only a large empty
hole containing the bones
of various animals.

Ꝺie facht sich an gar ein grauſſen

liche erſchꝛockenliche hyſtoꝛien von dem wilden wütrich.
Ꝺꝛacole wayde. Wie er die leüt geſpiſt hat. vnd gepꝛaten.
vnd mit den haübtern yn einem keſſel geſoten. vñ wie er die
leüt geſchunden hat vñ zerhacken laſſen als ein kraut. Jtez
er hat auch den müterñ ire kind gepꝛatē vnd ſy habēs müſ/
ſen ſelber eſſen. Vnd vilandere erſchꝛockenliche ding die in
diſſem Tractat geſchꝛiben ſtend. Vnd in welchem land er
geregiret hat.

Frontispiece of Dracula pamphlet printed by Ambrosius Huber in Nuremberg, 1499. The text above the woodcut translates: "Here begins a very cruel frightening story about a wild bloodthirsty man Prince Dracula. How he impaled people and roasted them and boiled their heads in a kettle and skinned people and hacked them to pieces like cabbage. He also roasted the children of mothers and they had to eat the children themselves. And many other horrible things are written in this tract and in the land he ruled."

"Here occurred a frightening and shocking history about the wild berserker Prince Dracula." Impalement scene and text page from a Strasbourg pamphlet dated 1500.

Hie facht sich an gar ein grauffen liche erschröckenliche hyftorien, von dem wilden wüt rich Dracole weyde Wie er die leüt gespist hot vnd gepraten vñ mit den haüßtern yn einē keffel gefotten

"An Extraordinary and Shocking History of a Great Berserker called Prince Dracula." Leipzig, 1493.

Petrus Gonsalvus of Tenerive, born in 1556 and popularly referred to as the "wolfman of the Canary Islands." Both he and his two children (a boy and a girl) were covered with hair and thus made medical history. Their portraits are located in the Monster Gallery, close to Dracula's portrait, at Castle Ambras.

Ivan the Terrible orders the cap nailed to the ambassador's head. Dutch gravure of the seventeenth century.

Dracula the Hero: statue of Dracula built by the National Tourist Office of Romania to attract attention to the gateway to the famous castle on the Argeş. The walls of the castle have been shored up and steps leading all the way to the castle built. The statue is located in the village of Copîţîneni.

The German actor Max Schreck playing Dracula (Count Orlock) in the film *Nosferatu — eine Symphonie des Grauens* (1922), directed by Friedrich Wilhelm Murnau, a master of the expressionist genre. This was the first vampire film based on Bram Stoker's novel and the characterization of the vampire most closely corresponds to the Romanian folkloric image of the *strigoi*.

before the Moldavians had time to reach Wallachia, the Turks caught and defeated them at Valea Alba on July 26, 1476. This forced the crusaders to march toward Moldavia and cross the Siret River, the old border with Wallachia, in order to aid Stephen of Moldavia in liberating his territory from the Turks. By August 18, Dracula was able to unite his forces with those of Stephen at the Oituz Pass at the Transylvanian border. They then pursued and defeated the Turks at the Siret River.

Once having secured the liberation of Moldavia from Turkish hands, the commanders were able to concentrate their efforts upon their main objectives — the elimination of Basarab Laiotă from the Wallachian throne and the restoration of Dracula to power. Consultations took place at Braşov. Though each of the chief officers was in charge of his own contingent, since Dracula, in fact, knew the terrain best, he took over command from this point onward.

Stephen the Great of Moldavia was to launch his attack on eastern Wallachia with about 15,000 soldiers. Dracula, Báthory, and Vuk Branković were to attack from southern Transylvania with an army of roughly 35,000 troops. Using the good offices of János Vitéz, the famous humanist and diplomat from the court of King Matthias, Dracula was able finally to assuage the ruffled feelings of the authorities at Braşov. By October 7, the Braşovians, in whose district Dracula had once committed so many atrocities, were wooed to his side by the promise of extensive commercial concessions and a renewal of trade relations favorable to them. Oxen, horses, and grain were to be sent from Wallachia in return for weapons and manufactured goods. None of the usual limitations were to be placed on the Braşovians with regard to the places where they were allowed to trade, as had been the case before. In return, Dracula, using two of his envoys, Ion Polivar and Mihai Log, was able to extract a promise from the citizens of that town not to protect any of Dracula's many political enemies who had sought refuge in Braşov. Another of Dracula's envoys, named Ladislas, was active in Buda; from there he sent regular reports to Dracula about the current state of Hungarian politics. Both Ladislas and János Vitéz were instructed to keep the Hungarian king, Matthias, well informed about the progress of the anti–Basarab Laiotă campaign.

The Dracula offensive from Transylvania into Wallachia began in early November 1476. A dispatch dated December 4, 1476, and addressed to the duke of Ferrara by his representative at the court of Buda, Florio de Reverella, reported that Basarab Laiotă, with an army of 18,000 made up largely of Turks and some of his boyars and their men, advancing along the valley of the Prahova, faced the combined forces of Báthory and Dracula. A battle was fought near the town of Rucăr at the Wallachian-Transylvanian border, and Basarab's army was defeated. It was a pyrrhic victory, since both armies lost about 10,000 soldiers, but nonetheless, Dracula and Báthory continued their progress. Coincident with this attack, Stephen of Moldavia launched his supportive campaign from Moldavia and succeeded in taking northeastern Wallachia away from the Turks. On November 8, Dracula himself had reported to the citizens of Braşov that his forces had captured the capital city of Tîrgovişte — a fact confirmed by the Austrian chronicler Jacob Unrest. Stephen of Moldavia met Dracula in his capital city, and the two sovereigns swore eternal allegiance to one another; they pledged as well, with Báthory present, to pursue the great crusade against the Turks.

Dracula continued mopping-up operations along the valley of the Dîmboviţa River all the way to Bucharest, his main objective at this point. Stephen Báthory reported to the town officials of Sibiu on November 11, 1476, that the greater part of Wallachia was already in Dracula's hands. He also added, "All the boyars aside from two are with us" and "Even the latter will soon join us." Báthory's army took Bucharest on November 16, and on November 26, Dracula was reestablished as prince of his land for the third time in his life.

King Matthias tried to take credit for this momentous achievement, since Dracula was his vassal. In a letter to Pope Sixtus IV, Matthias confirmed the fact that Dracula was again in control of his Wallachia. Venice was also informed and reassured that the return of Dracula signified the resumption of the long-delayed crusade against the Turks in Europe. The elector of Saxony learned of this happy circumstance from the Hungarian king. In a letter to the Venetian senate, Stephen of Moldavia's envoy, Ion Ţamblac, took pains to emphasize the great contribution of his master to this event, since Ţamblac knew that this news would be transmitted to the pope. Pope Sixtus IV was so impressed with the work of Stephen of Moldavia that he bestowed on him the coveted title of "Athlete of Christ" — an honor that had eluded Dracula. Only the great Albanian freedom fighter Skanderbeg had been given that title previously during the fifteenth century.

According to peasant tradition, within two months of his investiture as prince, Dracula's mangled and headless body was discovered by some monks from the monastery of Snagov in a nearby marsh. They secretly interred his remains in the chapel of Snagov in a crypt facing the altar of the principal chapel. One might say that every moment since Dracula's accession during his brief third reign was dominated by the certainty of death: the odds against survival were simply too great. That no chronicle speaks of a blood bath during these last few months may indicate that the dissident boyars chose to make themselves scarce during that time. The partisans of the Turks were still too close for comfort, and, as a Catholic convert, in the eyes of the Orthodox church, Dracula was a heretic, or at the very least a schismatic. Too many boyars had been deeply implicated in Radu's and Basarab Laiotă's reigns to hope for permanent reconciliation and mercy. To the sultan, Dracula was obviously cursed and unacceptable — the enormity of his crimes was simply unforgivable. Even the Transylvanian Saxons, in spite of temporary appeasement, continued to give comfort to Dracula's enemies. The moment that Báthory's main Hungarian contingent and Stephen's force left the country, Dracula was clearly exposed to great dangers, for he had not had time to consolidate his strength and rebuild a force loyal to himself. The fact that he was aware of these dangers is proved by his unwillingness to bring his wife and sons with him to Wallachia, where undoubtedly they too would have been exposed to the threat of assassination. Another indication of his pessimism is the peasant story about "hidden treasures" still related in the Snagov area and collected by Romanian folklorists. Sensing that his end was near and that he might need money for future contingencies, Dracula ordered some peasants to make cast-iron barrels, in which he placed the gold, silver, and precious jewels that he had hidden at his treasury at Snagov. To make certain that no one would find this booty, he ordered the course of a certain river (conceivably the Dîmboviţa near Bucharest) diverted by building a dam. Having buried the treasures in the river bed, he ordered his men to give free flow to the river again. All the peasants who partook of this operation were then ordered impaled. Having heard that one of these youths who was aware of the secret had escaped, Dracula had his men capture and kill him. As is the case with so many aspects of the Dracula story, no one knows precisely where these treasures were hidden, if indeed this popular tradition is true. In any event, this represents the last action recorded by the Romanian people before Dracula was killed. Stephen, now his loyal friend, shared this sense of foreboding. He had no great faith in the loyalty of the Wallachians to their newfound master and just for good measure left a small contingent of 200 Moldavian bodyguards to protect him. Perhaps he felt this was one manner of expiating his betrayal of 1462.

How did Dracula die? The determined vampirists will of course reply that he never died and that his spirit will haunt us perpetually. Romanian historians of the nineteenth century immortalized his spirit; in this sense

Dracula lives as the undying hero who in the moment of need will save the Romanian nation from destruction. One cryptic version concerning the scenario of Dracula's death comes from the Russian narrative of Kuritsyn, who alludes to a final battle in which "Dracula's army began to kill [the Turks] and to pursue them without mercy. Then out of joy Dracula ascended a mountain in order to see how his men were killing the Turks. Detaching himself from the army, one of those around him, taking him for a Turk, hit him with a lance. Dracula, seeing that he was being attacked by his own men, immediately killed five of his assassins on the spot with his own sword. However, many arrows pierced him and he died in this manner."

The real history of Dracula's final moments is more complex than the above account. It can be reconstituted with the help of a few foreign observers as well as the letters of Prince Stephen the Great to the king of Hungary. Perhaps one of Dracula's greatest mistakes following his victories at Rucăr, Tîrgovişte, and Bucharest was his failure to seize and kill Basarab III Laiotă as he had other Romanian rivals such as Dan III and Vladislav II. Laiotă's survival was a source of great danger, as the former prince was busy rallying the support of various Turkish frontier commanders on the Danube to organize the inevitable counterattack. Dracula, during his third reign, as noted, maintained his court at Bucharest, which was perilously exposed to a rapid attack from the south. According to most reliable sources, the final encounter took place near the monastery of Snagov in the last days of December 1476. Dracula was attacked by Basarab Laiotă and a Turkish contingent of 4,000 men, twice the number of his own defenders, which included Stephen's bodyguard of 200 Moldavians. It is entirely conceivable that Dracula disguised himself as a Turk, a practice he often resorted to in order to confuse his opponents. The Austrian chronicler Jacob Unrest helps to clarify the situation by confirming the fact that Dracula was killed by a hired assassin who came from the Turkish camp. He carefully explains the circumstances: "Dracula was killed with great cunning, because the Turks wished to avenge the enmity which he had borne against them for so long and also the great damages inflicted upon them. They hired a Turk [to act] as one of his servants with the mission of killing him while he served him. The Turk was apparently instructed to attack Dracula from the back. He was then to cut off his head and bring it back on horseback to the sultan." Dracula's head was later exposed on a high stake at Constantinople for the populace to witness that the great "Kazîglu" (the Impaler) was finally dead — a fact confirmed by the Hungarian chronicler Bonfini. Dracula and his small bodyguard of Moldavians must have fought like lions in this last encounter. We know that all but ten of Stephen's Moldavian bodyguards perished at the side of their master.

News of Dracula's death struck the conscience of Europe: one month after the event, Stephen, who had established his headquarters at Hîrlau in Moldavia, had news of a battle near the Danube, but no details. He wrote about his concern to the citizens of Braşov on January 5, 1477. Stephen finally had confirmation of Dracula's death three weeks later. His surviving ten veterans, who had taken several weeks to travel back to Suceava, relayed the sad news to their master. Stephen then informed King Matthias of Dracula's death, which was acknowledged in Buda during February, the month when information concerning that tragic event spread to the Italian capitals and western Europe. Leonardo Botta, the envoy of the duke of Milan at Venice, was the first diplomat to inform the doge Ludovico Moro and the Venetian senate that the Turks had conquered Wallachia and that Dracula had been assassinated. At the court of the Holy Roman Emperor in Wiener Neustadt, Dracula's death was dismissed in a very terse statement: "The captain named by King Matthias, Dracula, together with 4,000 men, was butchered by the Turks." There was no official reaction from the emperor, who had never been Dracula's friend.

Death came to Dracula in a little clearing of the Vlasia forest in the marshes near Bucharest. Again, according to local tradition, pious monks from the Snagov monastery, seeing the headless and bloodstained body of the Impaler exposed to the birds of prey, decided to bury his remains on the island monastery of Snagov, which, as we will see, perhaps more than any other structure bears the imprint of Dracula's tortured personality. They placed the body in a crypt at the foot of the main altar with the customary inscriptions regarding his three successive periods of rule. Judging from the date of birth given, 1431, he was only forty-five years old at the time of his death.

Only in distant Holy Russia were there some feelings of indignation, not because Dracula had died but because, in becoming a Catholic, he had betrayed his Orthodox religion. As the Russian narrative put it: "Dracula loved the sweetness of the earthly world much more than the eternal world, and he abandoned Orthodoxy and thereby forsook the truth and the light and accepted darkness, ending his life in heresy." Since abandonment of the true Orthodox religion, in the eyes of many believers of that church often entails some form of punishment — in the eyes of the superstitious — he would never be able to rest in peace in his grave, though the progressive vampirization of this prince is a far more complex story, to which we will now turn.

CHAPTER 8

The Mystery of the Grave

S TRANGE is the fate of the Dracula epic. The legend was born in Transylvania; it spread westward to the German lands and then eastward toward Russia. The heroic moments took place on the Danube; the dramatic ones at Castle Dracula and in Hungary. What makes the bloodstained history of Snagov, the place of death, unique is the fact that, unlike castles, essentially edifices built for war, it was a monastery — admittedly at one time a fortified monastery, but nevertheless a place of worship. According to the old Romanian chronicles, the monastery of Snagov was rebuilt by Dracula; the chronicles are very precise on this point, and most of the older Romanian historians have accepted this as fact. Just as we discussed the development of a "castle epic," there also exists a "Snagov saga," equally vivid and still alive in the minds of the peasants in the villages surrounding the lake. In the superstitious imaginations of these people, the terrible figure of the Impaler still dominates the little church. Dracula has succeeded in stamping his whole personality profoundly upon the bricks and stones of the only surviving chapel on the island, which he allegedly built and in which, according to tradition, he lies buried.

As popular folklore would have it and archaeological excavation on the island has confirmed, the monastery of Snagov originally occupied an area immeasurably larger than that occupied by the church one can see today. The original monastic complex must have extended to the full length of the island. It was evidently fortified. The original walls, which reached to the edge of the lake, were for added protection, for it was known that in a time of peril both princes and boyars stored their treasures at Snagov. In addition to three chapels, which included the Chapel of the Annunciation, by far the largest (built by Vladislav II in 1453), the monastery contained cloisters for the monks, residences, dependencies for the boyars and their servants, a small princely palace, probably a prison, the treasury, and a mint (coins have been found on the island). Snagov, in fact, like many medieval fortresses, was a little town in itself, naturally limited by the size of the island.

The original monastery of Snagov is much older; its foundation can be traced back to the fourteenth century. What is of interest to us is the extent of Dracula's contribution to the monastery. Here, as in the case of his castle, Dracula was partly responsible for the structure's completion. Snagov is certainly not the first ecclesiastical edifice in Romania founded by one prince and completed by another, and, as very often happens in the erection of larger buildings, the name that history associates with it is not that of the founder, but of the person who completed it.

Many of the popular folkloric traditions in the Snagov area are clearly fictitious: one popular ballad relates that Dracula had a vision from God telling him to establish a place of prayer near the scene of his father's assassination at Bălteni. Other stories are more specific and may contain an element of truth. One ballad relates that Dracula's contribution was the completion of another church on the island monastery, added just to compete with his enemy Vladislav II, who was responsible for the construction of the Chapel of the Annunciation. As noted above, it is far more likely that it was Dracula who converted Snagov from a poorly defended monastery into an island fortress. Given his morbid concern with having a "refuge," he could find no better natural fortification than the island surrounded by the dense Vlasia forest; the island commanded a view and was protected on all sides by water. Even in winter, when the lake is frozen, a cannon shot from the island could break up the ice and thus drown any incoming enemy. The fortress-monastery was seized by pro-Radu boyars following the collapse of Dracula's campaign in 1462. At that time, the monastery had been taken over by some of Dracula's boyars, who had hidden their treasures in the vault of the church. According to the peasant stories, the monks, fearful for their lives, threw some of these treasures, some of which belonged to Dracula, into the lake to avoid tempting the Turks, and these ill-gotten riches remain at the bottom of Snagov Lake. It is likely that Radu and his partisans also used the monastery to store their treasure, where it was comparatively secure, when he became prince.

Other peasant narratives make mention of Dracula's crimes on the island. Apparently Dracula's intention had been to transform the island monastery into a prison and establish a torture chamber for political foes. In a tiny cell, the prince would invite his intended victims to kneel and pray to a small ikon of the Blessed Virgin. While the prisoners were praying, a secret trapdoor controlled by Dracula would open, sending them deep into a ditch below, where a number of pales stood erect waiting to pierce the bodies of the unsuspecting penitents. The discovery of several decapitated skeletons, with each skull placed alongside the pierced body, lends further credence to the theory that the monastery was used as a place of punishment in Dracula's time. Yet another story relates how a great storm blew up on the lake on the day of Dracula's interment, a storm that tore the Chapel of Annunciation from its very foundations and blew it into the lake. To this day, the peasants in neighboring villages say that whenever the waters of Snagov become unduly agitated, one can hear the muffled noises from the bell of the chapel's steeple tolling at the bottom of the lake. Only the heavy, beautifully carved oak door of the chapel—one of the most beautiful legacies of fifteenth-century Romanian sculpture—which tore itself loose from its hinges, was seen, according to legend, floating down to the village of Turbaţi. There the archaeologist and novelist Alexandru Odobescu found it, when he was visiting a convent. The nuns had apparently used it for their own chapel. When he read the inscription on the door, he was amazed to find it was dated 1453, during the reign of Prince Vladislav II, Dracula's predecessor. The carved door is now located at the Bucharest Art Museum.

Many of the immediate members of Dracula's family were in some way connected with Snagov. We have already mentioned Radu's role there in 1462. Perhaps simply for reason of filial piety, Dracula's son Mihnea repaired the monastery after the extensive damage done to it by the Turks during the campaign of 1462 and endowed it with additional land. Vlad the Monk, Dracula's half-brother and political enemy, for a time became abbot of the monastery. He is listed only by his religious name, Abbot Pahomie. Vlad the Monk's second wife, Maria, took the veil and lived at Snagov as a widow, with her sons, assuming the same religious name, Eupraxia, as the Monk's mother. One of her sons, Vlad V, or Vlăduţ, spent all his early years at the monastery before becoming prince in 1510, reigning until 1512. The son of Vlad V, yet another Vlad, known to history as Vlad VII, "the Drowned," briefly ruled between 1530 and 1532, and owned his nickname to his drowning in the lake.

A great deal of violence has occurred at Snagov since Dracula's time, wrought both by man and by the elements of nature. Storms of great intensity have occurred on the lake, doing inestimable damage to the buildings on the island. During the winter, the place is heavily snowed under. The peasants say that when the waters freeze over and the cold, merciless *crivăţ* from the Romanian steppes blows hard, the wind scoops the snow from the lake and hits the island with such violence that it can bury the whole place several feet deep. The present abbot told the authors that in preparation for winter, food has to be stored, since the island becomes completely isolated from the mainland. Like other places in the vicinity of Romania's capital, Snagov has felt the tremors of earthquakes. The monastery, however, has suffered far more from the violence of men. Only a small portion of this brutal history is enshrined in the inscription on the walls and the cold stone tombs of the existing church.

Dracula carried the mystery of his life to his grave. In his death, as on so many occasions during his turbulent lifetime, Dracula left many enigmas. Among a number of puzzles, one of the most perplexing is the precise location of Dracula's tomb within the monastery of Snagov, if indeed he lies there, as popular tradition would have it. During the year 1931–1932 the archaeologist Dinu Rosetti and the genealogist George Florescu were officially assigned by the Romanian Commission on Historic Monuments to dig around the monastery and elsewhere on the island and to make certain investigations at the site of the princely stone just by the altar, where Dracula's decapitated body was supposed to have been laid to rest. Many interesting finds were made, which were publicized in a monograph edited by the Bucharest History Museum, directed by Dinu Rosetti, entitled *Diggings at Snagov*. Among these were archaeological remains that indicated that the island monastery was a very ancient historical settlement. The quantity and variety of coins that were dug up also confirm the use of Snagov as a treasury and mint since earliest times. One of the most interesting of the Florescu-Rosetti discoveries, however, centered upon the place where, in the eyes of the people, Dracula lay buried, in front of the altar of the church. Popular legend offers various reasons for choosing the altar site as the location of Dracula's grave, quite apart from its preeminent position. It is claimed that the monks purposely had Dracula's remains placed at the foot of the altar — contrary to usage. They say the tombstone rests in a north-south direction so that the priest and the monks could read the Gospel and say prayers for the permanent repose of his troubled soul while standing above the tomb. The constant trampling of the clerics' feet while officiating at the lengthy Orthodox liturgy may have helped erase all inscriptions. Among the many graves in the monastery, this particular tombstone, though not of princely proportions, was more ambitious than most. When the stone was removed, however, to the utter amazement of the researchers, there was not even a casket beneath it. Dracula's presumed tombstone covered a huge empty grave-pit containing the bones of various animals, some ceramics, and other archaeological finds dating back to the Iron Age.

Further exploration in various parts of the church revealed an unexcavated tombstone, on the right side of the entrance near the door, a most unusual place of burial in an Orthodox church. What struck the researcher team immediately was the identical size of the tombstone with the one that faces the altar, and the solidity of the crypt, built of heavy brick and mortar. Within this tomb was a casket still partially covered by a purple pall embroidered in gold. Much of the casket, as well as the remains of the cloth cover enclosing it, had rotted away. Within the coffin lay the bones of a headless skeleton still clothed in tattered fragments of a thick, yellowish-brown garment of silk brocade. The sleeves, originally crimson, the color of the dragon cloak, were clearly discernible, with large round silver buttons linked to filament cord. Judging by the position of the sleeves, what was left of the fingers of the skeleton were resting on the right of the pelvis. Not far away were the remains of a crown worked in cloisonné, with terracotta-colored claws, each holding a turquoise. Adding to the mystery, hidden in the fold of the cloak was a woman's ring, bereft of its adorning gem. A small cup and a buckle decorated with golden threads were also found in the coffin. All of these items could be dated back to the middle of the fifteenth century. The late archaeologist Dinu Rosetti was convinced that this tomb represented the last resting place of Dracula. The coffin, he said, had simply been transferred by some abbot who felt that Dracula, too evil to be close to God at the altar footsteps, should suffer the humiliation of having the faithful walk over his unworthy remains.

Some years after these discoveries, during a visit at a museum in Nuremberg, Rosetti discovered a ring and a buckle identical to the ones he had found in Dracula's tomb. They were typical of the kind of gift a noble woman of high standing would make to her favorite knight, victorious in a tourney. Indeed, this precious trophy from an unidentified lady was undoubtedly the one acquired by Dracula's father on the night of his successful tournament following his investiture in the Dragon Order at Nuremberg on November 8, 1431. Dracul later bequeathed the trophies, together with his cherished Toledo sword, to his oldest surviving son, Dracula, at the time an exile in Turkey. The precious relics in the tomb represented the sole surviving legacy from the murdered father to his son.

The irony lies in the sequel to this story. During World War II, these relics, housed in the City of Bucharest History Museum, were removed by convicts for safekeeping to the mountains at Văleni de Munte, where they were to be left in custody of one of Romania's greatest historians, Nicolae Iorga. The famous ring, as well as Rosetti's other finds, simply disappeared during the transfer. It seems that the vagabonds of another generation had finally avenged their earlier peers, who had been burned alive by Dracula in the fifteenth century.

Were these the last earthly remains of Dracula? Those responsible for the find, notably Dinu Rosetti and George Florescu, believe they were; so does Father Dumitriu, an Orthodox clergyman from the neighboring village of Turbaţi, who has done a good deal of research on the problem of the tomb. He is equally convinced that Dracula's Hungarian-born wife was also eventually interred at Snagov, which is highly unlikely. Doubts concerning Snagov will continue to haunt historians and archaeologists, as well as local peasants. In 1975, a monk at the monastery, who happened to be a tour guide, gave a lengthy interview to an Associated Press correspondent; he held the theory that the Florescu-Rosetti team had not dug deep enough in the original location. He implied that Dracula's remains lay underneath the empty hole, deep burial being a precaution not entirely unusual in the case of important personalities; they were often entombed very deep in the soil, with a suitable camouflage added to mislead and discourage the usual grave robbers. This story was picked up by the international press and led to a flurry of excitement and repeated requests for reopening the Snagov excavations. The co-authors informally approached the Romanian government with the thought of leading an American team of archaeologists in collaboration with the Romanians in reopening the grave, but the offer was never taken up seriously, mostly on the grounds that the monastery's foundations had been weakened by the earthquakes of 1940 and 1977.

Speculations will continue, but there is no need for learned scholarship to find plausible explanations for the desecration of Dracula's grave. Given both the terror that Dracula's name inspired and the vandalism that was permitted on the island during the latter part of the nineteenth century, when the monastery lay virtually abandoned, it would have been little short of a miracle for Dracula's tomb to have survived intact. Dracula's remains could have been removed from the more exalted position near the altar and reinterred at the rear of the church because the celebrants felt disturbed in their daily liturgy, standing so close to the body of a man who had performed so many cruel deeds. It could also be argued that because Dracula was a convert to Catholicism — thus, in the eyes of the Orthodox church, "a schismatic," it was against the Romanian church law to have his tomb at the altar footsteps. Those monks responsible for what can only be described as an act of "desecration" may have taken the precaution of carefully removing all inscriptions from the original gravestone and substituted for it a plain unmarked slab of identical size. As an additional symbolic gesture of contempt, the bones of various animals and other ancient remains present on the island were thrown into the empty grave. At the back of the church near the portico, unknown to all, they finally may have laid the earthly remains of the tyrant, where any visitor could trample him under his feet. (It is also symptomatic of such probable sentiment that there exists no mural or portrait of Dracula in Snagov, the church traditionally linked to his name. If such a portrait existed at one time, as is the custom when a ruling prince is buried, it was either washed away or painted over.)

No one knows for certain when the opening of the original grave first took place, and it would be unprofitable to go into the great variety of theories that have been advanced on the question of who was actually responsible for it. Some have suggested that it occurred when Snagov was under the control of the Greek monks during the eighteenth century. The Greek clergy were not interested, as were their Romanian colleagues, in praying for Dracula's soul near the altar. Others think that the desecration took place on the orders of Metropolitan Filaret, who became the head of the Romanian church in 1792, on the pretext of making some repairs to the monastery. A similar action could have been taken by Ilarion, bishop of Argeş, another who spoke ill of the prince, at the beginning of the nineteenth century. In fact, any bishop, archbishop, or abbot, Romanian or Greek, might have given the necessary orders. It could also have been the result of vandalism by the peasants themselves from villages in the vicinity of the lake, who looted many invaluable relics, including priceless illuminated Gospels, during the early nineteenth century when the monastery was partially abandoned. The enigma of Snagov remains unresolved and awaits the historian brave enough to pick up the slender clues that archaeologists have thus far provided.

Quite apart from the problem of the grave, there are other mysteries that remain unresolved, and perhaps defy a rational solution, thus giving rise to innumerable legends related by the peasants living in villages surrounding the lake. Stories of murders and assassinations of boyars and abbots at the monastery persist to our times. During the nineteenth century, the abbey was eventually converted into a prison. A bridge was constructed linking the island to the mainland to facilitate the transportation of convicts. Shortly after it was built, the bridge collapsed, dragging the line of chain-linked prisoners to their doom at the bottom of the lake. In the late nineteenth century the monastery was totally disestablished — as noted, looting and grave desecration followed on an increasingly more devastating scale. This lasted until the monastery was formally reclaimed by the Patriarchy of Bucharest at the beginning of the century. Untoward events, however, continued to occur. In 1940, during an earthquake, the main tower of the surviving chapel toppled and the monastery was badly damaged. Its foundations were also badly undermined during the earthquake of 1977. Given these circumstances, it is difficult to shake the peasants' belief that Dracula's curse clings to the place.

The Institute of Folklore in Bucharest has begun conducting surveys in the various villages on the lake's shores to collect the oral traditions of the elderly folk (the young are increasingly moving to Bucharest). The ethnologists hope to compile a complete record of the Snagov saga. One fascinating ballad recently collected suggests that it was at the bottom of Snagov Lake, rather than on the sands of the Dîmboviţa, that Dracula hid his gold treasure enclosed in barrels — the last surviving popular tale connected with him shortly before his assassination. Stories such as these provide a superb incentive for professional treasure hunters and scuba divers to fathom the murky, reed- and algae-infested waters of one of the deepest lakes in Europe. In spite of such commendable efforts, for the time being, the riddles of Snagov remain unresolved, to the delight of the vampirologists.

CHAPTER 9
Dracula's Descendants

SINCE the rediscovery of the real Dracula, many so-called descendants have emerged from the penumbra of relative obscurity and made headlines on popular tabloids and magazines, both in the United States and Europe, vaunting their so-called Dracula ancestry either for publicity's sake or monetary gain. They have ranged from notorious charlatans such as a Turkish bloodbank promoter who typically titled himself "Vlad Tsepeshi," with obvious reference to the Romanian word for the Impaler (Țepeș); his claim: "Blood is in the family business." Others, mostly Romanian families of boyar descent, and a few Hungarian aristocrats, have chosen to advertise their Dracula lineage to gain access to gossip columns, or to become members of jet-set "Dracula Societies," such as the one organized by the socialite Günther Sachs at Saint Moritz in Switzerland. Publicity stunts such as these have aroused the interest of serious-minded students of the very precise science of genealogy. Invariably they ask: "Are there in fact Dracula descendants alive today?"

The fate of Dracula's immediate descendants is a matter of record. Some were, in fact, the chief informants of the Russian ambassador Kuritsyn who met them at Buda.

Ambassador Kuritsyn wrote of them: "The king [meaning Matthias Corvinus] took his sister [that is, his cousin, Dracula's wife, Ilona Szilágy] with her two sons to Buda in Hungary. One of these sons is still in the retinue of the king, the other, who was residing with the Bishop of Oradea [Transylvania], died in our presence [presumably he was brought back to Buda mortally ill]. I saw the third son, named Michael [in Romanian Mihnea, sometimes Mihail], here in Buda. He had fled from the sultan to the Hungarian king [he had temporarily been captured by the Turks shortly after Dracula's death]. Dracula begot him on a young lady when he was not yet married.'' (Possibly this was the Transylvanian noblewoman who committed suicide in 1462.) This description, undoubtedly accurate, describes the events which followed Dracula's death, in February 1477. Ilona Szilágy, Dracula's Hungarian wife, had two children, the elder and only surviving of whom was called Vlad. During his brief third reign, the whole family stayed at Sibiu, where Dracula owned a mansion, thence for added security moved to Buda, where they became distinguished refugees at the Hungarian court. It was logical for the ambitious Ilona and her cousin King Matthias to consider her elder boy, Vlad, as the official pretender to the Wallachian throne. They could hardly accept the legitimacy of Basarab Laiotă, who belonged to the rival Dănești family. Yet the first member of the Dracula line to attempt to assert his rights as the legitimate successor was Vlad the Monk, Dracula's half-brother, who in 1468, in his early manhood, had attempted a coup against him.

Though some detractors have labeled him an imbecile, Vlad, the former monk and abbot, had a comparatively long and successful reign, which lasted thirteen years, from 1482 to 1495, twice as long as that of his half-brother Dracula, quite an achievement for these troubled times. He was buried in the monastery of Glavacioc, now largely in ruins, not very distant from Bucharest.

The eldest of Dracula's sons, Mihnea, made a serious attempt to succeed his father, notwithstanding his illegitimacy. In accordance with Wallachian custom, ''with a rib from the royal bone'' he was a legitimate claimant to the throne. Ambitious and eager to rule, Mihnea probed his chances by organizing several raids across the border with the support of dissident boyars. He finally succeeded in gaining the throne in 1508, but reigned only a scant two years, from April 1508 to October 1509. A strong, impulsive personality like his father, he soon fell into conflict with boyars — particularly the powerful Craiovescu faction, who avenged themselves by coining the epithet Mihnea the Bad or the Evil One. Among Mihnea's most vocal enemies was the monk Gavril Protul, an abbot and chronicler of the period, who spoke of Dracula's son in the following manner: ''As soon as Mihnea began to rule he at once abandoned his sheep's clothing and plugged up his ears like an asp. . . . He took all the greater boyars captive, worked them hard, cruelly

Romanian Branch
Descendants

VLAD THE IMPALER (DRACULA)
(Prince of Wallachia 1448, 1456–1462, 1476)
m. (1) Transylvanian noblewoman

Mihnea "the Bad"
(Prince of Wallachia 1508–1510)
m. (1) Smaranda
m. (2) Voica

Milos

Mircea II
ruled 1509–1510
co-regent with father 1509
m. Maria Despina

Alexandru II Mircea
ruled 1574–1577
m. Catherine Salvarezi

Mihnea II "the Islamized"
ruled 1577–1583
m.(1) Neaga
m.(2) Voica

Radu Mihnea
ruled intermittently 1611–1623
in Wallachia and Moldavia
m. Arghira Minctti

Alexandru "the Cocoon"
ruled 1623–1627
died 1632 without known heirs
m. Ruxandra Beglitzi

Peter the Lame
Prince of Moldavia
1574–1577
m.(1) Maria Amirali
m.(2) Irina the Gypsy

Ştefăniţă

Hungarian Branch
Descendants

VLAD THE IMPALER (DRACULA)
(Prince of Wallachia 1448, 1456–1462, 1476)
m. (2) Ilona Szilágy, relative of
Matthius Corvinus,
King of Hungary

Vlad Dracula m. (?)
claimant to
Wallachian throne

(son) name unknown
died ca. 1482;
lived with Bishop
of Oradea
(no heirs)

Ladislas Dracula
m. member of Vass de
Czege family (land in Banat)

Ladislas
Dracula de Sinteşti
(patent of nobility 1535)
m. Anna Vass de Czege

John Dracula m. (?)
(patent of nobility 1535)

George Dracula
(land in Szekler region)

John Dracula de Band
(land in Szekler region)
m. Anna
no heirs

Daughter
m. Getzi family,
which kept Dracula name
(land in Borgo Pass)

Line dies out
in seventeenth century

confiscated their property, and even slept with their wives in their presence. He cut off the noses and lips of some, others he hanged, and still others drowned.'' Mihnea evidently fought back as best he could, resorting to the terror tactics he had learned from his father. If Mihnea's crimes never assumed the proportions of Dracula's it was simply because of lack of time and opportunity. Shortly after he fled Wallachia in 1510, Mihnea, pursued by his Craiovescu opponents, who had their own pretender to the Wallachian throne, was cornered in the Roman Catholic church of Sibiu where he was attending Mass. As he was emerging from the service he was stabbed by a hired Serbian assassin, Dimitrije Iaxici, a partisan of the Craiovescu boyars. Mihnea the Bad is buried in a crypt of this church (now the city's Evangelical church), and his effigy and an ornate inscription can be admired there to this day. He was over sixty years old at the time of his death, quite an advanced age for one of the Dracula line.

History records the names of two women whom Mihnea married: the first was Smaranda, who died before 1485, and the second Voica, who was left a widow by her husband's assassination. She raised two sons, Miloš and Mircea, as well as a daughter, Ruxandra. The entire family continued to live in Sibiu. Mihnea showed preference for his younger son, called Mircea (in honor of Dracula's grandfather), briefly selected to be co-ruler and destined to succeed him in October 1509. He took the title Mircea II, but was otherwise undistinguished by any adjective describing his characteristics. We know that he was physically a strong and brutal man, since he caught some of the boyars involved in his father's assassination and killed them with his own bare hands. After being expelled by his boyar enemies, Mircea once again sought refuge in Transylvania; he twice unsuccessfully attempted to recapture the throne.

Of Dracula's numerous great-grandchildren, only two became princes of the land: Alexandru II (Alexandru Mircea), the fifth child of Mircea II, and Peter the Lame, the tenth. Both were raised in Istanbul by the Turks and hardly knew their country of origin before ascending the throne. During their long stays in the Turkish capital, both married into powerful Greco-Italian families, members of an increasingly influential community who lived in the wealthy lighthouse section of that city — the Phanar (hence the line's future name, Phanariots).

Alexandru II and his wife, Catherine Salvarezi, were greeted as the first lord and lady of the land in Bucharest in June 1574. Having inherited or acquired many of his great-grandfather's traits, Alexandru II can be considered one of the cruelest of all Wallachian princes, if anything, more sadistic than Dracula himself. He began his rule with the wholesale slaughter of dissident boyars, many of whom were then buried at Snagov monastery. Atrocities of this kind convinced even the sultan to try to depose him in 1577, though Alexandru II was in the end poisoned by his boyars. Like Dracula, he thought he could redeem himself in the eyes of God by founding churches and monasteries — a distinctive trait of misguided religious fervor characteristic of many members of that family. Among his best known edifices are the Church of Saint Troiţa in Bucharest (now called the Church of Prince Radu), where the visitor can still admire his portrait and that of his wife.

The second ruling son of Mircea II was Peter, who had a physical deformity, hence his nickname, ''The Lame.'' He was so proud of his Hungarian ancestry that he styled himself ''of the royal Corvinus family,'' a clear reference to Dracula's wife. Since he was ambitious and anxious to rule, and given the fact that his brother Alexandru occupied the Wallachian throne, Peter got himself elected prince of Moldavia in 1574. Unlike most of the Draculas, Peter was a weak prince, a tool in the hands of the boyars. In the end he gave up the throne, preferring a comfortable exile in the west to the struggle for power. He was known largely for his amorous pursuits. Prearranged in early youth, his marriage to his first wife, Maria Amirali, was not a success. Subsequently Peter fell in love with a beautiful gypsy woman named Irina, who became his mistress. Marriage to a gypsy slave was inconceivable. Peter nevertheless had Irina freed and baptized, hence she was nicknamed Botezata (the Baptized).

When Peter sought asylum in the territories of the Habsburg emperor Rudolph II, he took his gypsy wife, Irina, with him. They were given a suitable residence in the city of Bolzano, today located in the Italian Tyrol. In less than a year our aging Lothario fell in love again, this time with a seductive Circassian lady called Maria, the lady-in-waiting at his mini-court. The jilted gypsy died of a broken heart, barely twenty-five years of age. She was buried at Bolzano in a small cemetery located near a thirteenth-century Franciscan church in the heart of this picturesque Austro-Italian city. On her tombstone one can still read the Latin inscription written by the repentant husband: ''Princess Irina, who followed her husband in exile from Moldavia and converted to his religion. She died in the twenty-fifth year of her life [that is, aged twenty-four]. I, Prince Peter, have erected this tombstone in honor of a much beloved and honest wife. She died in Christ's love and in the belief that she will be resurrected with him at the end of time.'' Two years later, this ill-fated descendant also breathed his last, following a lengthy illness — poetic justice, one might say. Not even the good clean air of Zimmerlehen Castle, which had been placed at his and his mistress's disposal by the emperor, could save him from syphilis, a traditional plague of the Draculas. Peter the Lame's body was laid to rest beside that of his gypsy wife, and on his tomb lies the following inscription: "I, Prince Peter, descendant of the royal Corvinus family of Wallachia . . . who abandoned the throne of my own will, having obtained asylum from the House of Austria, [breathed my last] on July 1, 1594." These humble words were hardly worthy of his proud Dracula ancestry.

The reader will excuse a brief aside concerning the numerous possessions inherited by Peter the Lame from Dracula himself. One was the original of the Dracula portrait now hanging at Castle Ambras near Innsbruck. On Peter's death, it fell to the local Society of Jesus, who donated it to the archduke of the Tyrol, Ferdinand II, a nephew of Emperor Charles V, protector of Peter the Lame. The archduke had a passion for collecting portraits of moral and physical degenerates, people afflicted with strange diseases or infirmities that made medical history, as well as celebrities of doubtful moral standards. Some freaks of nature, such as giants, dwarves, and wild men, even became permanent fixtures at the archduke's castle, a source of distraction for his guests. Among the portraits in his collection were ones of "the savage Baron of Müncken," with his family, living like animals in a cage, and Gregor Baci (or Baxi), a Hungarian nobleman who made medical history by surviving for a year with the end portion of a stake piercing his head through the right eye. There was the "Wolfman" from the Canary Island of Tenerife, Petrus Gonsalvus, who had a strange infirmity that covered him with hair from head to toe, late in life. His two pathetic hairy children, a boy and a girl, one blond, the other brunette, were also covered with hair, while his melancholy Dutch wife is depicted beside him with an expression of quiet resignation. What had particularly aroused the curiosity of the medical world — more specifically that of one of the physicians of the period, Dr. Felix Plater of Basel, was the transmission of hirsutism, which had never occurred before. Dracula's portrait thus came to have interesting company.

After the death of Peter the Lame, some boyars attempted to get his son Ştefăniţă (young Stephen) to assert his rights to the Moldavian throne. Holy Roman Emperor Rudolph, however, resisted that move. Instead, the boy was raised as a Catholic and placed in a Jesuit seminary in Innsbruck. The young boy was seemingly a most obedient student and devout Catholic. He became prefect of a Jesuit congregation at Innsbruck and, had he lived, would have entered the Society of Jesus after termination of the lengthy years of study. Unfortunately, he died of tuberculosis some eight years later, in 1585. He was buried beside his father and mother in the cemetery of Bolzano. A portrait of Peter the Lame and Ştefăniţă also eventually found a home in the Ambras collection. According to Nicolae Iorga, who saw Stephen's portrait, it is the most beautifully finished portrait of any Romanian prince. However, like many of the crucial souvenirs of Dracula and his period, this portrait has disappeared as mysteriously from the "monster gallery" as the original painting of Dracula. (We are fortunate, however, in having a photograph copy of it made by the great historian.)

From the death of young Stephen, the Romanian line continued in the person of Mihnea, the only son of Alexandru II and Catherine, born in 1559. Following his father's assassination in 1577, Mihnea precariously maintained himself on the throne up to 1583, when, barely eighteen years of age, he was toppled by a boyar plot. His wealthy mother's family, the Salvarezi, finally made sufficient gifts to various officials of the sultan to purchase back the throne for a period of time. However, one year after the death of his powerful mother, Catherine, the Turks deposed Mihnea for a second time. He returned to the Turkish capital and, in a desperate attempt to curry favor, adopted Islam, together with his eldest son. This is why the second Mihnea became know in Romanian history as "the Islamized." He died in Istanbul and was buried in an unmarked grave in 1601.

His only surviving son was an interesting character named Radu Mihnea, born in 1585 or 1586 in Istanbul. After completing his studies in the Turkish capital, Radu Mihnea became prince of Wallachia at a very important time in Romanian history: following the union of the three principalities, Wallachia, Moldavia, and Transylvania, under Michael the Brave (1593–1601). With interruptions, Radu Mihnea ruled no fewer than four times in Wallachia and twice in Moldavia, a remarkable success during this early period. The reason for his success, by way of contrast to his cruel or weak predecessors, was that this representative of the Dracula family was a splendid worldly Renaissance-style prince and a patron of the arts, having been brought up by the monks of Iveron at the holy mountain of Athos, in Greece. When Radu Mihnea died in 1626 at Hîrlău in Moldavia, his body was carried triumphantly to Bucharest, and he was interred at the Church of Prince Radu, begun by Alexandru II and finally completed under Radu Mihnea's own rule. Because of his loyalty to his educators, the monastery was placed under the protection of Greek monks from Mount Athos.

Radu Mihnea's only legitimate wife was Arghira Bartholomeo Minetti, an Italo-Greek, by whom he had five children, three boys and two girls, who must be considered the last surviving direct Romanian descendants of Dracula. The eldest boy, another Alexandru, was nicknamed "the Cocoon" (Coconul), because of the tender age when he assumed the throne. Alexandru Coconul ruled on two occasions: first in Wallachia from 1623 to 1627, then in Moldavia from 1629 to 1630. Two years before his death, Radu Mihnea, the boy's father, had arranged for what appeared to be a brilliant match: the bride-to-be was Ruxandra Scarlat Beglitzi, daughter of a wealthy Greco-Italian "prince maker" at Istanbul. Then, while the bridal party was traveling through Bulgaria on their way to Bucharest, Ruxandra, who was reputedly one of the most beautiful women in Istanbul, contracted the dreaded smallpox, which disfigured her for life with horrible facial scars. During the wedding ceremony she covered her pockmarked face with a veil to hide her shame. However, Alexandru soon discovered her terrible secret. For political purposes and because of the need of the Beglitzi money, Alexandru kept her hidden at court for a time. He eventually repudiated her, and she returned in disgrace to Istanbul. He never married again, nor did he have any children. After losing the throne for the second time on April 28, 1630, Alexandru the Cocoon fled to Istanbul, where two years later there disappeared from the world stage the last Romanian male descendant of the Dracula family, heirless, penniless, unpraised, and unsung, in essence a minion of the Turkish masters. We possess no details of any kind on the fate of the Cocoon's two brothers. They are certainly lost to Romanian history.

Meanwhile, Dracula's Hungarian lineage carried on the name. According to new finds gleaned by a prominent Romanian heraldist, Dan Cernovodeanu, Dracula's eldest son by his Hungarian wife, Vlad, educated at the Hungarian court, though claimant to the Wallachian throne, never actually ruled. We know little about Vlad beyond the fact that he had a son called Ladislas, whose wife, a Transylvanian lady, had properties in the area of Sinteşti, in the Banat region of southwestern Transylvania; the name of the property was thus added to his title. As befitted a member of the Corvinus family, Ladislas Dracula was appointed administrator of Castle Hunedoara, originally built by John Hunyadi's father. His two sons, yet another Ladislas Dracula, and John, were born in that castle.

It was in part in recognition for Dracula's valor and courage as a Christian crusader, and in part due to Ladislas and John's being indirect descendants of the former Hungarian royal family of Corvinus (which became extinct following King Matthias's death in 1490) that the Holy Roman Emperor, Ferdinand I, responded favorably to the petition of Ladislas Dracula and his brother John. On January 20, 1535, they were granted a patent of nobility. The emperor specifically granted this request in Vienna on January 20, "after considering the merits of his [Ladislas Dracula's] ancestors, which were recorded as being neither small nor obscure." The new coat of arms consisted of a sword covering three wolf teeth on a blood-red crest: the arms of the Báthory family. Was it conceivable that Dracula's eldest legitimate son, Vlad, had married into the Báthory family? The hypothesis of a Dracula-Báthory marriage sounded very implausible when first advanced by the novelist Raymond Rudorff in *The Dracula Archive*, published in 1972. It simply suited his plot to suggest that the most cruel woman in history, "the Blood Countess," Elizabeth Báthory, had the blood of Dracula in her veins, and that at some point in time a Báthory-Dracula marriage had been arranged. The merit of the novelist's so-called "intuition" can be ascertained only by further meticulous genealogical research. It should be remembered that Stephen Báthory, a member of that illustrious but eccentric Transylvanian Hungarian family, was Dracula's commander-in-chief during the victorious campaign that led to Dracula's third reign in 1476, also that in the Holy Roman Emperor's patent specific mention was made of "the ancient insignia of his [Ladislas Dracula's] family," which was in effect the Báthory coat of arms (three wolf teeth).

We know that the two new barons of the empire, Ladislas and John, moved from the Banat to Transylvania proper, shortly after receiving their patent of nobility. They settled in the Mureş region, which is basically Szekler country. Ladislas married a Hungarian noblewoman, Anna Vass de Czege, with properties in the Band region of Transylvania, adding yet another title to the family name (Dracula de Band). In due course a son was born, John Dracula de Band. Ladislas's brother, John, also married, undoubtedly a Hungarian, and had a son given the name of George Dracula. Both these heirs were very much involved in the affairs of the Szekler counties and townships, which were not invariably loyal to successive Transylvanian princes appointed by the king of Hungary. Both Draculas opposed the rule of Steven Báthory, who was prince of Transylvania before he became king of Poland, and an enemy of Ivan III of Russia. The Dracula family suffered adverse consequences as a result of their opposition. Since George Dracula did not marry, and John, who married a woman called Anna, had no known descendants, the male

Hungarian Dracula line dies out by the end of the sixteenth century. Recent genealogical investigation in the Cluj archives suggests that the female Dracula line continued to survive under the name of Getzi, since a Hungarian landowner, Stephen Getzi or Gyzcy, from St. Gothard, married a female descendant of Dracula. This female Dracula line continued until the seventeenth century. Some of the family had properties in the region of the Borgo Pass, Bram Stoker's location, of course, for the fictitious count's castle.

The only descendant of Dracula's extended family to have achieved international fame was Nicholas Olahus, who perhaps exaggeratedly boasted of his Dracula ancestry, describing himself: "ex sanguini Draculae" ("of the blood of Dracula"). Dracula would undoubtedly have been prouder of him than of any other direct descendant. He ended his career as primate and regent of Hungary, having in the course of his life served as secretary to the last king of free Hungary, Louis II, shortly before the ill-fated battle of Mohácz (1526), acted as principal adviser to Louis's wife, Mary, the sister of the Emperor Charles V, who became regent of the Low Countries and befriended the king of the humanists, the great Erasmus of Rotterdam. In Dracula's sense, the greatest contribution of Olahus to his country of origin was having been the first scholar of world repute who upheld the theory of the ancient origins of the Romanian people, of which he as a descendant of Dracula was justly proud.

CHAPTER 10

Beyond the Grave
The Many Faces of Dracula

The German View: A Gruesome Psychopath

THE Dracula legend, which has so often been associated with Bram Stoker's *Dracula* and horror films, did not begin in 1897, when the novel was published, but started when Dracula was alive, then gradually spread throughout the Germanic world, becoming a unique phenomenon that certainly has no parallel in Romanian history and very few in world history of that period. The story of the fifteenth-century "Dracula phenomenon," this legend beyond the grave, is a complicated one that has not as yet been pieced together fully, and it is as fascinating as any other segment of Dracula's life.

Those responsible for starting the legend were hardly gothic authors, but German Catholic monks from Transylvania, refugees who fled the country because of Dracula's brutal attempt to destroy the Catholic institutions and confiscate their wealth within his territories. Like all escapees, they had a story to tell, and, as so often happens in these instances, the story tended to exaggerate their plight.

Altogether four manuscripts, copies of an original perhaps written at the Holy Roman Emperor's court at Wiener Neustadt in 1462, which has unfortunately disappeared, have survived. The oldest manuscript was at one time housed in the library of Austrian Benedictines at the monastery of Lambach; it has since disappeared. Two recent visits to that monastery and an exhaustive examination of the vast collections in their library, along with repeated conversations with the chief archivist, have thus far yielded little information concerning what is yet another mysterious Dracula disappearance. This was due in part to the utter disorganization of this once proud monastery; it had housed hundreds of monks — now it is reduced to a mere eleven. It was fortunate indeed that a German scholar, W. Wattenbach, was able to make a copy of the Lambach manuscript in 1896 — one year before the publication of Stoker's book. The other German manuscripts are now located at the British Museum, the public library in Colmar, France, and the former Benedictine abbey of Saint Gall, the monastic library, in Switzerland, which belongs to the Catholic archbishopric of that city. All these manuscripts are copies of a presumably missing original, transcribed in meticulous and ornate calligraphy in the Low German dialect spoken by the masses (Plattdeutsch or Nierderdeutsch). The manuscripts were clearly meant for the consumption of the monks themselves, since there was no reading public at the time.

The 32 separate segments of the Saint Gall narrative, all very similar in style and composition, initially strike the reader as short horror stories, undoubtedly among the first of their kind. They seem to be designed for an unsophisticated audience. Dracula is portrayed as a demented psychopath, a sadist, a gruesome murderer, a masochist, "one of the worst tyrants of history, far worse than the most depraved emperors of Rome such as Caligula and Nero," who fiddled while Rome burned. The crimes this Dracula allegedly committed included impalement, boiling alive, burning, decapitation, and dismemberment.

With the help of the research kindly placed at our disposal by our colleague and friend Matei Cazacu of the University of Paris, a fellow Dracula hunter of many years standing, and using — with caution — the poem of Michael Beheim as a genuine historical source, we now find it possible to reconstitute the route followed by one of these persecuted monks and describe the precise circumstances of his meeting Frederick III's poet laureate, Michael Beheim, at the emperor's palace in Wiener Neustadt.

Beheim relates that in 1461 Dracula met three barefoot Benedictine monks who had accepted the reforms of Saint Bernard, and as a result had been chased out of their abbey, called "Gorrion," in the northwestern part of present-day Yugoslavia. The two co-authors undertook a journey to the Benedictine abbey located in the Slovenian mountains only about thirty miles northwest of Ljubljana, the capital of the Socialist Yugoslav Republic of Slovenia. What had struck Professor Cazacu was the similarity of the name that Beheim cites, Gorrion, and the name of the town where the abbey is located: Gornijgrad. Our visit confirmed the fact that the bishop of Ljubljana, at the time Sigismund of Lamberg, on the pretext that the monks had accepted Saint Bernard's reforms, chased them out of the monastery, and appropriated the imposing edifice for his private use. Even today, the abbey serves the archbishop of Ljubljana as a summer retreat. When the reformed monks were obliged to disperse, most of them sought refuge in Benedictine houses located in neighboring lower Austria, or Styria, just a few miles across the border. However, by a quirk of fate, three of the lay monks crossed the Danube and fled northward towards Wallachia, where they found asylum in a fifteenth-century Franciscan monastery still extant in Tîrgovişte, not very far removed from Dracula's palace.

Michael Beheim mentions the names of these monks. They were Brother Hans the Porter, Brother Michael, and Brother Jacob. The lay brothers had just returned from a journey collecting alms for their abbey from neighboring villages and were undoubtedly proselytizing, a circumstance that offended Dracula, who until his forced conversion was an enemy of the Catholic church. As they returned, we are told, "at a distance about a quarter of a league" (about a mile) from the monastery, the chance encounter took place. Addressing Brother Michael, Dracula invited him to his palace, warning him to hasten "without delay."

Michael Beheim relates the subsequent conversation that took place in the lofty throne room: "Dracula asked the monk many questions but mostly he wished (with his twisted sense of humor) to find out from the monk [whether] the many victims for whose death he was responsible and for whose soul presumably the holy man was praying, God had a place reserved for him in paradise. 'In a way,' added the prince, 'could he in the eyes of God be considered a saint, since he had shortened the heavy burdens of so many unfortunate people on this earth?' " What concerned Dracula most was the expiation of his own crimes after death — a concern also implicit in his attention to "good works" (construction of monasteries, gifts to the Holy Mountain of Athos, services for the dead). Obviously intimidated in the presence of the awesome impaler, Brother Michael attempted to assuage Dracula's fears of hellfire. " 'Sire, you can obtain salvation,' replied the monk, 'for God in His Mercy has saved so many people, even when his Divine Mercy was belatedly expressed at the moment of death.' " By such meek, hypocritical words Brother Michael undoubtedly succeeded in saving his own life. But Dracula wished additional reassurance, and he hastily called for the other friar, Hans the Porter, asking him more bluntly this time, "Sire monk, tell it to me straight, what will be my fate after death?" The latter, with the courage of his convictions, was far more forthright in his answers, and reprimanded the prince for his crimes: "Great pain and suffering and pitiful tears will never end for you, since you, demented tyrant, have spilled and spread so much innocent blood. It is even conceivable that the devil himself would not want you. But if he should, you will be confined to hell for eternity." Then, with a pause, Brother Hans added: "I know that I will be put to death by impalement without judgment for the honesty of my words devoid of flattery, but before doing so, give me the privilege of ending my sermon." Annoyed yet fearful, Dracula allowed the friar to proceed, replying: "Speak as you will. I will not cut you off." Then followed what surely must have been one of the most damning soliloquies that Dracula ever allowed anyone to utter in his presence: "You are a wicked, shrewd, merciless killer, an oppressor, always eager for more crime, a spiller of blood, a tyrant, and a torturer of poor people! What are the crimes that justify the killing of the pregnant women you have impaled? What have their little children done, some of them three years old, others barely born, whose lives you have snuffed out? You have impaled those who never did any harm to you. Now you bathe in the blood of the innocent babes who do not even know the meaning of evil! You wicked, sly, implacable killer! How dare you accuse those whose delicate and pure blood you have mercilessly spilled. I am amazed at your murderous hatred! What impels you to seek revenge upon them? Give me an immediate answer to these charges." These extraordinary words both amazed and enraged Dracula. However, he contained his anger and replied calmly, reasserting his own Machiavellian political philosophy, particularly as applied to the killing of innocent children, the mention of which had struck a raw nerve. "I will reply willingly and make my answer known to you now. When a farmer wishes to clear the land he must not only cut the weeds that have grown but also the roots that lie deep underneath the soil. For should he omit cutting the roots, after one year he has to start anew, in order that the obnoxious plant not grow again. In the same manner, the babes in arm who are here will someday grow up into powerful enemies, should I allow them to grow into manhood. I wish to destroy and uproot them. Should I do otherwise, the young heirs will otherwise easily avenge their fathers on this earth."

Hans, who knew his fate was sealed, insisted on having the last word: "You mad tyrant, do you really think you will be able to live eternally? Because of the blood you have spilled on this earth, all will rise before God and His kingdom demanding vengeance. You foolish madman and senseless unhearing tyrant, your whole being belongs to hell!" Dracula then became mad with fury. The monk had pricked him where it hurt most, in his conscience and in his misguided belief that because of his being anointed, God in His mercy would have pity on his soul. He seized the monk with his own bare hands and impaled him on the spot. Forsaking the usual procedure, by which the stake was introduced from the buttocks up, he forced the monk to lie down on the floor, and repeatedly struck him through his head. After Hans quit writhing in pain on the bloodstained floor and expired, Dracula had him hanged by a cord by the feet, head downward. He then hoisted the unfortunate wretch in front of the Franciscan monastery on a high stake. For good measure he impaled his donkey as well.

One can well imagine the effect of this gruesome sight on the remaining monks. They were terrified and abandoned their monastery. Brother Michael and Brother Jacob crossed into Transylvania and then sought refuge, like many of their colleagues from Gorrion, in various Benedictine houses in lower Austria. Since Lambach was the oldest and the most prestigious Benedictine establishment, the two lay brothers sought refuge there first. There they related their unsavory adventures to scribes, and the tales were undoubtedly colored by the anguish of a close escape. It is in this manner that the first Dracula horror story was born, at the end of 1462.

From Lambach, we know that at least Brother Jacob moved to Melk, a far larger abbey, which in fact had been founded by the monks from Lambach. This abbey, the inspiration for Umberto Eco's detective thriller *The Name of the Rose,* still sits in a commanding position on a hill dominating the Danube and is one of the most palatial Benedictine houses in Europe. It houses more than a hundred monks, who run a most prestigious secondary school. In the fifteenth century, the more elegant and elaborate quarters of the abbey were reserved for the members of the imperial family, which included the Holy Roman Emperor Frederick III. His own palace at Wiener Neustadt lay but a few miles away.

It was at Melk that Brother Jacob met other Benedictine refugees from Transylvania, whose records can still be found in the archives of the monastery. One who signed himself Johannes de Septem Castris (meaning John of the Seven Fortresses, the German name for Transylvania), was likely another Benedictine, born a year before Dracula. Eventually he became prior of the monastery. Another refugee was a certain Blasius from Bistriţa, a township that had been severely attacked both by Dracula and Mihály Szilágy. Dracula's "horrors" undoubtedly became a conversational highlight among the Romanian and German Catholic monks now attached to this grandiose monastery. Proof of their interest is the fact that the Dracula story was inserted into the history of the abbey, composed by the Romanian prior covering the events of the years 1461 to 1477. Dracula horror tales could have been read to the monks at mealtime, during which the law of silence prevailed, as a break from the habitual reading of the lives of saints.

Michael Beheim, by his name clearly of Bohemian origin, was the son of a simple weaver, born on September 27, 1416, in Sulzbach, in the German state of Württemberg. A typical ambitious young man without money, from early youth onward he led a life of travel and adventure. First, he enrolled as a soldier of fortune; he then studied music and even indulged in religious and biblical studies. His main avocation, however, was that of singing poems to the accompaniment of various musical instruments, as a minstrel at the courts of the powerful patrons he served. He also developed a gift for writing historical ballads. Beheim first worked for the powerful Count Ulrich Cilli when the latter accompanied King Ladislas V Habsburg, after the liberation of Belgrade. Following the assassination of the count, which he described in some detail in a tome entitled *Ten Poems on the History of Austria and Hungary*, he returned with King Ladislas V to Vienna, and served him as a court poet during 1457. It was sometime before the death of Ladislas that Beheim decided to switch his allegiance to the Holy Roman Emperor Frederick III, residing at his court in Wiener Neustadt. The poet witnessed the emperor's humiliation when he was besieged in his palace by the Viennese people. Beheim nevertheless remained true to his master and was duly rewarded with the post of poet laureate and imperial page — a risky proposition at a time when the insurgent populace made a habit of assassinating the imperial sycophant. After the emperor's liberation by the Bohemian king George Poděbrady, Beheim served various masters in Hungary and Bohemia. He later accompanied the emperor to Wiener Neustadt, and for some years accepted the post of court historian and troubadour. By that time Beheim's skill at writing history in verse had been refined. He had composed, among other works, a fairly accurate description of the Varna crusade, based on the eyewitness account of a volunteer in the Christian armies, Hans Mägest. As we have seen, the latter often spoke of the important role played by Dracula's father and his brother Mircea in that campaign.

Clearly Beheim's appetite had been whetted for work on yet another member of that extraordinary family. Circumstances abetted this choice of subject. It was at Wiener Neustadt that Beheim first met the perambulatory monk Brother Jacob. The monk often went marketing in

Wiener Neustadt, the most important center southeast of Melk. Knowing
that the monk was a refugee from Wallachia, Beheim deliberately sought
out Brother Jacob. The first interview apparently took place at the
imperial palace on December 12, 1462. They met many times more at an
unnamed monastery within the city. Jacob was acting as an informant,
much in the manner of Mägest for the Varna crusade, on the strange life
and deeds of Dracula. The interviews took place during the spring and
summer of 1463, continuing for roughly four months — enough time for
the accumulation of solid notes on Beheim's part. Likely the poem was
completed in the winter of 1463.

This poem represents by far the most extensive contemporary account
of Dracula's life story. Totaling 1,070 lines, the original manuscript was
deposited in the library of the University of Heidelberg, where most of
Beheim's other original manuscripts are located. They ended up there
because Beheim finished his career in the service of Count Frederick I of
Heidelberg. He entitled the poem the *Story of a Bloodthirsty Madman
Called Dracula of Wallachia* and read it to the Holy Roman Emperor
Frederick III during the late winter of 1463, like a good troubadour,
accompanying his reading with music. The story of Dracula's cruelties
was evidently to the taste of the diseased mind of the emperor, for it was
read on several occasions from 1463 to 1465 when the latter was
entertaining important guests. There is no question that deliberate
distortions were introduced into the German text by Beheim for dramatic
effect or for the benefit of the emperor's audience.

We have dwelt on the manner in which this German propaganda was
exploited by the chancellery of the Hungarian king Matthias, who needed
incriminatory material to justify Dracula's arrest and to avoid the crusade
that he had promised to the papal curia. It is likely that the Hungarian
chancellery decided to print its own version of the Dracula story, which
came close to Brother Jacob's account at Vienna in the same year
(1463) — though the actual work has never been found. Its contents,
however, were uncritically incorporated in the work of the Viennese
professor Thomas Ebendorfer, *Chronicorum regum romanorum*, one
year before his death in 1464. In addition, this very negative view of
Dracula was cited by a number of German and Hungarian humanists such
as Leonardus Hefft, a notary from Regensburg, John Pannonius, a
propagandist and panegyrist of the Hungarian king, and János Vitéz,
bishop of Oradea and later primate of Hungary. The German story,
systematically spread by the Hungarian chancellery throughout the
various capitals of Europe for propaganda purposes, was thus also

disseminated in the guise of university lectures, aimed at a relatively small and sophisticated audience.

The progressive popularization of the Dracula story, however, was due to the coincidence, in the second half of the fifteenth century, of the invention of the printing press and processes for the cheap production of rag paper. In effect, the idea of writing books for profit was introduced. The first Dracula printing destined for the public at large, undoubtedly copied from the Lambach manuscript, was produced in 1463 in either Vienna or Wiener Neustadt in the form of a news sheet, an early newspaper of sorts. It was published by a certain Ulrich Han, a disciple of Gutenberg, who had founded his German printing press at Mainz.

Following the former prince's rehabilitation and marriage into the Hungarian royal family, the anti-Dracula propaganda campaign had outlived its usefulness; King Matthias lost interest in subsidizing these hostile tracts. However, this change of attitude in no way prevented money-hungry printers from seeing the commercial possibilities in popularizing the original narratives. The continued publication of the sensational tales confirms the fact that the horror genre conformed to the tastes of the fifteenth-century reading public. We suspect that Dracula stories, in fact, became, during the late fifteenth and early sixteenth century, the first best-sellers on a nonreligious motif — under various catchy and unsavory titles such as *The Frightening and Truly Extraordinary Story of a Wicked Blood-drinking Tyrant Called Prince Dracula*. Sales of each would have been upwards of 300 to 400 books a year. (Bibles, as usual, sold more copies.) In order to prove this point conclusively, bibliophiles and eminent scholars such as our colleague Matei Cazacu, who has already completed a remarkable bibliography of all the German prints, must continue their search among the earliest of them by contacting antiquarians, bibliophiles, or simply private families who are not always aware of the precious relics in their possession.

Besides the lost Vienna print of 1463, no fewer than thirteen different ghastly fifteenth- and sixteenth-century Dracula stories have been discovered in print thus far, all of them in the various German states within the former empire. Two were published in Nuremberg by the printer Mark Ayrer in 1488, followed by another edition by Peter Wagner, and one in Lübeck by a typographer named Bartholomaeus Gothan, all in the same year. The year 1491 saw an edition printed in Bamberg by Hans Spörer; one was issued in 1493 in Leipzig by Martin Landsberg. In 1494, Christoph Schnaitter took his chance with an edition in Augsburg; Ambrosius Huber published one in Nuremberg in that same year. Interest may have been particularly strong in Nuremberg, because the older citizens remembered Dracula's father, who had journeyed there to be invested in the Dragon Order, or else because of its trade connection with Transylvania. In 1500 there was a publication by Mathias Hupfuff at Strassburg, indicating that there was also interest on the subject in this imperial city far removed from Transylvania. Hamburg, in the sixteenth century, was a Baltic city equally removed from Transylvanian trade, but a Dracula narrative by Des Iegher [Eiger] was printed there in 1502. Augsburg was linked by strong banking and financial interests with the Transylvanian Saxons; Melchior Ramminger published several editions of the story there, and he was evidently successful, since Matheus Francken reprinted the book nine years later. Jobst Gutnecht committed yet another edition to print in Nuremberg in 1521.

The business of collecting Dracula pamphlets, begun by Romanian bibliophiles such as Ion Caradja, was continued more recently in the United States by Abraham Samuel Wolf Rosenbach. He was successful in finding a rather unusual version of the Dracula story, printed in Nuremberg in 1488 with a colored woodcut of the prince on the cover, not very dissimilar from the Ambras portrait. The early printers of the fifteenth and sixteenth centuries were apparently beginning to learn the art of packaging their works with appropriate images or engravings to catch the eye of their readers. Gutenberg himself had shown the way in a book entitled *Türkenkalender*, urging the Christian world to embark on a crusade, printed in 1462, the year of Dracula's arrest. It had a striking picture on its first page, portraying gruesome Turkish atrocities, meant to encourage his readers to take up the cross. The printers of the Dracula tales, who had begun using on their title pages woodcuts of the prince modeled upon the original Ambras portrait, began, with time, and presumably to enhance sales, to take liberties with this original portrait, distorting the prince's features and throwing his face out of proportion. The Nuremberg and Augsburg prints of 1520, for instance, lend him a far sterner and more cruel countenance than the prints of the 1480s. In the Leipzig edition of 1493, Dracula, portrayed in a military outfit, looked particularly somber and ferocious. The image that appeared on the cover of the Nuremberg edition of 1499 and the Strassburg one of 1500 was especially suggestive — it referred to an incident that took place at the foot of Tîmpa Hill in Braşov. The prince is depicted having a meal; the food is laid out in front of him on a table. Around him are strung innumerable dead or dying impaled victims in a variety of grotesque positions, the poles penetrating either their chests or their buttocks.

Beside Dracula are his henchmen, using axes and hacking off the limbs of yet other victims; heads, legs, arms, and memberless torsos are strewn haphazardly around Dracula's chair. In other Dracula tracts, woodcuts with religious themes appeared alongside the horrible images, either to arouse the reader's indignation or else to induce thoughts of divine retribution. Providing a suitable ending to one Dracula tract was the image of the crucifixion of Christ, with Mary Magdalen and the Blessed Virgin standing by.

The net result of the anti-Dracula propagandistic efforts subsidized by the Hungarian king and the commercialization of the subject by German printers of the fifteenth and sixteenth centuries was the blackening of Dracula's reputation following his death. This dreadful image took root mostly in the Germanies. Popular acceptance of it was reflected in the arts. In recent years W. Peters, a German art historian from Saxony, chanced to visit an exhibition of fifteenth-century paintings at the Belvedere Museum in Vienna; he came across one of Saint Andrew in which the saint was crucified in a particularly cruel fashion. Upon examining the witnesses whom the artist had introduced as plausible personalities likely to enjoy the macabre scent, Peters recognized the features and costume of Dracula. The co-authors have visited the famed Cathedral of St. Stephen in Vienna, where, in a small chapel at the rear of the church, a series of paintings depict Christ's Calvary on stations of the cross. In one painting the unknown artist, presumably wishing to include the familiar face of someone who might enjoy the sorrowful Calvary, chose a figure very reminiscent of Dracula as a witness.

Since the Dracula stories were best-sellers in fifteenth- and sixteenth-century Germany, it was but natural that they should find their way into popular literature and history from the sixteenth century onward. Although Dracula did not figure in major works, his story was inserted in anonymous German novelettes such as *Fortunatus* (Augsburg, 1509), Valentin Schumann's *Nachtbüchlein* (1599) and in the satiric poem *Flöhaz, Weiber Traz,* by Johann Fischart (1573), in which Dracula is briefly dismissed as embodying the spirit of evil. In Hungary, Dracula's negative image also lived on, in minor compositions such as a poem printed by Gaspar of Heltai in Cluj in 1574. In this instance the author's purpose was to praise Hunyadi and defame both Dracul and Dracula, as Hunyadi's enemies. A poem that made similar reference to Dracula was written in 1560 by Matthias Nagybánki, a priest from upper Hungary, and printed in 1574 at Debrecen. Dracula was portrayed as a villain also in a play by Adam Horváth, published in 1787 at Györ, first performed at

Buda on July 15, 1790, and rewritten as a drama in three acts at Pest in 1792. An obscure Hungarian writer, Miklós Jesiku, wrote a novel, published in 1863, that takes place at the time of Dracul, in which Dracul and Dracula are confused and Dracul is thus the criminal. Finally, the Calvinist priest Ferencz Kóos published in 1890 a work in which Dracula was depicted as a villain. Like the Germans, Hungarian authors have played up the image of a basically evil Dracula.

Reinforcing the view that Dracula was an enemy of humanity were, of course, Turkish historians, who as panegyrists of Sultan Mehmed II were paid to denigrate the character of the Impaler. Their anger was heightened by the fact that Dracula at one time had been the friend and the protégé of the sultan and had betrayed this sacred trust, inflicting enormous losses, cruelties, and humiliation on his erstwhile protector. He was, in fact, the only European ruler responsible for inflicting a crushing defeat on Mehmed, and this defeat compelled the sultan to abandon the conquest of Wallachia in a shameful manner. Dracula's Turkish detractors coined the most damaging epithet of all by referring to Dracula as "Kazîglu Bey," "The Impaler Prince." The same negative standpoint was taken up by the historians, such as Michael Critobulos, among those Greeks who had made their peace with the sultan: Critobulos was richly rewarded as a result with the gift of the governorship of the island of Imbros.

Among the most respectable sixteenth-century historians who helped perpetuate the portrait of Dracula the villain was Sebastian Münster, a German scholar of some academic integrity who wrote a famous history entitled *Cosmographia universalis* (*Description of the World*) first published in Latin in 1544, in German during his lifetime, and then reprinted many times in a variety of languages, including English (1552). The work enjoyed a unique success as a kind of reference work on eastern Europe. Unfortunately, there was a temptation to repeat distortions, as he had become famous. It was in this manner that the negative image of Dracula gained a wide degree of acceptance in most of the German and Austrian universities and centers of learning. It would be a thankless task to enumerate the names of prominent historians who accepted this view. One who drew wide readership simply because he wrote the first scholarly history of the Romanian lands in German (*A History of Moldavia and Wallachia*, published at Halle in 1804) was Johann Christian Engel. In his work Dracula remained a ruthless and relentless tyrant and psychopath, a portrait that he had inherited from Münster and the fifteenth-century humanist Pannonius. Engel's viewpoint was in turn taken up by two of the foremost German scholars of the nineteenth century, Joseph von Hammer-Purgstall and Leopold von Ranke, and even a few Romanian historians educated in Germany. And when William Wilkinson, appointed English consul in Bucharest in the early nineteenth century, began looking for sources to help him compose one of the first surveys of Moldavian and Wallachian history in English, he must have used the works of these German precursors.

Gradually, however, a more positive view of Dracula also came to be expressed by some scholars. Among the first was the Polish Romantic historian Adam Mickiewicz, who lectured at the prestigious Collège de France in Paris, founded by Francis I. In a lesson devoted to Slavic literature in the 1840s, Mickiewicz astounded his students by paying unqualified tribute to Dracula ''as the ideal of a despot.'' Perhaps because of his Slavic origins, the Polish scholar had become familiar with the Russian Dracula narrative, to which we shall now turn.

The Russian Narrative: "Cruel but Just"

We have noted that German and Turkish writings about Dracula aimed in essence to blacken Dracula's reputation in the eyes of posterity. Other authors, while admitting his crimes, saw Dracula as a just ruler. The latter line of thinking, which was never publicized in the west, was the approach of a remarkable Russian diplomat, in a sense the founder of the modern Russian diplomatic system, Fedor Kuritsyn, whose reports we have often cited.

Kuritsyn was sent by his master, the grand duke of Moscow, Ivan III, with a large retinue on a mission to the west in the year 1482. Its avowed aim, rather like Peter the Great's famous embassy of 1689, was to ''open the windows'' that closed Russia to the west. In Ivan III's mind, Buda represented the gateway to Europe, where the impact of the Italian Renaissance, with its scientific inventiveness and humanistic revolution, had been fully felt. In current parlance, the Russian ambassador's mission could be labeled industrial spying. The grand duke was in desperate need of artisans, architects, artists, and professional people to help modernize Russia. For diplomatic purposes, Ivan also wished to sign a treaty of alliance with the Hungarian king against the Poles, Russia's Tatar overlords, and rival city-states such as Novgorod, which were threatening the duchy of Moscow.

Kuritsyn reached Buda in the early portion of 1482 and stayed until the beginning of 1483, spending almost a year in Hungary. In the course of his stay he met King Matthias, Bonfini the court historian, and countless officials, diplomats, merchants, and bankers. Among the many courtiers to whom he was introduced at the royal palace were Dracula's Hungarian wife and his three children, Vlad, Mihnea (the eldest son of a different marriage), and an unnamed third, who habitually resided with the bishop of Oradea in Transylvania. In the retinue of these Dracula family members there were a number of boyars who had remained loyal to their former master. It was fortunate for Kuritsyn that in his delegation there was a Transylvanian, Martinco, familiar with the Hungarian and Romanian languages, who probably acted as an interpreter. In the course of such conversations Kuritsyn's attention was drawn to the German narratives that were still circulating at court. Kuritsyn was intrigued to the point of absorption by what he heard and read about this remarkable Prince Dracula, who had died only six years earlier.

When the moment for his next diplomatic mission came, Kuritsyn made a point of making a detour to Braşov, the scene of some of Dracula's most spectacular crimes, where he spent several months. He was seeking additional details about Dracula. From Braşov he crossed the northern Transylvanian Alps at the Borgo Pass and sojourned at Bistriţa, the bailiwick of the Hunyadis, where, near his castle, Dracula's memory was also enshrined. Here Kuritsyn was introduced by a special letter of recommendation by King Matthias to the mayor in February 1483. His lengthy stay in Bistriţa gave him ample time to collect additional details provided by the Saxon citizenry, who had little fondness for the prince. Kuritsyn finally reached Suceava, the capital of Stephen the Great's Moldavia, only a day's distance from Bistriţa in the spring of 1484. The ambassador's journey to Moldavia was intended to solidify the final details of a treaty of alliance with Stephen the Great, which had been signed at Moscow a few months earlier, following the celebration of a marriage between Princess Elena, daughter of Steven's second wife Evdochia of Kiev (Ivan's cousin), and Ivan's eldest son, the future heir to the throne, yet another young Ivan. Still obsessed with the Dracula story and knowing that ten surviving veterans in Stephen's army had actually witnessed the last days of the Impaler near Bucharest, Kuritsyn took the opportunity of questioning them, as well as Stephen himself, who had known Dracula since boyhood. Another person of great interest to Kuritsyn was Stephen's third wife, Maria Voichiţa, the daughter of Radu the Handsome (who had inherited her father's good looks).

Having spent over a year in the Moldavian capital, Kuritsyn's delegation left Suceava for Moscow by way of what was then Akkerman, early in 1485, apparently unaware that the Turks had just captured that important fortress on the Danube delta a few months earlier, in August 1484. The whole embassy, its baggage, servants, and retinue, as well as numerous priceless gifts Kuritsyn had received for the grand duke from both Matthias and Stephen, were seized by a band of marauding Turkish irregular forces. A high ransom was demanded for Kuritsyn's liberation. He and his suite were detained at Akkerman from 1485 to 1486. The whole Russian party was eventually freed, through the mediation of the khan of the Tatars, Mengli Giray, a vassal of the Turks, who wished to ingratiate himself with his increasingly powerful Muscovy neighbor to the north. Kuritsyn finally reached Moscow with the drafts of the Hungarian and Moldavian alliances before September 1486.

Kuritsyn's lengthy stay on the Danube had given him ample time to study the notes he had gleaned from all Dracula sources during his stays in Hungary, Transylvania, and Moldavia. He finally put his account to paper, under a simple title bereft of any partiality. He called his report *The Story of Prince Dracula* (*Povest' o Drakule*), much in the manner of a diplomat writing a dispatch. Kuritsyn's original report has thus far never been found. But at the end of the existing copy researched by Professor McNally at the Saltykov-Shchedrin Library in Leningrad there is a brief note written by the scribe who transcribed the original, first in 1486 and later in 1490. The scribe simply signed himself "I, the sinner Eufrosin." Eufrosin was evidently a monk attached to Kuritsyn's service, who had likely accompanied him during his mission to the west. His diplomatic capacities are further attested to by the fact that he later became abbot of the Saint Cyril Monastery of the Lake, which served as the official repository of foreign correspondence (a kind of state archive) for fifteenth-century Russia. Unlike his master Kuritsyn, who had no great fondness for the power of the Orthodox Church, Eufrosin described himself simply as a "sinner." The note he inserted at the end of the manuscript was equally discordant. Eufrosin felt compelled to condemn Dracula for "preferring the pleasures of this world" as evidenced by his conversion to Roman Catholicism and said Dracula thereby deserved the punishment of hellfire.

Scholars have, so far, found no fewer than twenty different copies of this document, some of them dating back to the seventeenth and eighteenth centuries. Though not printed until the nineteenth century, the Russian Dracula narrative had a deep and long impact on Russian political theory.

Why was Kuritsyn so fascinated with the subject of Dracula? We can immediately discard motives of political propaganda (the Hungarian incentive), or making money (the objective of the German printers); Kuritsyn's report, which was never published in his lifetime, served as an internal document for the exclusive benefit of the grand duke Ivan III and his successors, to enrich the political education of the Russian head of state, much in the manner of Machiavelli's *Prince*. From this viewpoint, Dracula, far from being an irrational killer, provided an example of an effective ruler, who threatened torture and death to advance the principles of justice and good government. The boyars, rival candidates to the throne, competing independent townships, the Orthodox church, and the alien Roman Catholic church constituted so many threats that had to be repressed by terror. Kuritsyn's account taught that the principal objective of the despot must be to create a new nobility, faithful bureaucrats, and an army loyal to himself alone.

As one of the founders of the Russian state department, Kuritsyn was also anxious to teach the grand duke, by way of Dracula's example, concern for good diplomatic etiquette at his court in Moscow. He stressed the need for selecting brilliant and intelligent men who must not only be taught the rudiments of protocol, but who must also learn to weigh their words in the presence of a great leader. Kuritsyn was very conscious of the fact that Russia was still a second-rate power, not accepted as an equal within the European community of nations. Westerners still poked fun at the unusual attire of occasional official delegations from Moscow, and at international conferences, the representative of the grand duke usually came last in terms of precedence. Dracula's insistence on the need for a great prince to be respected by other powers thus struck close to home. The grand duke of Moscow had barely recovered from the abject humiliation of having to kneel in front of the Tatar khan with gifts of precious fur, as a token of submission. Taking his cue from Dracula's practice of nailing the hats on the heads of haughty ambassadors, Ivan III of Moscow now began to punish disrespectful Tatar representatives with equal severity.

Dracula's vendetta against the Catholic church and its numerous religious orders, which he considered as "papal enclaves" that subverted his own supremacy, also provided a suitable model for the ruler of the Russian state, who saw himself equally threatened by the Catholic priests and monks working in the interests of the Catholic Polish-Lithuanian kingdom. Though the Turks did not as yet directly threaten Russian power because of Moscow's remoteness from the shores of the Black

Sea, Dracula's crusade against the infidel, on which Kuritsyn laid a good deal of stress, provided a good precedent for liberating Holy Russia from the Muslim Tatar yoke. Since the Tatars occupied the Crimea, a successful liberation of that territory held incalculable potential for future Russian expansionism.

Kuritsyn and his brother Ivan Volk may also have been influenced by their study of Dracula's relationship with his own church, where he attempted to subordinate the all-powerful bishops and abbots to the will of the prince (which was not as yet the case in the duchy of Moscow). The two Kuritsyn brothers tried to implement this particular lesson in a tantalizing underhand manner aimed at obtaining long-term results. They claimed that they had become converted to an obscure sect started by a Jew from Novgorod, who wished to convert the Russian people to principal tenets of the Jewish religion. Their adherents denied the divinity of Christ, rejected the Trinity, and revived the ritualism and iconoclasm of Orthodoxy, though they advised against circumcision for fear of being discovered by the Orthodox authorities. Rather than theological controversy, Kuritsyn's interest focused on the Judaizers' revolt against the overwhelming political power and ecclesiastical privileges of the Russian Orthodox church. In order to gain adherents, the Judaizers began to criticize the many abuses practiced by the upper ecclesiastic hierarchy, the duplicitous and immoral lives of individual bishops and abbots; they denounced the monasteries that cared little for the pious works for which they initially had been intended. The secretary of state soon recognized that in an Orthodox country that was not theologically minded, the social and political aspects of the Judaizers' protest were far more significant than its religious appeal. The head of the Russian Orthodox church, together with his bishops and abbots, constituted a state within a state, which competed with the authority of the grand prince. As such the church was most alarmed at Kuritsyn's conversion to the Judaizers' point of view, which promised to undermine their own authority. On the other hand, now the head of Russia's foreign office, Kuritsyn sensed that he might use the Judaizers as a tool to convince his master, a despot by temperament, to curb the power of the Russian church, thereby gaining power himself.

In this respect, the Russian foreign minister managed quite deftly, gaining allies within the small circle of Ivan's immediate family. Having befriended Stephen the Great of Moldavia during his stay at Suceava in 1484, and as a partisan of the Moldavian alliance, what more natural than that Kuritsyn should approach Stephen's daughter Elena ''the Moldavian,'' as she was dubbed in Moscow, Ivan's daughter-in-law, who had just given birth to a son, Dmitri, who was next to her husband in the line of succession? Making use of the enormous prestige that he had gained at her father's court, Kuritsyn pointed out to Elena the overwhelming advantages that conversions to the Judaizers' point of view would entail both for her husband Ivan and their son Dmitri in order to curb the power of the Russian hierarchy. Kuritsyn was eventually successful in converting Elena to his views.

Subsequent events played admirably into the ambassador's hands. Unexpectedly, young Ivan, the grand duke's son, died in February 1498. This left Ivan III with a grave constitutional crisis over who would succeed him. He had recently married the ambitious Sophia Paleologus, a niece of the last emperor of Constantinople; she had given him a son, Basil. The problem was: Who should be his rightful heir? Dmitri, the son of Ivan's deceased son, whose mother was Elena, or the eldest son of his Byzantine wife, Sophia? Faced with the horns of this unprecedented dilemma in Russian history, Ivan III cut the Gordian knot by choosing Dmitri the son of Elena the Moldavian as his heir and co-ruler — a remarkable triumph for Kuritsyn and the Judaizers.

Kuritsyn, the all-powerful foreign minister, and his brother, Ivan "the Wolf," were certainly involved in this plot, for they knew that once Dmitri (then seventeen) was chosen as the official heir, they and Elena could dispose of him as they wished. The success of this "coup" proved that the grand duke himself had been converted to Kuritsyn's and Elena's viewpoint concerning the need to further emasculate the Orthodox church in the interest of centralized government. In addition, Kuritsyn had pointed out to his master the advantages he would derive from the confiscation of the vast landed wealth of the church; he could begin financing the armies and bureaucracies he so badly needed to found a modern Russian state. Most persuasive in Kuritsyn's arguments was the premature formulation of the doctrine of "the divine right of kings" (a theory of government that became fashionable elsewhere only two centuries later).

This view of the "divine" origin of the prince's power was derived from Dracula's view that "anointment," meaning the prince's being touched by the holy relics of some saint, was ordained by God, and thus the ruler was implicitly akin to the Divinity. Therefore God alone could judge his actions. Since Ivan III had every interest in strengthening the power of the central government against the Orthodox church, he was easily won over to this view of his own "divinity," against the arguments of Sophia Paleologus, who supported the Orthodox church.

The victory of Dracula's viewpoint was symbolized by the splendid ceremony that took place at the Cathedral of the Assumption in Moscow, when the youth Dmitri, brought up in the traditions of his mother's Judaizing friends, was recognized as Ivan's sole legitimate heir — while Sophia Paleologus and her son Basil were sent away in disgrace into house arrest.

Kuritsyn and Elena, however, had not reckoned on the unusual resiliency and talent for intrigue of her clever rival, the ambitious Sophia. She staged a remarkable comeback, by cleverly insinuating that Elena and Kuritsyn were planning a coup against the aged grand duke, hoping to poison him in order to hasten the rule of the young grandson. Ivan III, who was ill, and suspicious of his daughter-in-law, abruptly changed his mind. He had Elena and Dmitri arrested barely four years after his grandson had been crowned, while Sophia's son Basil, reemerging from his confinement, became heir.

Elena was probably murdered in jail in 1504. Her unfortunate son Dmitri lingered for another five years and died in circumstances that have never been satisfactorily explained. Equally mysterious was the end of Kuritsyn and his brother Ivan the Wolf and their Judaizing followers, who suddenly disappeared from the political scene in 1501. They were condemned by the powerful Orthodox hierarchy in a special synod convoked in 1503.

Though the power of the Russian church survived intact until the more radical reforms of Peter the Great, Dracula's political philosophy, inherent in Kuritsyn's narrative, continued to hold sway among a number of successive tsars. Particularly strong was its impact upon the deranged mentality of Ivan IV (1533–1589), nicknamed "the Terrible," the grandson of Ivan III. The Dracula narrative was probably read to the young heir to the throne during the impressionable years of childhood. His biographers inform us that one of his chief pleasures was torturing animals, particularly plucking the feathers of birds, eccentricities that match those committed by Dracula, mentioned in Kuritsyn's story. Especially after the poisoning of his beloved wife, Anastasia Romanova, in 1558, Ivan IV prosecuted the old Russian boyars whom he knew to be disloyal to his person with cruelty inspired by pages from the Dracula manuscript. Like Dracula, he chose new elements to serve him, pliable and loyal to his person. Even his infamous *strelsy* guard, responsible for his most dastardly crimes, were closely modeled on Dracula's hired armaşi. He taught disrespectful ambassadors the lessons of protocol by nailing their hats onto their heads — the precise method used by the Wallachian prince. Dracula's standards for diplomatic protocol found their way into the *Chronicle of Kazan*, drafted upon the tsar's orders. Ivan made frequent use of impalement in killing boyars and other political enemies — a method of imposing death rarely used in Russia before his time and obviously inspired by Dracula. Ivan showed Dracula's intolerance for idle priests and monks who did not live up to the moral standards of the church; he subjected them to punishments that included impalement. Contemporaries observed that he, like Dracula, enjoyed seeing men twist in pain before they died in a variety of grotesque postures.

Though the Dracula narrative continued to serve as an internal court document for some time, it lost its appeal over the course of the centuries. It became irrelevant with Russia's progressive emergence on the European stage as a major power in the era of Peter the Great. In the long run, the Russian Dracula narrative acquired the legendary and even mythical aura of the German tales. In the eighteenth century, Kuritsyn's account began to be disseminated in various popular, literary, and even religious writings.

The Romanian Tradition: Dracula the Hero

Contrary to the gruesome Dracula depicted in the German and Turkish writings and, in contrast to the "cruel but just" characterization of the prince exploited by successive Russian rulers, a much kinder picture of the Wallachian ruler has emerged in Romania. Over the course of time, his heroic traits prevailed. This process has reached the point where some western readers accustomed to the vampirization of Dracula and Romanians who have witnessed his gradual deification believed for a while that they were dealing with two different personalities. This wide gulf was accentuated by the use of different names: "Dracula" in the west and "Vlad the Impaler" in Romania. Most confused by this double identity are tourists visiting the various sites associated with Dracula's name. To the inquisitive visitor asking for additional information concerning Dracula, the response of the national tourist-office guide is invariably "Oh, you mean Vlad the Impaler!"

The sources for the Romanian story must be sought in oral folklore, since Romanian did not exist as a written language until the sixteenth century—only Church Slavonic, the language of the liturgy, was in use at Dracula's court. The original authors of the Romanian Dracula narratives, mostly peasants, came from those regions of Transylvania and Wallachia associated with places where Dracula had sojourned, where he fought, and where he prayed. As noted, the majority of the population in Transylvania spoke the Romanian language. Living among the German Saxons, they were familiar with their anecdotes and included many of them in their own sagas. In regions of mixed ethnic origins, such as Bulgaria and Serbia, similar accounts of Dracula's exploits have recently been collected by folklorists.

The manner in which these Dracula ballads began was in essence no different from the beginning of oral traditions of any people: bards, minstrels, poets, drawn from the peasant class, would convert these stories to verse and compose songs, often accompanied by the music of rough wooden musical instruments like the bagpipe or Pan pipes, on festive occasions such as Easter or on the feast days of certain saints. There was a tendency to give the ballad a local flavor, connecting it with a familiar place or landmark. Dates of succession of princes and precise locations are rarely mentioned in the collective memory of the people. As tales are repeated from generation to generation, embellishments are naturally introduced with the passing of time. However, from the viewpoint of our research, these oral traditions of the Romanian people have provided an invaluable source to close the many gaps in our study of Dracula where documents were missing.

Although folklore has to be used with caution by the historian, it can become a legitimate tool. There are perhaps more reasons to trust collective folk wisdom, because people can be more discriminating in what they chose to remember, than the memoirs of statesmen, diplomats, and kings, who often chose to deceive posterity to enhance their reputation. What is worth stressing in connection with the rich folkloric tradition Dracula has generated is the fact that, although several Romanian princes had more distinguished careers and ruled for more extensive periods of time, Dracula, whose total reign lasted barely six years, is remembered most reverently by the people.

''The Dracula Castle Epic'' first appeared in an old historical chronicle known by the name of its presumed author, Cantacuzino. Since written sources on Dracula were scanty, the earliest chronicler inserted a popular narrative concerning the construction of Dracula's castle, using the language of the Romanian people in the Slavonic script still current at that time in the seventeenth century. Cantacuzino related the story of the punishment of the citizens of Tîrgovişte for burying Dracula's brother Mircea alive. ''After the death of Prince Mircea, Prince Vlad, whose name was 'the Impaler,' came to rule. The latter built the monastery of Snagov and the castle of Poenari. He inflicted a severe punishment on the citizens of Tîrgovişte, because they committed a great injustice to one of his brothers. For these reasons he sent his retainers, who, striking on Easter Day, apprehended the husbands and their wives, their sons and daughters in their gaudy clothes, and took them to the castle of Poenari, where they toiled until their clothes fell off their backs.'' This detail is revealed in no historical document of the period. The first traveler to the region who recorded in the Romanian language the story of the construction of the famous castle was the head of the church at the time, Metropolitan Neofit. In the course of a journey he undertook to the source of the Argeş River in 1747, he discovered Dracula's abandoned fortress. He left us yet another account, gathered from the tales of local peasants, of its construction by boyar slave labor.

One of the earliest nineteenth century collectors of peasant stories who focused on the Dracula legend was Petre Ispirescu. He had little training or background for this formidable job, being an artisan in a Bucharest print shop, with little knowledge of the subject of folklore. Instead of trying to understand the local peasant dialect of the castle region, he used the slang of his native Bucharest suburb to compile a faulty transcription.

A far more accurate account of Dracula peasant stories was compiled by C. Rădulescu-Codin, who was a native of the Muscel district, in which Dracula's famous castle is located. As a village teacher, he knew the local dialect well. In recent years the Institute of Folklore in Bucharest has made a most commendable effort in organizing research surrounding the castle area, subjecting it to rigorous scientific evaluation. Most notable in this respect was the work done by a group of professional researchers, led by Mihai Pop, at the time director of the Folklore Institute, an internationally recognized authority on the subject, who has worked closely with the two co-authors. By far the best work so far published on the Dracula castle epic is owed to Georgeta Ene, who wrote a dissertation on the subject under the direction of Mihai Pop. She refers to the siege, the suicide of Dracula's wife, and Dracula's escape across the mountains, which are not otherwise documented.

Serious folkloric work at the other sites connected with Dracula's name, such as Snagov, Tismana, Bucharest, Sibiu, Bistriţa, the Danubian battlefields, Tîrgsor, Mediaş, even small villages like Ghergheni, and the many Transylvanian townships, has not as yet begun in earnest. A comprehensive survey in villages near Snagov such as was conducted at the castle site might yield important new discoveries to help resolve the problem of his death and entombment. Such a work is all the more essential, since with the current industrialization of Romania, the exodus of young people to the city, and the dying out of old people, it is increasingly difficult to find genuine ''storytellers.'' The problem has been compounded by the Romanian regime's recent decision to destroy village communities in order to make additional land available for agricultural production. This devastation of the rich cultural legacy of village life in the name of modernization is nothing less than a sacrilege.

The image of Dracula that has emerged from this vast compilation of Romanian folklore is in marked contrast to the two views we have described so far, those of the German and Russian narratives, in spite of the coincidence of many themes. The contrast is greater with reference to the German stories, in which Dracula is depicted as killing and torturing people without rational cause. Closer to the man revealed in Kuritsyn's original report, the "Romanian Dracula" is indeed a law-upholding statesman who is implacable in punishing thieves, liars, idlers, or people who otherwise cheated the state. He was a rational despot attempting to centralize his government by killing unpatriotic anarchical boyars. Dracula's crimes are further justified on a variety of counts. From a peasant point of view, because of his antiboyar stance he acquires the characteristics of a social leveler, a Robin Hood type of character, who plunders the rich in order to help the poor. In justifying his harsh punishment of unfaithful wives, there is a strong moral flavor to the stories (not fully in tune with the psyche of the Romanian people, who, like the French, are fond of "wine, women, and song"). Even the burning of the sick and the poor is condoned by the peasants on the grounds that Dracula was getting rid of undesirables and useless mouths to feed in times of war. Above all, his anti-German and anti-Turkish exploits gave a boost to the patriotic ego, in the dawn of the era of nationalism. All in all, the Romanian peasant narratives harnessed a law-and-justice theme to aid in the incarnation of a national hero. The tales were thus a powerful source for the Romantic historians of the late eighteenth and nineteenth centuries, who sought heroic and just precursors to pave the way for the establishment of an independent Romanian state. The task of transcribing the spoken language of the peasants, which was rough, ungrammatical, and limited in vocabulary, into a written language was difficult in the extreme.

Through a remarkable coincidence, the first fictional work in this new Romanian language, written by Ion Budai-Deleanu (1760–1820), was a poem that centered on Dracula. Deleanu gave his work the deceptive title of *Țiganiada* (*Gypsy Epic*). In the poem Dracula leads an army of gypsy slaves in a campaign against the Turks. The manuscript, dormant for almost a century, was finally published in its original form only in 1875.

Born not very far away from Hunyadi's castle at Hunedoara, Budai-Deleanu was educated at the College of Santa Barbara in Vienna, which was then experiencing the full bloom of the Enlightenment of the eighteenth century; and he completed his doctorate at the University of Erlau in Germany. He then settled at Lvov in Poland, where he finished his remarkable work. He consulted long-forgotten archives, among them narratives about Dracula in German, Slavonic, Latin, and Greek, as well as his native Romanian folklore. Like Homer in his *Iliad,* Budai-Deleanu sought in Romania's past a hero to be immortalized above all other heroes and found him in the person of Dracula. He refused to use the nickname Dracula, which in his view had been exposed to excessive abuse by his German detractors; Deleanu instead opted for ''The Impaler,'' initially coined by the Turks but adopted by Romanian chroniclers since. In Deleanu's presentation, the Impaler Prince, far from being a villain, appeared as one of Romania's first great national heroes, fighting the Turks, the boyars, and legions of Satan, with a motley army of gypsies and angels, in essence representing the forces of good.

Narrated in a powerful orchestration of words perhaps unequaled until the nineteenth century, this poem, which contained satire, other forms of humor, sarcasm, and also political philosophy, was critical of despotism and absolute monarchy. It was also Voltairean in its distrust of men and revolutionary in its attacks on the boyars and the establishment. In this respect, Dracula was being used for purposes entirely contrary to those of the Slavonic narrative, which aimed at the justification of absolute monarchy.

The whole plot of the German stories and of Bram Stoker's famous novel is turned topsy-turvy in Deleanu's work, since the vampires and other evil spirits are Dracula's enemies. Deleanu, in fact, introduced, in written form, the Romanian equivalent for the word *vampires:* the *strigoi,* derived from the Latin word *strix,* meaning a hag or goblin. *Vampire,* adopted in English and in other western languages, is a word used by the Slavic peoples. In the poem Deleanu had these vampires (*strigoi*) ''fly in the direction of Retezat toward a certain mountain that lies between Wallachia and the Banat,'' a moonscaped ridge 100 miles distant from the authentic location of Castle Dracula. Deleanu also introduced the female vampire to his readers, creatures ''who fly at nightfall when beautiful ladies take their walks, breaking people's bones.'' Such evil spirits, of which the vampire is but one species, were of course familiar to Deleanu from his knowledge of the superstitions of the Romanian people of Transylvania. (In the course of time, such beliefs became the subject of scholarly investigations by a succession of English and other foreign travelers to Transylvania. Perhaps the most famous among them was the Scottish lady Emily Gerard, whose works were consulted by Bram Stoker in the composition of *Dracula.*)

When the current of nationalism that had started in Transylvania crossed the mountains into the principality of Wallachia, it was natural that the heroic figure of Dracula should in turn be exploited by Romanian nationalists to give precedence and paternity to the movement for independence. Most of the Romantic historians (G. Lazăr, N. Bălcescu, I. Eliade Rădulescu, Aaron Florian, A. Treboniu Laurian) responsible for organizing the revolution of 1848 (which aimed at securing total freedom from Turkish and Russian domination) took part in romanticizing Dracula's deeds and explaining away his crimes.

Beyond having nationalist motives, the men of the generation of 1848 were interested in presenting Dracula's career in literary rather than historical form. Since it was dangerous to teach Romanian history in the schools at a time when the country was under combined reactionary Russian and Turkish control, plays, poems, and novels with nationalistic themes were an effective, permissible way of reaching a wider audience. For instance, the public was bound to recognize the obvious message contained in Dracula's spectacular anti-Turkish campaign in 1462. Under cover of writing literature, one could successfully overcome the severe Russian censorship.

The Dracula heroic theme is best exemplified by the poets of the period. One of the most prominent figures of the generation of 1848, Dimitrie Bolintineanu (1819–1872), sounded the trumpet call, praising Dracula's military valor. In highly stylized but beautifully versified rhymes, and with a sense for the musical sounds of the Romanian language, Bolintineanu recalled the highlights of Dracula's career in his "Battles of the Romanians." The episode of the nailing of the turbans to the heads of the Turkish envoys is dismissed in the following manner:

> The assembly of soldiers
> Shout with people:
> "Long live the Impaler!"
> The terrified boyars jump through the window
> While Dracula drives spikes into the Turkish
>   envoy's heads.

In 1863 Bolintineanu wrote in the same nationalistic vein a historical novel based on Dracula's life.

However, the greatest of all Romanian poets of the late nineteenth century (one of the few whose works have been translated into English) was undoubtedly Mihai Eminescu (1850–1889), whose life was tragically cut short at the age of thirty-nine. Eminescu represented an isolated voice crying in the wilderness, protesting the amorality of politics, the perfidy of politicians, the faithlessness of diplomats, the crass materialism and iconoclasm of the literary men who took in vain the name of heroes of the past. Like Hamlet, he felt that times were out of joint. In despair, in a great historic ballad called *The Third Letter*, he appealed to the giants of old to rise from the dust under which they had been laid to rest in order to regenerate Romanian society and political life. They alone, he said, understood the true meaning of patriotism and had shown genuine love of the fatherland. The poem opens by recalling the manly virtues and military valor of Wallachia's early medieval princes, notably Prince Mircea the Old, Dracula's grandfather, who, when summoned to surrender his country to the great Sultan Bayezid, then at the height of his power, defied him at the Battle of Rovine (1394) with the following proud words:

> *"Oh,*
> *But the man you see here stand*
> *Is no common mortal; he is Prince*
> *of the Romanian land."*

Eminescu immortalized Vlad with an often quoted stanza. He recalls the great Dracula from the grave to save the Romanian nation and asks him to do away with the Philistines in the land:

You must come, O dread Impaler, confound them to your care.
Split them in two partitions, here the fools, the rascals there;
Shove them into two enclosures from the broad daylight enisle 'em,
Then set fire to the prison and the lunatic asylum.

Only during recent decades in Romania has Dracula made a full comeback even among Socialist historians. Heretofore, Romania's historians had dismissed Dracula in only a sentence or two along the lines of "cruel but heroic and just."

The occasion chosen for this belated awakening of a scholarly interest was the celebration of the five hundredth anniversary of Vlad's death, "Dracula Year," proclaimed in 1976. Panegyrics, commemorative eulogies, discussion panels, lead articles in the press and in scholarly journals (the popular *History Magazine* dedicated its entire issue of November 1976 to Dracula), radio and television commentaries, and films were devoted to the subject. Even Romania's president Ceauşescu invoked the memory of Vlad. A special commemorative stamp was issued. Dracula became a national hero par excellence, one who defended the nation's independence against overwhelming odds — a kind of George Washington of the Romanian people, who had been maligned by his political enemies in the west, from his own period to our times, when he had finally degenerated into a vampire. In the view of some Romanian authors, the progressive vampirization of Dracula by western novelists and movie producers had all been a "Hungarian plot," originally inspired by King Matthias, continued by Vambery, Stoker's Hungarian informant, and given its most masterful stroke by Bela Lugosi, a Hungarian who adapted his name from the town where he was born, Lugoj, in the Banat region of Transylvania (his real name was Béla Ferenc Blasko).

One last factor in the extraordinary Vlad/Dracula dichotomy is Romania's reaction to Stoker's best-selling novel, which has been printed in virtually every European language and many Asian ones. To date, the book has not been translated into Romanian — nor have Lugosi-style vampire films been shown in Bucharest. Even the National Tourist Office, in its legitimate attempt to earn hard currency by encouraging the so-called Dracula Tours, has decided to divide Romania into two segments — the southern and western tiers, Wallachia and southern Transylvania, are "Vlad country," associated with genuine historic sites connected with the Romanian prince: the castle on the Argeş, the monastery of Snagov, the palace of Tîrgovişte, et cetera. Beautiful sound-and-light spectacles have been held at such locations at night. Ruins like these are as sacred to the Romanians as the Washington Monument or Plymouth Rock to Americans and the tours are aimed at the serious-minded history buffs. For the vampire hunters — and this includes many Dracula societies that have flourished in the west — the government has created an artificial Disneyland-style vampire scenario centered in Stoker's Borgo Pass region in northeastern Transylvania, where the plot of the famous book was laid. Like Jonathan Harker, Dracula's solicitor's clerk in the novel, a visitor can book a room at the Golden Crown Hotel in Bistriţa, which has been rebuilt; there he can enjoy "paprikash chicken" and "Mediasch" wine, which is fermented not far away, and then proceed to the not-so-sinister Borgo Pass in quest of the ruins of an insignificant castle that once belonged to Dracula. This was the concession the Socialist government of Romania was willing to give to what they considered decadent western vampirologists, on the condition that they not fraternize too closely with the local population, many of whom still believe in the dreaded *strigoi*.

CHAPTER 11

Stoker's Count Dracula, the Vampire

T HERE can be no question that the best-selling novel *Dracula*, published by the Anglo-Irish writer Bram (Abraham) Stoker in 1897 (and published in no fewer than 85 editions between 1897 and 1971) was responsible, after a prolonged period of silence, for giving the Romanian prince a kind of fame he had never enjoyed in the fifteenth century, projecting him onto the world stage. Though historically this new image can be linked to the earlier traditions of the German stories associated with the historical Dracula — which, as noted, were best-sellers of a kind during the fifteenth century — it is Stoker's fictitious creation, the ultimate metamorphosis of the many images of Dracula, that has most successfully anchored itself in the public mind and immortalized that name, largely through the mass media and forms of communication not widely available during the earlier period.

Even though it is a work of fiction, some of the strength and many details of Stoker's creation are derived, as we suggest in our prologue, from what can be described only as a prolonged period of study and research — not least about Dracula the man — extending over some six years, from 1890 to 1896, before the final draft was completed in Scotland at Cruden Bay a year before publication. Evidence for these facts was gathered by the two co-authors, who were the first to discover Stoker's notes (some 75 pages in all) during a visit to the Philip H. and A. S. W. Rosenbach Library at Philadelphia. (Others, such as Professor Phyllis Roth of Skidmore College, Dr. Joseph S. Bierman, and Bernard Davies, president of the English Dracula Society, have since researched these same documents.) Pending possible new finds in the possession of the Stoker family (Stoker's granddaughter, Anne Dobbs [née Stoker] is now the honorary president of the Bram Stoker Society founded at Trinity College, Dublin, in 1980), the existence of an original manuscript remains a subject of speculation. In its absence, the notes available at the Rosenbach Library provide invaluable insights into some of Stoker's sources of information, the general conception of the novel, and the various stages of adaptation it underwent. In addition to extensive bibliographies on vampirism and the occult, there are copious notations on such diverse subjects as the appearance of Whitby Abbey and the cemetery (Stoker was particularly interested in sailors who died in nautical disasters), countless meteorological observations about tides, winds, et cetera, a few remarks about and sketches of the symptoms of insanity garnished from one of Stoker's brothers, Sir William Thornley Stoker, a former president of the Royal College of Surgeons, and a short bibliography dealing with eastern European history.

To understand the significance of this detailed research, one must first place *Dracula* within the general context of the gothic novel and trace Stoker's indebtedness to that tradition, which dates back to Horace Walpole's *Castle of Otranto* (1764) and Ann Radcliffe's *Mysteries of Udolpho* (1794). Unlike Mary Shelley, who kept extensive bibliographies of gothic works she consulted for *Frankenstein*, many of them loaning some element to her novel, Stoker makes no specific acknowledgment in his notes to any of his English, Irish, or French gothic precursors.

According to a story known to every English schoolboy, the famous foursome of Lord Byron, Percy Bysshe Shelley, Mary Shelley, and Byron's doctor, John Polidori, were confined because of heavy rainstorms to Villa Diodati in the small village of Cologny outside Geneva. On the particularly stormy night of June 16, as a thunderbolt of lightning struck down a tree outside, Lord Byron began reading ghost stories in his stentorian and dramatic manner, while Polidori was discussing the latest inventions in the field of electricity. Under the impact of copious doses of the drug laudanum (opium), Lord Byron issued his famous challenge, daring all assembled to write a truly terrifying story that would frighten generations to come. Mary Shelley eventually wrote *Frankenstein*. With relevance to the vampire, Byron's young lover Polidori, taking his cue from a vampire plot that Byron had sketched out but never finished (derived from his various readings on vampirism in Arab countries and China and his experiences with folkloric superstitions in Albania), published the first vampire story in the English language, *The Vampyre*, in April 1819. The story, wrongly attributed to Byron (Goethe thought it was the best thing that Byron had ever written), led to a vampire craze in English and French theaters during the 1820s. Operettas and stage plays were quite popular. The German composer Heinrich Marschner wrote *Der Vampyr* (*The Vampire*), a successful opera that may have influenced Richard Wagner.

Vampire serial novels became the rage in English popular literature during the 1840s. The most famous was *Varney the Vampire or, The Feast of Blood,* written by Thomas Peckett Prest in 1847. Varney is a reluctant vampire aristocrat who sucks the blood from young Flora Bannerworth, captures her lover, and inadvertently brings havoc wherever he goes. The novel ends spectacularly when Varney throws himself into the hissing mouth of Mount Vesuvius.

The vampire novel *Carmilla*, by the Irish author Joseph Sheridan LeFanu (1814–1873), published in 1871, was the most important literary inspiration for Stoker's *Dracula*. It is a story of a strange, almost lesbian, relationship between the young heroine Laura and the mysterious countess, Carmilla, who turns out to be a female vampire. When Carmilla's body is discovered in her crypt, the traditional wooden stake is driven through her heart to pin her to her coffin and she is beheaded. Her friend Laura remains haunted by the countess and imagines hearing the soft footfall of Carmilla coming to see her again. LeFanu's story made a deep impression on Stoker, who was then an unpaid Dublin theater critic.

Two foreign works in particular could have drawn Stoker's attention to the vampire's folkloric connections with Romania and Transylvania. One was Alexander Dumas's *Mille et un fantômes* (*A Thousand and One Ghosts*), published in 1849 under the initial title *Les Monts Carpathes* (*The Carpathian Mountains*), which centered on the castle (located not very far from the site of that of Stoker's vampire count) of a Prince Brancovan. A member of that princely family had dealings with a vampire who refused to stay in his grave. Only five years before the publication of *Dracula* there appeared Jules Verne's *Château des Carpathes* (*Castle of the Carpathians*), published in Paris in 1892. It is the story of wicked ghosts who haunt the Jiu Valley of Transylvania. Like Stoker's *Dracula*, the novel has references to early princes in Romanian history, notably to Radu I, one of Dracula's precursors, and to his palace at Argeş.

Another important influence on Stoker that cannot be ignored is his friendship with Sir Richard Burton, the prominent orientalist. Burton had translated into English the *Thousand Nights and One Night,* which included a tale about a vampire originating in Hindu sources. It is fascinating to note that in his *Personal Reminiscences of Henry Irving,* about the famous Shakespearean actor for whom Stoker worked most of his life, Stoker wrote how impressed he was not only by Burton's accounts but also by his physical appearance — especially his "canine teeth." Sir James George Frazer's *Golden Bough*, which mentions the "walking dead," and Stoker's friendship with fellow vampire specialists, such as members of the "Hermetic Order of the Golden Dawn," though secret by their very constitution, are obviously relevant in gauging his fascination with the occult.

There are innumerable other works on the gothic and/or vampire traditions that Stoker might have read, though we have no proof of such readings from gleanings in his notes that are at the Rosenbach Library. The notes are precious, because we can follow the progression of Stoker's research in a more or less precise fashion by observing the letterheads of the various hotel stationeries or other papers on which he took them down, such as the Stratford Hotel in Philadelphia (where he stayed with Sir Henry Irving while on his tour of the United States) or the Lyceum Theatre in London, which Stoker managed for Irving. Quite apart from precise citations from books, Stoker seems to have jotted ideas as they came during his travels or in his idle moments away from managing the theater or going on tours. Most of his period of study and perhaps the preliminary outlines for the book were completed during his summer holidays at Whitby in Yorkshire, where he went to escape the London heat in 1890, 1892, and finally in 1896, upon his return from America. He then began writing the final draft, which was completed, as we said, at Cruden Bay in Scotland. (From our experience, at least until a few years ago, the landlady of the house that Stoker rented in Port Erroll, that quaint Scottish town, was still willing to relate anecdotes about the eccentric Englishman's daily program and behavior.) The length of time it took to write the novel provides additional proof of the gradual adaptations it underwent and the seriousness with which the author digested the many facts he had accumulated in the course of his research.

Stoker's primary interest was the vampire and the occult, and the list of books he consulted on that theme, available in his notes at the Rosenbach Library, is extensive. It includes titles such as Sabine Baring-Gould's *Curious Myths of the Middle Ages* and *The Book of Were-Wolves*; this author is perhaps best known for having penned the words to that rousing hymn "Onward, Christian Soldiers."

Stoker's interest in vampirism and the supernatural was by no means restricted to the traditions of Transylvania. Indeed, the readings attest to the worldwide origins of vampire superstitions, spanning not only continents but centuries as well. Dr. Van Helsing makes this point clear in his halting English: "Let me tell you, he [the vampire] is known everywhere that men have been. In old Greece, in old Rome; he flourish in Germany all over, in France, in India, even in the Chersonese; and in China, so far from us in all ways. . . ."

Progressively, however, Stoker began to focus on the superstitions of eastern Europe in general and Transylvania in particular. This narrowing tendency can be traced from copious notes from his reading of yet other books, mostly travelogues and pseudoscientific books dealing with folklore. Most extensive of all were those from Emily Gerard de Laszowska (a Scottish lady who had married a Polish-born Austrian officer), who wrote an article entitled "Transylvanian Superstitions" for the *Nineteenth Century Magazine* (of July 23, 1885, published simultaneously in London and New York) — a periodical to which Stoker also contributed articles. Her work was later expanded into a widely read two-volume travelogue entitled *The Land beyond the Forest*.

With few exceptions, most of Stoker's information on Transylvanian vampirism and other superstitions were transcribed literally from Emily Gerard's article. Comparing several crucial passages from that book with the novel's content on the parallel subject will make our point quite clear. Describing many forms of evil spirits thought to exist among the Romanians of Transylvania, Gerard writes: "More decidedly evil, however, is the vampire *nosferatu*, in whom every Romanian peasant believes as firmly as he does in heaven or hell. The very person killed by a *nosferatu* becomes likewise a vampire after death, and will suck the blood of other innocent people till the spirit has been exorcised . . . by opening the grave of the person suspected and driving a stake through the corpse. . . . In very obstinate cases it is further recommended to cut off the head and replace it in the coffin with the mouth filled with garlic, or to extract the heart and burn it, strewing the ashes over the grave" (p. 142). In the novel, Van Helsing, when referring to Lucy's vampirization, makes the same point, warning her fiancé in his poor English: "Last night when you open your arms to her, you would in time, when you had died, have become *nosferatu*, as they call it in Eastern Europe, and would all time make more of these Un-Deads that so have fill us in horror." (In strict Romanian folkloric terms, *nosferatu* refers to the devil [*necuratul*] rather than the vampire, whom the peasants refer to as *strigoi* or [feminine] *strigoaică*.)

Stoker also picked out of Gerard's book the materials on the fearsome devil's school in the mountains, which some of the Draculas attended, according to the novel. In Gerard's essay one reads, "They learned the secrets in the Scholomance, amongst the mountains over Lake Herman-stadt, where the devil claims the tenth scholar as his due." Gerard continued, ". . . I may as well mention the *Scholomance*, or school supposed to exist somewhere in the heart of the mountains, and where all the secrets of nature, the language of animals, and all imaginable magic spells and charms are taught by the devil in person. Only ten scholars are admitted at a time, and when the course of learning has expired and nine of them are released to return to their homes, the tenth scholar is detained by the devil as payment, and mounted upon an *Ismeju* [the correct Romanian spelling is *Zmeu*, another word for dragon] he becomes henceforward the devil's aide-de-camp. . . . A small lake, immeasurably deep, lying high up among the mountains to the south of Hermanstadt, is supposed to be the cauldron where is brewed the thunder, and in fair weather the dragon sleeps beneath the water" (p. 136). Again, Stoker has Van Helsing state in the novel: "The Draculas were, says Arminius, a great and noble race, though now and again were scions who were held by their coevals to have had dealings with the Evil One. They learned his secrets in the Scholomance, amongst the mountains over Lake Herman-stadt, where the devil claims the tenth scholar as his due." This reference to the Scholomance is derived from the Romanian word *Şolomonari*, meaning "students of alchemy." It is a corruption of the name Solomon, the wise judge in the Bible, whom legend turned into an alchemist. Such students were thought to study and control the forces of nature. Near Sibiu (Hermannstadt), in the mountains close to the town of Păltiniş, there is a spot named Pietrele lui Solomon ("Solomon's Rocks"). That is where wandering students traditionally took oaths to uphold their scholarly way of life.

Referring to Emily Gerard's article, Stoker notes that perhaps "the most important day in the year is the feast day of St. George, 23rd of April, the eve of which is still frequently kept by occult meetings taking place at night in lonely caverns or within ruined walls, and where all the ceremonies usual to the celebration of a witches' Sabbath are put into practice. . . . This same night is the best for finding treasures. . . . On the night of St. George's Day (so say the legends) all these treasures begin to burn, or, to speak in mystic language, to 'bloom' in the bosom of the earth, and the light they give forth, described as a bluish flame resembling the color of lighted spirits of wine, serves to guide favored mortals to their place of concealment" (p. 134). Once again, Stoker incorporated these ideas into his book, when an old lady at the hotel in Bistriţa warns Harker, "It is the eve of St. George's Day. Do you not know that to-night, when the clock strikes midnight, all the evil things in the world will have full sway?"

According to many traditions, evil spirits are thought to hold sway on the eve of important holy days. Halloween, an ancient Celtic devotion to dead ancestors, was transformed by Christianity into the eve of All Saints' Day, hence the name All Hallows' Eve, popularly pronounced as Halloween; on this night, like Saint George's Eve, goblins are thought to roam and cause mischief.

On May 8, Harker notices about Dracula that there was "no reflection of him in the mirror!" The notion that vampires do not cast any reflection in a mirror is authentic Romanian folklore. Emily Gerard cites it in *The Land beyond the Forest*. The basic idea behind it is that the vampire has no normal human soul and hence cannot have the usual appearance in a mirror.

In his very unscientific vampire search, Stoker quite freely mixes authentic superstitious beliefs about various creatures, as when he ascribes werewolf characteristics to the vampire, which, though related, is quite distinct from the werewolf in Romanian folklore. When Harker meets Count Dracula on the night of May 5, he fixates on Dracula's "peculiarly sharp teeth," which "protruded over the lips." He is also struck by his hands: "Hitherto I had noticed the back of his hands as they lay on his knees in the firelight, and they had seemed rather white and fine; but seeing them now close to me, I could not but notice that they were rather coarse — broad, with squat fingers. Strange to say, there were hairs in the centre of the palm. The nails were long and fine, and cut to a sharp point." Characteristics such as these were freely borrowed by Stoker from Sabine Baring-Gould's *Book of Were-Wolves*, where the author, referring to a so-called authentic werewolf case, writes as follows: "The teeth were strong and white, and the canine teeth protruded over the lower lip when the mouth was closed. The boy's hands were large and powerful, the nails black and pointed like bird's talons" (p. 87). And again: "A werewolf may easily be detected, even when devoid of his skin; for his hands are broad, and his fingers short, and there are always some hairs in the hollow of his hand" (p. 107). With great poetic license, Stoker adapts these werewolf characteristics to his vampire count.

There are other instances of borrowings from sources, such as Stoker's citing the vampire's control over the animal world, particularly horses, who "smell blood," a reference derived from E. C. Johnson's *On the Track of the Crescent*. Examples such as these are sufficient to demonstrate the variety of themes drawn upon by Stoker in creating his composite vampire.

Beyond written sources, Stoker's vampire creation was also inspired by experiences in his life. He had to spend the first seven years of his life on his back in bed because of some mysterious childhood ailment that was never properly diagnosed. It is not by chance that interest in strange undiagnosed disease permeates the entire novel *Dracula*. The symptoms of the vampire attack remain undiagnosed for a good part of the novel. In addition, Stoker's confined existence was similar to that of the vampire, since he was as bound to his bed as Count Dracula to his coffin. Stoker tells us in his *Reminiscences of Henry Irving* that when he was a child, he never knew what it was like to stand up straight. Later in life, Stoker's mother told him horrifying stories about the cholera epidemic that had taken place in County Sligo when she was a child. She referred to this in a letter to her son in 1872: "One house would be attacked the next was spared. There was no telling who would go next, and when one said good-bye to a friend he said it as if forever. In a very few days, the town became a place of the dead. No vehicle moved except the cholera carts or doctors' carriages. Many people fled, and many of these were overtaken by the plague and died by the way." Count Dracula's attacks, as described by Stoker, resemble those of the plague, and they are just as unstoppable. (The similarity between the spread of vampire attacks and the Black Death, the dreaded bubonic plague, was exploited in the classic silent movie *Nosferatu*, the first Dracula film ever made, and also in the latest *Nosferatu*, by Werner Herzog. The rats seem to spread the Black Death in both of those movies, whereas it is the vampire who is in reality killing the people.)

Although he makes no reference to it in his notes, Stoker was always interested in Irish folklore. Long before *Dracula*, he wrote a series of horror tales, based on Celtic themes, for children. He spent time in the west of Ireland, his mother's home country, where Gaelic and the old traditions still held on in his day. The word for bad blood in Gaelic is *drochfhuil* and the genitive singular is *drochfhola*, which is pronounced very much like the word *Dracula*. Belief in the returning dead was very strong in Ireland. Stones were piled over the graves of the dead to try to discourage them from rising out of the ground.

However, in the last resort, it was the gloomy atmosphere of the Yorkshire moors, with which he was well acquainted from his many summer vacations, that seemed ideally adapted to the purposes of his gothic novel. (It had served the Brontë sisters equally well.) He was particularly struck by the stark and forbidding rocky coastline surrounding Whitby Harbour, a resort dominated by its Gothic cathedral, which overlooked a very desolate cemetery, where Stoker was fond of strolling, while he examined the inscriptions on sailors' tombs. By comparison, Gerard's descriptions of the Transylvanian countryside, which Stoker never visited, seem quite cheery.

Most relevant to our biography of the historical Dracula are Stoker's references to authentic Romanian history and geography. His concern for authenticity is demonstrated by two separate references incorporated in the novel to consultations with his "friend Arminius [Vambery]," professor at the University of Budapest, references to the library of the British Museum, and allusion to a document in which Dracula is described as a "vampyre." How serious or extensive was Stoker's interest in the life story of the authentic Prince Dracula? Judging from his notes and citations of the books in the Rosenbach foundation holdings, Stoker's knowledge of Romanian history and of Dracula in particular was sketchy, to say the least, and some of it was clearly erroneous. Other historical errors, however, were deliberately manufactured by him—for the search for historical truth was hardly his concern as a novelist. He did, nevertheless, make a serious and unique effort to give his novel and his principal character a definite historical reference point. Stoker's historical gleanings were principally derived from the following books of unequal worth: Nina Elizabeth Mazuchelli, *Magyarland* (London, 1881); Andrew F. Crosse, *Round about the Carpathians* (London, 1878); E. C. Johnson, *On the Track of the Crescent* (London, 1885); Charles Boner, *Transylvania: Its Products and People* (London, 1865); and William Wilkinson, *Account of the Principalities of Wallachia and Moldavia with Political Observations Relative to Them* (London, 1820). Of these books those of Charles Boner, William Wilkinson, and Major William E. C. Johnson can be described as more or less accurate history. Wilkinson, who liked to describe himself as English consul in Bucharest, though he was in point of fact merely the representative of the English Levant Company, wrote the first substantive survey of Romanian history in English, with a remarkable eye for detail, very different from other, superficial travelogues. In the historical introduction, and particularly referring to Dracula's period, Wilkinson adopted the largely negative German interpretation popularized in academic circles by Münster's *Cosmographia,* which had been translated into English and by that time had become a standard historical reference work. Dracula was described therein, essentially in the manner of the early fifteenth-century German pamphleteers, as an evil personality.

Stoker's acquaintance with Wilkinson's work came about in an accidental manner in August 1890, during his frequent trips to the local library at Whitby. Intrigued by the title, he checked the book out. The fact that it is the only work mentioned by a specific call number in Stoker's notes clearly indicates that he consulted the book repeatedly during subsequent visits in 1892 and 1895. No fewer than ten citations from Wilkinson's book have been incorporated into the novel.

Far more to the point, however, it was Stoker's reading of Wilkinson's book that was responsible for changing the title of the novel and giving it the specifically Romanian veneer concerning the historical Dracula. Until the summer of 1890, Stoker had been influenced chiefly by LeFanu's vampire story *Carmilla*. He had, in fact, chosen Austrian Styria as the locale for a book he entitled "The Wampyre Count," a takeoff on Polidori's *Vampyre*. This preliminary sketch of the novel was later published as a special essay in *Bedside Companion: Ten Stories by the Author of Dracula*, and is inserted as a first chapter in a few editions of *Dracula*. However, fascinated by the unusual feminine ring of the name *Dracula*, and no doubt influenced by the evil reputation of the prince that Wilkinson had reviewed, Stoker, in a moment of inspiration duly recorded in his notes, struck out the name "Count Wampyre" from the title and substituted the words "Dracula-Dracula-Count Dracula," as if he were savoring the sound of the name. Thus both Transylvania, the home of the vampire that he had adapted for his purposes from Emily Gerard's book, and Dracula, taken over from William Wilkinson, suddenly became magic words, instrumental in the final success of the book.

Most of the other citations that Stoker took over from Wilkinson's book were incorporated in one manner or another in the novel. They included some accurate historical details. Thus, Stoker knew that the name Dracula was that of the family, being applicable to both father (Dracul), son (Dracula), and his descendants: that is, the other "Draculas." Stoker cited the fact that Ladislas (Ladislas III, king of Poland) had embarked on the Varna crusade against the Turks and that "four thousand Wallachians under the command of Dracula's son (Mircea) joined him." He was informed of the details of Hunyadi's defeat at Varna; he learned of the murder of Dracula's father and his replacement by Prince Vladislav II (mistakenly identified by Wilkinson as Dan). As noted, in the prologue to the novel, Stoker used the defeat of the Hungarians and Vladislav II at the second battle of Kosovo, an episode that led to Dracula's first reign in 1448. Stoker also learned from Wilkinson that when Sultan Mehmed II was "occupied in completing the conquest of the islands in the Archipelago" the Wallachians found that this "afforded them a new opportunity of shaking off the yoke [of the Turks]. . . . Dracula, did not remain satisfied with mere prudent measures of defense; with an army he crossed the Danube and attacked the few Turkish troops that were stationed in his neighborhood; but his attempt, like those of his precursors, was only attended with momentary success." This is a clear reference to Dracula's Danube winter campaign of 1461, which found its way into the novel. Wilkinson adds that the sultan replaced Dracula with his brother Radu, another instance of historical fact, incorporated later into the fiction. We could find other examples of authentic history derived from Wilkinson which were inserted into the novel; mention of the Hungarian defeat at Mohácz in 1526, for one; a vague allusion to the victories gained by Michael the Brave, an indirect descendent of Dracula through his half-brother Vlad the Monk, who "defeated the Turks on their own ground," over a century after the historical Dracula's death, being yet another example.

Most puzzling, on the other hand, are Stoker's references to Dracula's so-called Szekler — Stoker uses the term *Szekely* — descent, clearly a historical error that requires some comment. Judging both from the notes and the contents of the novel, there is no question that Stoker was quite fascinated by the destructive power of Attila the Hun's inroads deep into western Europe in the fifth century and intrigued by the relationship of the Huns with both the Hungarians and the Szekler tribes of Transylvania. He derived most of this information from A. F. Crosse's *Round about the Carpathians* and E. C. Johnson's *On the Track of the Crescent*. However, Stoker also incorporated some material from Nina Elizabeth Mazuchelli's two-volume *Magyarland*. In order to give some respectability to her account, Mazuchelli was fond of quoting the prominent Oxford University Orientalist Max Müller (1823–1900), with whom Stoker later engaged in a correspondence, to support her views concerning the origins of the Szeklers: "Max Muller, by the unerring guide of language, has traced the original seat of this interesting people to the Ural mountains which stretch upwards to the Arctic ocean; and pointing out the close affinity the Magyar tongue bears to the idiom of the Finnish race spoken east of the Volga, declares that the Magyars form the fourth branch of the Finnish stock, viz. the Ugric" (p. 45). But why should Stoker be so insistent on the vampire count's so-called Szekler descent?

One might answer, Why would Stoker care about authenticity on this point? He was, after all, a novelist, not a historian, using historical references in his plot only to gain a certain flavor of authenticity or else to derive for his central character the kinds of attribute that fitted best. What would have more dramatic impact than to make Dracula an indirect descendant of Attila, a man wicked enough to be known in history as "the scourge of God"? Stoker needed a pedigree of evil for his vampire count.

However, it is also possible to probe the missing Szekler connection a little further by tackling Stoker's problematic relationship with the famous Hungarian orientalist, philosopher, and professor of Eastern languages, Arminius Vambery (Hermann Vamberger), whose role is highlighted in the novel by Professor Van Helsing, Stoker's real hero. There is not a single reference to Vambery in Stoker's notes; and though this Hungarian scholar wrote dozens of tomes about Matthias Corvinus (he studied at the famous library of the Hungarian king), the Hunyadis, Sultan Mehmed II, and other principal characters of our plot, apparently he wrote not a word on Dracula. This fact is confirmed by Vambery's most recent biographers, Lory Alder and Richard Dolby. We do know that Stoker met the famous orientalist on several occasions, first briefly at a reception at Sandringham House, where Sir Henry Irving staged a command performance in honor of Queen Victoria in 1889. Later, in 1890, the two men met at the Beefsteak Club, essentially an annex of the Lyceum Theatre, a club where dinners often prolonged themselves deep into the night. Pending any further disclosure from the Stoker family, one may only guess at the nature of Stoker's personal conversations with Vambery, which were never transcribed. Certainly Vambery was in a good position to answer Stoker's many queries about the real Dracula, with whom he, as an eastern European historian, was obviously familiar from the works of Engel and Münster to which we have earlier referred. Vambery would have been able to confirm Wilkinson's negative image of the authentic prince, for whom no Hungarian historian ever had much interest or respect, a very good reason for Vambery's slighting of Dracula in his own writings.

In regard to the Szekler issue, it is possible that in these conversations Vambery laid emphasis on the Hungarian connection of the Dracula family, some of whom still lived in Hungary and Transylvania. After all, they had been honored with a patent of nobility by the Holy Roman Emperor Ferdinand I in 1535 and had properties in what was essentially Szekler territory. Vambery may also have been familiar with the fact that this branch, which survived through its female line well into the seventeenth century, had acquired additional lands in the region of the Borgo Pass, in essence the site Stoker ultimately chose for his vampire castle. Referring to Dracula himself, Vambery undoubtedly knew that Mihály Szilágy had given the Wallachian prince a castle in that region for services rendered against the Saxons.

Encyclopedic a scholar that he was, it is at least conceivable that Vambery also had some knowledge of Beheim's poem, the source for Van Helsing's statement in the novel that he had found a document in which Dracula was described as a blood drinker — a clear reference to one of Beheim's verses. This in turn provided Stoker with a significant historical matrix on which to base Dracula's identification with the vampire. Our assumption that these particular Stoker-Vambery conversations must have had some sort of substance is linked to Vambery's repute and prestige in London society. It is highly unlikely that Stoker manufactured the "blood drinker" statement out of hand; this might even have exposed the author to a possible lawsuit by the Hungarian scholar, since Van Helsing cites him indirectly as a source.

As for the details in the novel concerning geographic and topographical place names (obscure villages), descriptions of countryside, details concerning the costume and ethnic origins of the people, and other minutiae such as the bad condition of the roads in Transylvania and Moldavia, these are easily accounted for by some of Stoker's above-mentioned travel books and consultation of travel guides readily available not only at the British Museum but at almost any major library. Mention in the novel of the British Museum library, one of the greatest collections of books, further illustrates Stoker's concern for scholarly credentials.

What manner of a creature is Stoker's Dracula, in the end? He certainly has a memorable character beyond his connection with the historical Dracula, the subject of the present biography. Nor does he correspond precisely with the genuine Romanian folkloric concept of the vampire, though Stoker took some of his trappings from his readings of Gerard's book, which includes the antivampire arsenal so often depicted on the stage (including the stake through the heart). For one, in the minds of the Romanian people, the *strigoi*, though he can take the shape of various evil animals (though not the bat), is neither immortal, nor does he possess the alluring and seductive qualities of Stoker's antihero. In fact, quite the opposite is true: the Romanian folkloric vampire, much in the manner of Max Schreck's characterization in *Nosferatu,* is a living corpse, essentially unattractive and reeking of blood.

Stoker's vampire count is indeed a composite creature, in the end the product of Stoker's imagination, his reading, and the result of his life experiences. He cannot be neatly explained away, as so many of his critics have attempted to do with complex a priori psychological clichés, which Stoker himself would have had difficulty in understanding. The personage is indeed the quintessential vision of evil, an anti–father figure of great potency. He is seductive, particularly attractive to women, though the sensual and erotic qualities of Stoker's vampire have been even further amplified by movie scriptwriters since. The count craves immortality and wishes to conquer a decadent and materialistic Victorian England in the first instance, but ultimately he wishes to dominate the world. With this objective in mind, he goes about his task in a systematic, calculating way, much in the manner of his historical counterpart.

Having stated this, one cannot question that the count's aristocratic Romanian background and the genuine historic trappings with which Bram Stoker chose to clothe him, as well as the precise Transylvanian geography gleaned from Stoker's readings and possibly strengthened by his conversations with Vambery, added to the novel a powerful sense of realism otherwise absent in the older gothic tradition. This undoubtedly contributed to the ultimate success of *Dracula*.

CONCLUSION
Who Was the Real Dracula?

DRACULA is by no means the only controversial personality of history. Many other historical personages such as Henry VIII, Richard III, or Gilles de Rais were destined to suffer similar fates at the hands of posterity. As in the case of Dracula, writers of fiction, sometimes even historians, have preferred to lay emphasis on the villainous aspects of their respective characters. Henry VIII is often described as a flabby, gluttonous, cruel "killer of women." This, at least, is the popular image generally conveyed. Very much the same is true of Richard III, the Yorkist king of England, who shared much of Dracula's fate as an archetypal villain in the eyes of his Tudor detractors, largely because he is thought to have had murdered his two cousins, Edward VI and his brother Richard, in the Tower of London. Yet, when we penetrate more deeply into the lives of such controversial figures, we are invariably confronted with a serious problem. If Henry VIII was indeed so sanguineous a tyrant, how can we account for the fact that he was successful in achieving almost every major action that he undertook, which included getting rid of his popular first wife, Catherine of Aragon, with whom the public sympathized, and breaking away from Roman Catholic doctrine, in which the untheologically minded English people believed? On the whole, modern history has attempted to rehabilitate such characters that have been excessively reviled. In fact, societies have been formed for their total rehabilitation, against the hostile traditions of the past. Much the same is true of the historical Dracula.

For most vampire buffs, Dracula is the fiend who comes to haunt us and suck our blood at nighttime. For a few others, he is the aristocratic Transylvanian count from eastern Europe who wishes to conquer England and the rest of the world. For the Romanian nationalist, he represents the immortal hero of the race, ready to rise from his grave in defense of the fatherland at the hour of need, to paraphrase the poet Eminescu. It is the essential immortality of both hero and antihero that provides a trait common to both these extreme images of Dracula and Vlad the Impaler.

Taking his cue from German fifteenth-century narratives, Bram Stoker simply put the finishing touches to the most permanent fictional vampire horror tale of all times. In this sense the "vampire count" is indeed immortal and will in his various guises live on forever on the large and small silver screens. The tribute we pay to the German-inspired Stoker creation is to concede unabashedly that without the vampirism, the historical personality of Vlad the man would have languished permanently in the shadows of obscurity. Our final compliment is best expressed in the simple statement that without the vampire element, the present book would never have seen the light of day.

Looking at the realities of the heroic personality, though, we are equally unable to dismiss from our minds the portrait of Dracula created by the Romanian people, which again enjoys great vogue today, particularly since the celebration of the five hundredth anniversary of his death. Romania is certainly not the only nation to have mythologized semiobscure figures unearthed from its past. Each country needs heroes of the stamp of the undying German Frederick Barbarossa, or the saintly patriot of France, Joan of Arc. This very strong image of Vlad Ţepeş (The Impaler) the hero has prompted every schoolteacher in Romania to explain away his crimes and idealize his actions, not only to encourage pupils to pass their exams, but because a nation still threatened by foreign domination needs the weight of its mythical heroes to survive. Idealizing national symbols is hardly a sinful practice, particularly among those states that cannot afford the luxury of historical impartiality because they are still threatened with extinction.

The two separate and extreme portraits of Vlad, the villain and the hero, therefore deserve both mention and recognition, and in that sense they are equally real. Nonetheless, the two faces of Dracula have contributed to a serious historical problem that is detrimental to the historian's quest for truth. It is the historian's duty to attempt to reconcile the many images of Dracula drawn by contemporaries and other chroniclers.

We must honestly acknowledge the paucity of sources for a detailed biography of Dracula. Detailed biography is possible for some of his fifteenth-century contemporaries, such as Charles VII, Ludovico Sforza, Emperor Frederick III, or even Matthias Corvinus. But lack of historical documentation is more characteristic of fifteenth-century eastern Europe and Russia because of the massive destruction of records and the absence of court chroniclers. We have very little knowledge of the personal life of Vlad, of his family relationships, of his mistresses and his wife, and of the more intimate character of his court. Such lacunae make the task of the historian all the more challenging. To compensate for the small number of primary sources, we have used the reports of foreign diplomats, sources drawn from personal narratives, folklore, portrait analyses, study of coins, archaeological investigation, and genealogical research.

Most tantalizing are, of course, the contemporary anecdotal accounts that provide the material for a substantial portion of our presentation of the historical Dracula. They can certainly not be dismissed as pure fiction, as some have suggested, for a variety of reasons: they are solidly based on identifiable eyewitness accounts, detailed in their knowledge and nomenclature of a given geographic area, precise about the names and dates. They have all the ingredients of a purely factual document in spite of the distortions to which they are often prone. One should further stress that each narrator provides only the details of the plot with which he is most intimately connected: for instance, Beheim focuses his attention on Transylvania, because his informant, Brother Jacob, was familiar with this area. Kuritsyn, the Russian envoy, relates the story of Dracula's career in exile, and informs us of his family, with which he was best acquainted. By way of contrast, the Turkish chronicles as well as the Byzantine writers focus their attention on Dracula's military campaign, which they either witnessed or heard about. In point of fact, the documentation referring to Dracula's campaign against Mehmed in 1462, because of the abundance of eyewitness accounts on both sides, represents one of the most comprehensive sources for the study of a major campaign fought during the fifteenth century. Nothwithstanding the differences of opinion expressed by various writers on many aspects of Dracula's life, there exists a remarkable coincidence of facts and themes among narrators, official court historians, and diplomats. This concord expressed in many languages (Italian, Latin, Russian, German, et cetera), could hardly have been the result of some cleverly concocted plot to be explained away by those who enjoy conspiratorial theories of history.

Most convincing is the fact that the oral Romanian tradition, in spite of its attempt to rationalize Dracula's crimes, coincides to a large extent with German, Greek, Turkish, Slavic, and even South Balkan narratives — also composed at the time when the Balkan language did not exist in written form. Though folklore has to be used with caution where no other documentation exists, it is a legitimate tool of study, particularly for events occurring within a span of two hundred years or less, when the recorded tales of Dracula were first noted by the chroniclers (for example, the construction of Castle Dracula). In spite of the subsequent distortions, why distrust the songs and poems of the people and place exaggerated reliance on official historians or memorialists, who almost invariably praise the masters in whose pay they were? The panegyrist who lies in order to preserve a favorable image of his master is hardly a fifteenth-century phenomenon. What is most fascinating in connection with Dracula is the fact that though assuredly greater princes ruled in Romania, he is one of the few who are remembered reverently in the collective conscience of the people, engendering a rich folklore that has not as yet been fully studied. On the whole, we have tended to give most credence to those events that are recorded by a wide variety of different sources, as opposed to those facts mentioned in only a single narrative.

From these sources, there is no escape from the conclusion that we are dealing with a cruel artist in crime, who, though he principally used impalement for disposing of his enemies, also employed a great many other techniques, such as death by fire, by boiling, skinning people alive, and sawing off their limbs, without distinction of sex, nationality, or age. We certainly challenge the staggering statistic provided by the papal legate, the bishop of Erlau, of Dracula's having caused 100,000 deaths, at the time when the total population of his land numbered merely 500,000. If true, the statistic would qualify Dracula, in terms of numbers alone, as one of the greatest butchers of all times. We discount this particular figure on the simple grounds that wholesale statistics of this kind are almost invariably false and that no other reference confirms that number. In other instances, as in the case of the 20,000 boyars slain within the courtyard of Tîrgovişte at the beginning of the reign, a very simple measurement of the foundations of the palace courtyard, which could at most hold a few hundred people, helped us reject that particular figure. Mass murders at the castle of the Argeş, which housed a garrison of not much over a hundred men, are equally inconceivable.

Having dismissed the figures, one could still suggest that Dracula's crimes may have exceeded those of the other Renaissance tyrants, at least in terms of numbers. However, did he kill for the pleasure of killing, as his detractors have attested when comparing him with the most depraved emperors of Imperial Rome? Was there the kind of morbid enjoyment at the sight of his victims writhing in pain, more familiarly associated with the crimes of Ivan the Terrible of Russia or Gilles de Rais, the prototype of the notorious Bluebeard? Was he, in a word, the psychopath that the German narratives suggest, who destroyed lives without rationality? Was he a sadist? These are questions we have at least the right to pose, even in the absence of more pertinent documents concerning Dracula's psychological makeup.

The problem of Dracula's cruelties, irrespective of statistics, is heightened by the methods by which he imposed death, and by his reputed presence at the moment of execution, implying pleasure at the sight of blood. In addition, the use of various forms of psychological torture mentioned in the narrative is revealing.

In no sense can such crimes be lightly explained away (though Romanian historians have tried to do so). One line of possible defense already sufficiently alluded to is the low standards of political ethics prevailing in fifteenth-century Europe, even before the days of Machiavelli. Further, we must take into account that Dracula's whole life must be viewed across prison bars — he actually spent almost twice as many years in jail as he did on the throne, and during any one of these moments his own life was threatened. This fact assuredly provides the historian with a pertinent clue as to why Dracula held life in such low esteem. One may add to these explanations that as a child he had virtually no family existence. When a young boy, he was sent off to a distant alien court as a hostage, knowing that his father was pursuing policies incompatible with promises made; he witnessed the sexual abuse of his younger brother, Radu, and the blinding of other hostages. Later in life, he learned that his father had been assassinated; his elder brother was buried alive; he witnessed the assassination of his uncle Prince Bogdan (the father of Stephen the Great); faced mass defection of the boyars and conspiracies by members of his family, including his cousin Stephen. Finally, the Hungarian king Matthias, upon whom he had placed his trust, betrayed him. Factors such as these are, however, insufficient by themselves for the twentieth-century historian to give Dracula absolution.

The problem of the sanity of historical characters, particularly for that early period, is a most difficult one to resolve, this in spite of the progress of psychohistory or even psychological analysis of historical personalities. Bereft of the science and training of the psychologist, the historian is naturally limited by the exigencies of his trade: the written document, in this instance, is of little help for detailed psychoanalysis of Dracula's personality. Those few psychoanalysts who have hazarded Freudian or other explanations of Dracula have not been particularly convincing. For lack of real historical knowledge, these "scientists" tend to fit the facts to suit their individual theories. One nineteenth-century Romanian historian, B. P. Haşdeu, made use of phrenology or the study of physiognomy to determine character traits in dissecting Dracula's personality.

Dracula was probably not insane — in the sense in which an Ivan the Terrible was. Most of his crimes had a certain rational purpose. Through his "terror tactics" he saved the Wallachian nation from Turkish conquest in 1462. The persecution of Catholic monks deterred defection from Orthodoxy, at a time of Hungarian proselytism. The struggle with the Dăneşti was a matter of survival, as crucial as the Wars of the Roses in England. Even Dracula's attack on the German Transylvanian merchants can be justified upon the grounds that he was encouraging the birth of a native middle class. Granted this intrinsic rationality, Dracula, like many tyrants of history who were the victims of adverse circumstances during their youth, may have been prone to temporary bouts of mental derangement, depressions that could lead to paranoia, induced by distrust of humankind. Our sources are explicit in revealing that Dracula sought solace and refuge in isolated castles or monasteries infinitely preferable to the hustle and bustle of his capital, Tîrgovişte. Like Ivan the Terrible, he liked to roam around the countryside, usually accompanied by very few others, to seek his inner peace in the natural beauty of the rural Wallachian regions.

With reference to Dracula's unusual relationship to his legitimate and illegitimate wives, we cannot, as noted, completely rule out impotency at an early period in life. The problem was presumably resolved with the birth of the three children that Dracula fathered by two different women. The problem of sexual inadequacy has been raised by some psychologists, who have speculated on the symbolism of the stake penetrating the buttocks of his victims as a substitute of genuine sexual satisfaction. However, Dracula's attitude toward women was not very different from that prevailing at the courts of other eastern European sovereigns, which includes the Sultan's court. Though they did have certain legal rights, women in fifteenth-century eastern Europe were looked upon as sex objects by those in a position of power. Marriage was not particularly significant. All that mattered was that an heir be provided from "the royal bone."

As counterpoint to his cruelty, we highlight the personal courage that Dracula allegedly displayed in battle. There are indeed some instances — the famous night attack in the summer of 1462 is one—in which Dracula risked his own life, as was attested to by his Turkish detractors.

Ultimately, we must see Dracula in many guises; the ecclesiast, the statesman, and the soldier. Following the fall of Constantinople, he, like many of his successors considered himself the only truly independent patron and defender of Eastern Orthodoxy, centuries before Russia assumed this traditional mantle. As a statesman, though very much like the characteristic condottiere who wished to acquire power for its intrinsic sake, Dracula, perhaps like Joan of Arc, had a vague notion of the spiritual unity of the Romanian people from all three provinces: Wallachia, Transylvania, and Moldavia. This idea was most eloquently expressed on the eve of his last reign, when volunteers from the three provinces united in the common pursuit of national goals in the face of the common Turkish danger. Beyond his country, however, was the much broader concept of a fatherland of European civilization that had to be defended from an alien creed. This mission he inherited from his mentor Hunyadi and the crusaders of old.

Failing to rally the powers of Europe in defense of the borderlands of European civilization, he was compelled, given the slender means placed at his disposal by a nation in arms, to carry out this task himself as a member of the Dragon Order. In that crucial conflict, Dracula can hardly be included among the great tacticians of war such as Napoleon or Alexander the Great. Nevertheless, making use of a mixture of truly extraordinary tactics, unusually well suited to the terrain of his country, he was able to repel an army three times the size of his own and inflict upon Mehmed the Conqueror one of the greatest humiliations of the latter's lifetime. It was essentially this military action, exploited by the diplomacy of Dracula's brother Radu, that saved his country from the onus and humiliation of being reduced to the status of a Turkish province. It also gained for Europe an invaluable breathing spell to marshal its defenses against the common danger. It is in that sense only that the backhanded compliment of Sultan Mehmed II must be understood: here was a man fully capable of conquering the universe — coincidentally, this challenge was almost identical to the goal attributed to Stoker's Vampire count!

A Brief Annotated Bibliography

with critical commentary provided by Radu R. Florescu and Raymond T. McNally

(Only works in English have been included; the primary sources are only those available at English and American libraries.)

Primary Sources

At the Philip H. and A. S. W. Rosenbach Foundation, Philadelphia:
   Anonymous German print: *Die Geschicht Dracole Waide* . . . (Nuremberg: Wagner, 1488). Color frontispiece.
   The notes, outlines, and diagrams for Bram Stoker's *Dracula,* containing lists of the secondary sources, books, et cetera, that he used for the composition of his novel.
At the Library of the British Museum, London:
   MS. 24315, F⁰⁵ 138–143. Fifteenth-century Dracula manuscript.

Anonymous German pamphlet *Ein wünderliche und erschröliche Hystorie* . . . 1A2673 (Bamberg: Hans Spörer 1491). For precise call numbers, see *Catalogue of Books Printed in the 15th Century Now in the British Library* (London, 1963).

Books

Carter, Margaret L., *Dracula the Vampire and the Critics* (Ann Arbor: University of Michigan Institute for Research Press, 1988). Anthology of studies; only reference to the historical Dracula is in Devendra P. Varma's "Dracula's Voyage from Pontus to Hellespontus."

Farson, Daniel, *The Man Who Wrote* Dracula: *A Biography of Bram Stoker* (New York: St. Martin's, 1976). A controversial book that highlights Romanian touristic exploitation of the historical Dracula.

Florescu, Radu R., and Raymond T. McNally, *Dracula: A Biography of Vlad the Impaler* (New York: Hawthorn Books, 1973). A preliminary study of the historical Dracula within the Romanian context.

Gerard, Emily de Laszowska, *The Land beyond the Forest* (London: A.M.S. Press, 1888). One of Stoker's main sources for the study of Romanian folklore.

Giurescu, Constantin C., *The Life and Deeds of Vlad the Impaler: Drăculea* (New York: Romanian Library, 1969).

Halecki, Oscar, *The Crusade at Varna: A Discussion of a Controversial Problem* (New York: Polish Institute of Arts and Sciences in America, 1943). Of interest in accounting for the Dracul-Hunyadi feud.

Held, Joseph, *Hunyadi: Legend and Reality* (Boulder: East European Monographs; distr. by Columbia University Press, 1985). The only work available in English with an excellent analysis of Hunyadi's character and aims.

Kritoboulos of Imbros, *History of Mehmed the Conqueror,* trans. Charles T. Riggs (Princeton: Princeton University Press, 1954). A mediocre translation of a pro-Turkish chronicle that discusses Dracula's campaign against Sultan Mehmed II.

Leu, Corneliu, *Dracula's Complaint,* trans. Victor Budeanu (Bucharest; Cartea Româneasca, 1978). A novel based on some authentic historical sources.

Ludlam, Harry, *A Biography of Dracula: The Life Story of Bram Stoker* (London: Foulsham, 1962). Although dated, still the most comprehensive of the Stoker biographies. The author was not acquainted with the notes at the Rosenbach Foundation.

McNally, Raymond T., and Radu R. Florescu, *The Essential Dracula* (New York: Mayflower Books, 1979). An annotated text of Bram Stoker's novel, based on the author's notes available at the Rosenbach Foundation.

————, *In Search of Dracula: A True History of Dracula and Vampire Legends* (Greenwich, Conn.: New York Graphic Society, 1972).

Münster, Sebastian, *Cosmographia universalis,* English ed. (London, 1558), vol. 6. Contains most of the early German anecdotes concerning Dracula's cruelties.

Myles, Douglas, *Prince Dracula Son of the Devil* (New York: McGraw-Hill, 1988). A purported biography that intermixes facts and fiction.

Ronay, Gabriel, *The Truth about Dracula* (also published under the title *The Dracula Myth*) (New York: Stein & Day, 1972). Essentially the history of Countess Elizabeth Báthory. Superficial on the historical Dracula.

Roth, Phyllis A., *Bram Stoker* (Boston: Twayne, 1982). The most recent biography of Bram Stoker. The author is acquainted with the notes available at the Rosenbach Foundation. A scholarly treatment.

Rudorff, Raymond, *The Dracula Archives* (New York: Arbor House, 1972). A fictionalized account of Count Dracula's past with interesting speculations on a possible Dracula-Báthory marriage alliance.

Stoicescu, Nicolae, *Vlad the Impaler,* trans. Cristina Krikorian (Bucharest: Romanian Academy, 1978). A very strict interpretation of the documents by one of Romania's leading medievalists.

Tappe, Eric, *Documents Concerning Romanian History, 1427–1601, Collected from the British Archives* (The Hague: Mouton, 1964). Includes the letter of the English pilgrim William of Wey, which reports a Dracula victory over the Turks in 1462.

Wilkinson, William, *An Account of the Principalities of Moldavia and Wallachia, with Various Political Observations Relative to Them* (London: Longmans, 1820). Interesting in that Stoker obtained most of his information on the historical Dracula from this book.

William of Wey, *The Itineraries of William Wey* (London: A.M.S. Press, 1857). The travelogue of an English pilgrim to the Holy Land who mentions Dracula.

Wolf, Leonard, *The Annotated Dracula* (New York: Clarkson Potter, 1975). Superficial on the historical Dracula and written with no apparent reference to Stoker's notes.

———, *A Dream of Dracula* (Boston: Little, Brown, 1972). Contains only one chapter on the historical Dracula.

Articles

Bierman, Joseph S., "Dracula: Prolonged Childhood Illness and the Oral Triad." *American Imago,* vol. 29 (1972).

———, "The Genesis and Dating of *Dracula* from Bram Stoker's Working Notes." *Notes and Queries.* N.S., 24, n. i (1977).

Czabai, Stephen, "The Real Dracula." *Hungarian Quarterly* (Autumn 1941).

Eddy, Beverly, "Dracula: A Translation of the 1488 Nürnberg Edition, with an Essay by Beverly D. Eddy." *Rosenbach Museum and Library* (1985).

Florescu, Radu R., "Dracula as a Hero: Apology for a Part-Time Monster." *International History Magazine,* vol. 1, no. 8 (August 1973).

———, "The Dracula Image in the Works of the Folklorists Petre Ispirescu and C. Rădulescu-Codin." *Cahiers roumains d'études littéraires,* vol. 3 (Bucharest, 1977). In English.

———, "Dracula in Romanian Literature: From Budai-Deleanu to M. Eminescu.'' In *Eminescu, the Evening Star of Romanian Poetry* (Ann Arbor: Michigan University Press, 1986).

———, ''The Dracula Search in Retrospect.'' *The New England Social Studies Bulletin,* vol. 43, no. 1 (Fall 1985–1986).

———, ''What's in a Name: Dracula or Vlad the Impaler?'' *Balkanistica* (1980).

Kirtley, B., ''Dracula, the Monastic Chronicle and Slavic Folklore.'' *Mid-West Folklore,* vol. 6, no. 3 (1956).

McNally, Raymond T., ''The 15th Century Manuscript of Kritoboulos of Imbros as a Source for the History of Dracula.'' *East European Quarterly,* vol. 21, no. 1 (March 1987).

———, ''Origins of the Slavic Narrative about the Historical Dracula.'' In *Romania between East and West,* ed. S. Fischer-Galati, Radu R. Florescu, and G. R. Ursul (Boulder: East European Monographs; distr. by Columbia University Press, 1982).

McNally, Raymond T., and Stefan Andreescu, ''Where Was Dracula Captured in 1462?'' *East European Quarterly,* vol. 23, no. 3 (September 1989).

Nandriş, Grigore, ''A Psychological Analysis of Dracula and Rumanian Place-names and Masculine Personal names in a/e.'' *Slavonic and East European Review,* vol. 37 (1959).

———, ''The Dracula Theme in European Literature of the West and of the East.'' In *Literary History and Literary Criticism,* ed. Leon Edel (New York: New York University Press, 1965).

———, ''The Historical Dracula.'' In *Comparative Literature: Matter and Method* (Urbana: University of Illinois Press, 1969).

Index